Paradoxes of Power

For Sarah, Rebecca, and Emily

Paradoxes of Power

David A. Baldwin

Basil Blackwell

First published 1989

Basil Blackwell Inc.
432 Park Avenue South, Suite 1503
New York, NY 10016, USA

Basil Blackwell Ltd
108 Cowley Road, Oxford, OX4 1JF, UK

Library of Congress Cataloging in Publication Data

Baldwin, David A. (David Allen), 1936–
 Paradoxes of power.
  1. Power (Social sciences) 2. Exchange theory (Sociology) I. Title
JC330.B323 1989 303.3'3 88–7739
ISBN 1–55786–005–X

British Library Cataloguing in Publication Data

Baldwin, David A. (David Allen), 1936–
 Paradoxes of power.
 1. Power. Social aspects
 I. Title
 303.3
 ISBN 1–55786–005–X

Typeset in 11 on 13pt Sabon
by Hope Services, Abingdon
Printed in Great Britain by
T.J. Press Ltd, Padstow, Cornwall

Contents

Preface

The essays in this volume represent the author's attempt to explore two of the most fundamental concepts in social science – "power" and "exchange." Although they were originally written over a period of fifteen years, each has been revised for publication in this volume. References have been updated, wording has been clarified, and critics have been noted; but the fundamental arguments remain.

Many people have helped to clarify the arguments in this book, including the following: Michael Banks, Colin D. Campbell, Roger Davidson, Harry Eckstein, Henry Ehrmann, Raymond Hall, Jeffrey A. Hart, Richard Joseph, Nelson Kasfir, Robert O. Keohane, David Kettler, David Kipnis, Robert Kleck, Nancy Marion, Joseph Massey, Roger Masters, Helen Milner, Felix Oppenheim, Robert Packenham, James N. Rosenau, Arthur Rubinoff, Bernard Segal, James P. Sewell, J. David Singer, Michael Smith, Melvin Snyder, Denis G. Sullivan, Richard Winters, and Oran Young. In the preparation of the manuscript, the staff of the Institute of War and Peace Studies, with the guidance of Jean Leong, have been an invaluable help.

The author and publishers are grateful for permission to reprint material from previously published material:

"Interdependence and Power: A Conceptual Analysis," *International Organization*, 34 (4) (1980), pp. 471–506, by permission of MIT Press.

"Power and Social Exchange," *American Political Science Review*, 72 (December 1978), pp. 1229–42, by permission of American Political Science Association.

"Thinking About Threats," *Journal of Conflict Resolution*, 15 (1) (1971), pp. 71–8, by permission of Sage Publications, Inc.

"The Costs of Power," *Journal of Conflict Resolution*, 15 (2) (1971), pp. 145–55, by permission of Sage Publications, Inc.

"Money and Power," *Journal of Politics*, 33 (August 1971), pp. 578–614, by permission of Southern Political Science Association.

"The Power of Positive Sanctions," *World Politics*, 24 (1971), pp. 19–38, by permission of Princeton University Press.

"Power Analysis and World Politics," *World Politics*, 31 (1979), pp. 161–94, by permission of Princeton University Press.

I

Introduction

Power, in the sense of someone getting someone else to do something they otherwise would not do, is all around us. Unless we live as hermits, there is no escaping it; we influence others and are, in turn, influenced by them many times each day. Human beings are social animals, and it is impossible to think seriously about social life without thinking about power. Thinking about power is *inevitable* in the sense that we cannot get through the day without doing it. "How do I get my boss to give me a raise (or refrain from firing me)?" "How do I get my son to mow the lawn?" "How do I get a taxi to drive me to the airport?" Such questions and hundreds like them fill our minds every day. Power does not always take the form of showdowns between heads of state with respect to important matters like nuclear disarmament; it may also take mundane and trivial forms.

Thinking about power is *ubiquitous* in the sense that all arenas of social life involve power. Families, churches, schools, social clubs, and businesses all require thinking about power.

Thinking about power is *difficult* because of the ambiguity of language, because power takes many complex and subtle forms, and because one can never be sure what would have happened in the absence of an attempt to exercise power. Although power analysis is never easy, this book attempts to help by discussing some important and often misunderstood dimensions of power.

In addition to being inevitable, ubiquitous, and difficult, thinking about power is also likely to be morally ambiguous. Because power can be, and has been, used for good or evil purposes, no simple moral judgment on power is justified. Even the act of thinking about power sometimes raises questions and eyebrows. Is it an indication that one loves power or that one is fascinated with power or that one wants to glorify it? Not necessarily. The approach in this book is not intended to praise or denounce power, but rather to promote realistic recognition of the role of power in social life. As Robert A. Dahl reminds us, "the analysis of 'power' is no merely theoretical enterprise but a matter of greatest practicality. For how one acts in political life depends very heavily on one's beliefs about the nature, distribution, and practices of 'power' . . . [To] be misled about 'power' is to be misled about the prospects and means of stability, change, and revolution."[1]

Finally, thinking about power is *paradoxical* in that statements about power that are true often seem to be false. The seemingly powerful are sometimes weak and vice versa. Much of the discussion in this book is intended to enhance understanding of such paradoxes.

The chapters that follow are concerned with *how* to think about power, not *what* to think. They are designed to help one ask the right questions rather than to provide answers. Although each chapter stands on its own, four themes weave them together.

THEMES

The "social power" literature

Discussions of power frequently begin by noting the absence of agreement on basic terminology. A student approaching the subject for the first time can easily get the impression that power analysis is characterized by intellectual chaos. Once this impression is implanted, it is tempting for the student to become impatient with the arduous process of familiarizing oneself with previous scholarship and to proceed to "go it alone." After all, if there is no consensus with respect to how to think about power, one might as well do it any way one likes. Why not?

[1] Robert A. Dahl, *Modern Political Analysis*, 2nd edn (Englewood Cliffs, N.J.: Prentice-Hall, 1970), p. 15.

While it would be folly to deny the existence of serious disagreements among students of power, it is equally wrong to deny that there is any consensus at all on major issues. Serious disagreement does not preclude equally serious agreement. The analysis in this book assumes that it is both meaningful and useful to refer to the scholarly literature on social power.

Examples of fundamental areas of agreement by large numbers of power analysts include the following: (1) agreement that power should be treated as a relationship between two or more people rather than as a property of any one of them; (2) agreement that the bases of power are many and varied; and (3) agreement that power is a multidimensional phenomenon that varies in scope, weight, domain, and cost.

Contributors to this literature include political scientists, economists, sociologists, psychologists, and philosophers.[2] The social power literature is an impressive scholarly edifice and cannot be ignored by the serious student. It is marked by rigor, familiarity with and respect for the work of others, and willingness to cross the boundaries of academic disciplines. Much of this work builds upon the landmark work of Harold D. Lasswell and Abraham Kaplan published in 1950.[3]

To assert that an impressive scholarly literature on social power exists is not to say that further refinements are impossible. It is not even to argue against the possibility of a revolutionary change in thinking about power that would invalidate that literature. It is to

[2] References to this literature are contained in the chapters that follow. For reviews of the literature, see Dorwin Cartwright, "Influence, Leadership, Control," in *Handbook of Organizations*, ed. James March (Chicago: Rand McNally, 1965), pp. 1–47; Robert A. Dahl, "Power," *International Encyclopedia of the Social Sciences*, 12 (New York: Free Press, 1968), pp. 405–15; Jack H. Nagel, *The Descriptive Analysis of Power* (New Haven: Yale University Press, 1975); and James T. Tedeschi and Thomas V. Bonoma, "Power and Influence: An Introduction," in *The Social Influence Processes*, ed. Tedeschi (Chicago: Aldine-Atherton, 1972), pp. 1–49; and Dennis H. Wrong, *Power* (New York: Harper & Row, 1979).

It should be specifically noted that the "social power literature" subsumes, but is not the same as, the "community power literature." The latter concerns a particular set of questions about democratic theory. For references on the community power literature, see Nelson W. Polsby, *Community Power and Political Theory*, 2nd edn (New Haven: Yale University Press, 1980).

[3] Harold D. Lasswell and Abraham Kaplan, *Power and Society: A Framework for Political Inquiry* (New Haven: Yale University Press, 1950).

argue that proposals for new ways to think about power must come to terms with that literature. Proponents of alternative approaches should be required to demonstrate that they have paid their scholarly dues by familiarizing themselves with that literature. In addition, they should be required to demonstrate why and how the approach to power analysis they favor is superior to the conventional literature. Thus, when Nicos Poulantzas proposes that power be defined as "the capacity of a social class to realize its specific objective interests," one is entitled – nay, obliged – to ask why such a notion is preferable to conventional concepts. The response that "it is, of course, impossible to undertake a detailed critique of the many concepts of power" is unacceptable. The expectation that a three hundred and fifty page book entitled *Political Power and Social Class* would spend more than two pages on a critique of alternative approaches is eminently reasonable. When the same author dismisses the most widely shared definition of power in social science by observing that "it is unnecessary to point out how mistaken" such a view is, he forfeits the right to be taken seriously as a scholarly student of power.[4] Likewise, when Kenneth N. Waltz dismisses this same definition of power as "practically and logically untenable," one expects more than three paragraphs of explanation.[5] Those who advance unconventional conceptions of power do not deserve the attention of scholars unless they make a serious effort to deal with the conventional social power literature.

The foregoing discussion should not be read as an attempt to discourage new modes of thought. Rather, it should be viewed as a warning that serious scholars have written much on the subject of power and as a plea for subsequent writers to show a decent level of scholarly courtesy by acknowledging and grappling with the arguments they have advanced. One need not agree with the conventional social power literature, but one cannot ignore it.

[4] Nicos Poulantzas, *Political Power and Social Classes* (London: NLB, 1973), pp. 104–6. The most widely shared definition of power among social scientists is Dahl's: "*A* has power over *B* to the extent that he can get *B* to do something that *B* would not otherwise do." See Robert A. Dahl, "The Concept of Power," *Behavioral Science*, 2 (1957): 201–15.

[5] Kenneth N. Waltz, *Theory of International Politics* (Reading, Mass.: Addison-Wesley, 1979), pp. 191–2.

The economic reference point

A second theme permeating this book is the comparison of economic with political life. Chapter 2, entitled "Money and Power," lays the intellectual groundwork for this comparison in the rest of the book. The value of such an exercise derives from clarification of both the similarities and the differences between these two spheres of social life. On the one hand, it is argued that it is wrong to depict threats, coercion, punishment, conflict, and power as peculiar to politics while viewing promises, rewards, cooperation, and exchange as the special province of economics. Such approaches impede understanding of both the polity and the economy. "Exchanges," as Dahl has noted, "are as ubiquitous in political as in economic life";[6] and power, one might add, is as common in economic as in political life. This analytical perspective paves the way for an attack on one of the more formidable obstacles to social inquiry – the assumption that thinking about conflict is fundamentally different from thinking about cooperation. On the other hand, it will be argued that economic and political life differ in at least one very significant way. In a market economy, economic exchanges are likely to be facilitated by a generally agreed upon medium of exchange that also serves as a standardized measure of value, i.e., money. No very close counterpart of money functions in most political exchanges, thus imbuing them with a degree of uncertainty and difficulty with far-reaching ramifications. One of the main purposes of the chapters that follow is to explore such ramifications.

The significance of money can be illustrated by comparing arms sales with disarmament negotiations. Both situations involve exchange, and both involve one country getting another country to give up some of its arms. One of the most insurmountable difficulties in arms negotiations is comparing the political value of long-range missiles, short-range missiles, big warheads, small warheads, bombers, and bombs. Even if each country has identical quantities of each type of weapon, differences in the strategic situation faced by each country make it unlikely that each will place the same value on the various weapons. Long-range missiles

[6] Dahl, *Modern Political Analysis*, 4th edn (Englewood Cliffs, N.J.: Prentice-Hall, 1984), pp. 43–4.

are more valuable to some countries than to others. In the absence
of a standardized measuring rod in terms of which the strategic
value of various weapons can be compared, one might expect arms
control agreements to be difficult. And they are! Arms sales,
however, are comparatively easy. That is to say, if one country
wants to induce another to give up a package of various types of
arms in return for money, it has only to translate the value of the
arms into the common denominator of money. To the extent that
going market prices exist for such weapons, the negotiations
should be relatively easy.

In order to avoid later misunderstandings, one caveat is in
order. Although the absence of a political counterpart to money as
a standardized measure of value makes the measurement of
political power difficult, it does not make it impossible. The
measurement of power is *both* difficult and necessary. Judgments
about the magnitude of power are made every day. The argument
in this book cautions against assertions that power can be
measured with a high degree of precision, and it urges intellectual
humility and appropriate qualifications when making such judgments. Arms control agreements may be difficult, but they do
occur.

Contextual analysis

Another theme in this book is the wisdom of specifying the context
within which power analysis is occurring. Precisely because of the
existence of an agreed upon measuring rod for economic value,
economists need not be as attentive to contextual variables as
political scientists. They can refer to a market basket of "things"
worth $100 with the expectation that others will know what they
mean even if they do not specify which "things" they have in
mind. After all, the idea that John Doe exercised $100 worth of
purchasing power is a reasonably meaningful statement for some
purposes. A statement that he has exercised 100 units of political
power, however, is less likely to be understood. Questions are
likely to arise as to the context and the manner in which this
power was used. Dahl has wisely noted that "because of the
necessity to convey meaning in political analysis, works that
convey the optimum understanding of power and influence in

concrete situations are often detailed, descriptive, subtle, and
employ a vocabulary of variety and nuance."[7]

Conceptual analysis

Some of the discussion in this book could be classified as
conceptual analysis, that is to say, the object is to clarify the
meaning of statements about power rather than to determine the
truth or falsity of such statements. This analytical approach is
sometimes belittled as "hair splitting" or "mere semantics."
Although conceptual analysis does sometimes degenerate into a
seemingly pointless series of distinctions, this need not happen.
Scholarly communication depends on understanding what people
mean, but discussions about power are often marred by mis-
communication. The empirical researcher would do well to acquire
a firm grasp of the basic concept of power before trying to
operationalize or measure it, and the normative theorist should be
sure to understand the nature of power before condemning or
applauding its use.

One way to avoid getting bogged down in the interminable
distinctions that sometimes plague semantic analysis is to focus on
fundamental concepts. Thus, this book does not try to distinguish
among a host of related terms, such as power, influence, control,
persuasion, manipulation, domination, or force. Instead, the
primary focus is on the underlying meaning shared by all of these
terms. This is not to deny the value of distinguishing various types
of power for some purposes; it is merely to affirm the value of
explicating a broad generic concept of power for other purposes.
Although some writers find it useful to distinguish between power
and influence, this book will use these terms interchangeably.

The concept of power explicated in this book has been called a
causal notion of power. This approach treats power relations as a
type of causal relationship in which the power wielder affects the
behavior, attitudes, beliefs, or propensity to act of another actor.
One important implication of this notion of power is the necessity
of specifying the scope and domain of an influence relationship.

---

[7] Ibid., p. 37. For an example of the author's attempt to analyze power in a concrete
situation, see David A. Baldwin, *Economic Statecraft* (Princeton: Princeton University
Press, 1985).

This point is often misunderstood by those who fail to distinguish conceptual from empirical analyses. The admonition to specify scope and domain does not concern the most useful level of abstraction on which to make empirical generalizations. From the standpoint of conceptual analysis, the specification of scope and domain is a requirement for a meaningful statement *at any level of abstraction*. The point is well put by Nagel:

> Anyone who employs a causal concept of power *must* specify domain and scope. To say "X has power" may seem sensible, but to say "X causes" or "X can cause" is nonsense. Causation implies an X and a Y – a cause and an effect. If power is causation, one must state the outcome cause. Stipulating domain and scope answers the question, "Power over *what*?"[8]

Some writers contend that power is one of a number of social science concepts that are "essentially contested."[9] From this point of view, there is no such thing as a concept of power that is not biased in favor of a particular ideological position. Radicals and conservatives, it is argued, cannot use the same concept of power. Any statement attributing power to someone is also a normative statement in the sense that the exercise of power always has implications for one's moral responsibilities. Without disputing the truth of this argument in some ultimate sense, there is still a case to be made for attempts to explicate a concept of power with as little ideological bias as possible. Just because perfect neutrality is impossible, it does not follow that "anything goes." The attribution of power, after all, not only has moral implications, it also has economic, educational, religious, psychological, and

[8] Jack H. Nagel, *Descriptive Analysis of Power*, p. 14. See the equally strong assertion by Dahl that "any statement about influence that does not clearly indicate the domain and scope it refers to verges on being meaningless." (*Modern Political Analysis*, 4th edn, p. 27.) For an example of a study that overlooks this fundamental point, see James Lee Ray and Ayse Vural, "Power Disparities and Paradoxical Conflict Outcomes," *International Interactions*, 12 (1986), pp. 315–42.

[9] See William E. Connolly, *The Terms of Political Discourse*, 2nd edn (Princeton: Princeton University Press, 1983); Steven Lukes, *Power: A Radical View* (London: Macmillan, 1974); Felix E. Oppenheim, *Political Concepts* (Chicago: University of Chicago Press, 1981); K. I. Macdonald, "Is 'Power' Essentially Contested?", *British Journal of Political Science*, 7 (1977), pp. 418–19; Barry Clarke, "Eccentrically Contested Concepts," *British Journal of Political Science*, 9 (1979), pp. 122–6; and Hugh V. McLachlan, "Is 'Power' An Evaluative Concept?", *British Journal of Sociology*, 32 (1981), pp. 392–410.

linguistic implications. We live in a world where everything has actual or potential implications for everything else, but this does not — and should not — prevent us from making some simplifying assumptions. Since we cannot think about everything at once, we often simplify. As a practical matter, judgments are often made about power by people who have no intention of implying a moral judgment. The debate over "essentially contested" concepts of social inquiry raises questions that go beyond the scope of this book. Even if the ideas about power advanced in this book are ultimately unacceptable to certain ideological positions, however, those holding such positions should at least be able to clarify their own views by consideration of the arguments in this book. For example, one may ultimately decide to reject the argument that rewards and promised rewards can be instruments of power; but one should at least do so in a self-conscious way after considering the arguments in favor of such a view. One may never be able to escape from one's ideological biases, but one can at least try to think about them.

ORGANIZATION

Chapter 2 explores the role of power in basic social processes of exchange. The following three chapters examine various means of exercising power and the costs and benefits associated with different means. Chapter 6 returns to the question of the relation between exchange and power and synthesizes the preceding chapters. The last two chapters apply the ideas developed earlier to the field of international relations.

2

Money and Power

Political scientists are fond of observing that "power is to us what money is to the economist: the medium via which transactions are observed and measured."[1] The analogy sometimes implies, as it does in this quotation, that money and power perform similar social functions. At other times it seems to mean that political scientists ought to spend as much time thinking about power as economists do thinking about money. At still other times one detects an envious tone that seems to say, "How lucky are the economists to have money, while our nearest equivalent is that slippery concept of power." The precise implication rarely matters, however, since the analogy is usually more a rhetorical than an analytical device. The article cited is typical in its use of the analogy as little more than a device to introduce a discussion of power.

If the analogy between money and power were confined to such offhand use, it would hardly merit scrutiny. Such is not the case. Serious and systematic use of the analogy as an analytical device was suggested and demonstrated by G. E. G. Catlin in *The Science and Method of Politics*.[2] His chapter entitled "The Process of Politics" is an extended comparison of the processes of political and economic exchange. Catlin believed that in the "attempt to reduce politics to the compass and system of that science which it

[1] J. David Singer, "Inter-Nation Influence: A Formal Model," *American Political Science Review*, 57 (1963), p. 420.

[2] G. E. G. Catlin, *The Science and Method of Politics* (New York: Alfred A. Knopf, 1927), pp. 206–79.

has long pretended to be, no subject is likely to prove more instructive for comparative study than that of economics."[3] He also believed that the key to progress in political science lay in the establishment of a political analogue for money:

> The *supreme difficulty* of a science of politics lies not so much in the establishment of a human constant, such as economics had in the "economic man," or in establishing analogues to the desire for consumption and the irksomeness of production, but in the establishment of a standard and unit of value. Without measurement physics, without money economics, could not have become sciences; both required first a numerical unit.[4]

It is clear that Catlin was not using the analogy between power and money casually. He wanted the comparison of economic and political processes to proceed on a serious and systematic basis.

Catlin's call for systematic development of the analogy between economics and politics has been renewed by Karl Deutsch and Talcott Parsons.[5] They see politics as a process of social exchange in which power plays a role similar to the role played by money in economic exchanges. Parsons conceives of political analysis as parallel to economic analysis "in the sense that a central place in it is occupied by a generalized medium involved in the political interaction process, which is also a 'measure' of the relevant values. [He conceives of] . . . power as such a generalized medium in a sense directly parallel in logical structure, though very different substantively, to money as the generalized medium of the

---

[3] Ibid., p. 206.

[4] Ibid., p. 251. (Italics mine.)

[5] Karl W. Deutsch, *The Nerves of Government* (New York: Free Press, 1963), pp. 116–27; Karl W. Deutsch, *The Analysis of International Relations*, 3rd edn (Englewood Cliffs, N.J.: Prentice-Hall, 1988), pp. 46–53; Talcott Parsons, "On the Concept of Influence," *Public Opinion Quarterly*, 27 (1963), pp. 37–62; Talcott Parsons, "On the Concept of Political Power," *Proceedings of the American Philosophical Society*, 107 (1963), pp. 232–62; Talcott Parsons, "Some Reflections on the Place of Force in Social Process," in *Internal War*, ed. Harry Eckstein (New York: Free Press, 1964), pp. 33–70; and Talcott Parsons, "The Political Aspect of Social Structure and Process," in *Varieties of Political Theory*, ed. David Easton (Englewood Cliffs, N.J.: Prentice-Hall, 1966), pp. 71–112. The conception of power as money is a late development in Parsons's thought. It represents a change from the conception of power that he employed prior to about 1960. See William C. Mitchell, *Sociological Analysis and Politics: The Theories of Talcott Parsons* (Englewood Cliffs, N.J.: Prentice-Hall, 1967), pp. 35–6; and Anthony Giddens, " 'Power' in the Recent Writings of Talcott Parsons," *Sociology*, 2 (1968), pp. 257–72.

economic process."[6] The extent to which Deutsch agrees with
Parsons is unclear. He does note, however, that the remarks on
power as a currency in *The Nerves of Government* are based on
collaboration between Parsons and himself.[7] The importance that
Parsons attached to the analogy is evident: "Perhaps the main
point of my analysis is the conception of political power as a
generalized medium of political process that parallels the role of
money in economic process."[8] Whatever one thinks about the
value of the analogy between money and power, one cannot
dismiss it by saying that Catlin, Deutsch, and Parsons did not
expect it to be taken seriously.

Another reason the analogy deserves serious attention is the
extravagance of the claims made on its behalf. William Mitchell
believes that Parsons' concept of power is a dramatic new usage
that is likely to generate considerable interest and controversy. He
sees Parsons as having "sponsored one of the most revolutionary
changes in recent political science."[9] Deutsch claims that Parsons
"has perhaps opened a path to a more fundamental reinterpretation
of power than has been possible since the days of Hobbes and
Locke."[10] Such claims as these indicate that close scrutiny of the
conception of power as money is in order. Let us not engage in
revolution until we have a firm idea as to the cause we are to fight
for and the weapons we are to fight with.

The following discussion will examine the Deutsch–Parsons
formulation of the analogy and other possible formulations. The
main questions to be asked are: Is the conception of power as
money compatible with other conceptions of power currently in
use by political scientists? What is the nearest political counterpart
for money? What is the nearest economic counterpart for power?
How much isomorphism is there in the power–money analogy?
How could the analogy be developed to make it more useful to
political scientists?

[6] Parsons, "Concept of Political Power," p. 234.
[7] Deutsch, *Nerves of Government*, p. 120.
[8] Parsons, "Political Aspect," p. 104.
[9] Mitchell, *Sociological Analysis*, pp. 87–90.
[10] Deutsch, *Nerves of Government*, p. 116.

COMPARING SUBSETS OF POWER

Robert Dahl has suggested that "power terms in modern social science refer to subsets of relations among social units such that the behaviors of one or more units . . . depend in some circumstances on the behavior of other units."[11] Noting that power so conceived spreads widely over the whole domain of human relations, he observes that students of power have tended to focus their attention on a few subsets of power relations. Given the ubiquity of power relations and the utility of the comparative method, it seems promising to compare one subset of power relations with another. This, in effect, is what Parsons and Deutsch are proposing. Parsons identifies a "family" of ways by which one social unit can get another social unit to behave in desired ways, and he proceeds to compare and contrast these mechanisms.[12] The labels he chooses for these "ways of getting results" – influence, power, money, and generalization of commitments – are unnecessarily confusing. Parsons' "ways of getting results" correspond closely to what Dahl might call "ways of exercising power." We should not, however, let Parsons' terminology obscure the fact that he is calling for a comparison of the subset of power relations (in Dahl's sense) associated with economic exchange and the subset of power relations associated with political exchange. The analogy between money and power invites us to search for political counterparts to money and economic counterparts to political power.

Purchasing power

An obvious candidate as an economic counterpart to political power is purchasing power. It is possible to conceive of purchasing power relations as a subset of those social relations in which A gets B to do something B would not otherwise do. The economists, who have conducted most of the discussions of purchasing power, have shown little interest in or awareness of the political science

[11] Robert A. Dahl, "Power," *International Encyclopedia of the Social Sciences*, 12 (New York: Free Press, 1968), p. 407.
[12] Parsons, "Concept of Influence," pp. 42–5.

literature on power. The conceptual apparatus developed for the analysis of political power, however, appears to be adequate for describing purchasing power. In fact, economists could probably benefit from using this apparatus more than they do.

Purchasing power can be considered as a subset of the power relations conceived by Dahl without distorting the conventional meaning of the term. Although rarely made explicit, the following perspectives are often implied in common usage:

1 *Purchasing power is a human relation.* Although we sometimes refer to it as "command over goods and services," this can be misleading. One can acquire goods without purchasing them, e.g., the person who acquires apples by picking them from a tree. A purchase, however, requires both a buyer and a seller. Robinson Crusoe could have neither political nor purchasing power until the arrival of Friday. Purchasing power is a relation in which A gets B to sell him or her something.

2 *Purchasing power is not money.* Although economists are prone to say that money *is* generalized purchasing power, this merely indicates a lack of interest in distinguishing between power and the bases of power. A comparable lack of interest is exhibited by the political scientist who carelessly refers to an army as power, thus blurring the distinction between power relations and power bases. The relation between money and purchasing power could be described in conventional power terminology as follows: Money is a power resource (power base or base value) that will very probably allow the possessor to exercise purchasing power that is generalized in scope and domain.[13] Such a definition makes "moneyness" a matter of degree, since probability, scope, and domain are all variable. The higher the probability and the wider the scope and domain, the more "moneyness" a given power base has.[14]

3 *Money is neither a necessary nor a sufficient condition for the*

[13] Cf. Harold D. Lasswell and Abraham Kaplan, *Power and Society* (New Haven, Conn.: Yale University Press, 1950), pp. 83–6.

[14] Defining money as a matter of degree is not unusual. Cf. Albert Gailord Hart, "Money," *International Encyclopedia of the Social Sciences*, vol. 10 (New York: Free Press, 1968), p. 426; Peter M. Blau, *Exchange and Power in Social Life* (New York: John Wiley, 1964), p. 269; and Kenneth E. Boulding, *Economic Analysis*, vol. 2, 4th edn (New York: Harper & Row, 1966), pp. 71–2.

exercise of purchasing power. Money does not guarantee the exercise of purchasing power. A blind deaf mute may find it difficult to exercise purchasing power no matter how much money he possesses. Like any other power resource, money is used with varying degrees of skill. Money is only one of many base values that can be used to exercise purchasing power. In some situations the following resources can serve almost as well: (a) an honest face, (b) personal acquaintance with the seller, (c) reputation for honesty, or (d) goods or services to barter. Lasswell and Kaplan have advised us of the crucial importance of recognizing that political power may rest on a variety of bases.[15] This advice applies to purchasing power as well.

4 *Purchasing power varies in scope, weight, and domain.*[16] Variations in the weight of purchasing power are evident to anyone who can tell a dollar from a dime, but variations in scope and domain are less obvious. Because money enables us to exercise generalized purchasing power so easily, we tend to forget about the limits on scope and domain. In our daily lives most of us, if we have the money, can buy whatever we want from whomever we want. We rarely think about the things outside the scope of the buying power of our money, such as (dare I say drugs?) atomic bombs, nerve gas, or certain kinds of friendship. Likewise, variations in domain are not very salient unless one travels abroad a great deal. He who tries to insert an American coin in a French vending machine will become keenly aware of variations in the domain of purchasing power. Like other kinds of power, purchasing power varies in scope, weight, and domain. If we are going to compare money with its political counterpart, we should be careful to specify these three dimensions of power.

The above discussion was designed to show that conceptions developed for analyzing political power, such as those suggested by Dahl, Lasswell, and Kaplan, can be used to analyze purchasing power as well. Purchasing power can plausibly be viewed as one of Dahl's subsets of power relations. It is this conception of purchasing power that will be used as a touchstone in the discussion that follows.

[15] Lasswell and Kaplan, *Power and Society*, p. 85.
[16] These terms are used in the sense Lasswell and Kaplan used them. Ibid., p. 73.

Power and exchange

The analogy of power and money is almost invariably linked with the conception of politics as an exchange process. This is not surprising since there is widespread agreement that the most important function of money is to facilitate economic exchange.[17] Exchange models of politics may well be the wave of the future,[18] but they are certainly not new in political analysis. Thomas Hobbes, John Locke, Edmund Burke, and others conceived politics as a kind of exchange between the rulers and the ruled. More recently, Catlin and Lasswell have suggested explicit comparisons between politics and the process of economic exchange.[19] Although Parsons and Deutsch help to focus our attention on the continuing nature of the exchange process, there would appear to be nothing very revolutionary about the use of a political exchange model.

There are, however, some important implications for power analysis in the comparison of the role money plays in economic exchange with the role power plays in political exchange. If there is one point on which most power theorists have come to agree, it is the utility of treating power as a relation rather than as a possession.[20] The failure to distinguish between power as a relation and the resources (base values or power bases) that may be used to bring about such a relation has been a source of great confusion in political science.[21] It has led to many fruitless discussions of such paradoxes as "the power of the powerless," "the powerlessness of the powerful," and so on. Those who think that it is useful to distinguish between power bases and power

[17] The following passage taken from a standard textbook is typical: "Money has but one fundamental purpose in an economic system: to facilitate the exchange of goods and services – to lessen the time and effort required to carry on trade." Lester V. Chandler, *The Economics of Money and Banking*, 3rd edn (New York: Harper, 1959), p. 2.

[18] See William C. Mitchell, "The Shape of Political Theory to Come: From Political Sociology to Political Economy," in *Politics and the Social Sciences*, ed. Seymour Martin Lipset (New York: Oxford University Press, 1969), pp. 105ff.

[19] Catlin, *Science*, pp. 206–79; Lasswell and Kaplan, *Power*, pp. 80–1.

[20] Dorwin Cartwright, "Influence, Leadership, Control," in *Handbook of Organizations*, ed. James March (Chicago: Rand McNally, 1965), p. 40.

[21] See Robert A. Dahl, *Modern Political Analysis*, 4th edn (Englewood Cliffs, N.J.: Prentice-Hall, 1984), pp. 21–2.

relations should be wary of the version of the power–money analogy propagated by Deutsch and Parsons, since it blurs this distinction.

Parsons has explicitly complained that Dahl's concept of power makes it logically impossible to treat power as a *"specific mechanism operating to bring about changes in the action of other units."*[22] Throughout Parsons' later writings on power one finds the conception of power as a "means," a "mechanism," or a "medium," that can be possessed and used in order to get things done. Power, for Parsons, is not a form of social interaction; it is a "generalized mechanism operating in social interaction."[23] It is not the *process* of A getting B to do something B would not otherwise do; it is merely one of several *means* by which A can affect the behavior of B.

This concept of power as a means rather than a relation is embedded in the analogy between power and money. Thus Parsons writes: "I conceive *power* to be a generalized symbolic medium which circulates much like money, the possession and use of which enables the responsibilities of an office with authority in a collectivity to be more effectively discharged."[24] And Deutsch suggests: "Just as money is the currency of economic life, so power can be thought of as the currency of politics. Here, power is the currency or medium that makes easy the exchange of more-or-less enforceable decisions for more-or-less dependable support."[25] It is rather easy to argue, as Deutsch does, that power is neither the center nor the essence of politics if one *defines* power as a specific mechanism instead of as a relation.[26] Now we see why it is so important to distinguish between money and purchasing power. Whereas purchasing power is a relation, money is but one of

---

[22] Parsons, "Concept of Political Power," p. 232.

[23] Parsons, "Concept of Influence," pp. 38–42. James S. Coleman indicates that he objected at first to "the analogy of influence to money, on the grounds that the term 'influence' refers to an effect, while the term 'money' refers to a medium by which this effect may be obtained." Coleman apparently abandoned this objection after reading the paper several times. He does not say why. James S. Coleman, "Comment on 'On the Concept of Influence,'" *Public Opinion Quarterly*, 27 (1963), p. 81. In a later article Coleman appears to have accepted the definition of power as a resource. See James S. Coleman, "Political Money," *American Political Science Review*, 64 (1970), pp. 1076–7.

[24] Parsons, "Political Aspect," p. 79.

[25] Deutsch, *International Relations*, p. 47.

[26] Deutsch, *Nerves of Government*, p. 124.

several means by which such a relation can be created. It is one thing to conceive of power as a *kind* of exchange; it is quite another to conceive of it as a *medium* of exchange. Those who define power as a relation may find it more useful to compare political power with purchasing power rather than with money.

Barter If political power is considered the counterpart of purchasing power, what is the political counterpart of money? If we are to find a political counterpart to money, we must first understand what money is; but we cannot understand what money *is* unless we know what money *does*. Sometimes woodpecker scalps are money; other times they are not. "Anyone who begins his study of money with the belief that there is some one thing that 'is by nature money' and that has been used as money at all times and in all places will find monetary history very disconcerting . . ."[27] There seems to be general agreement that, as a medium of exchange, money is that which differentiates barter transactions from other transactions. It would seem, then, that one's conception of the role of money as a medium of economic exchange will depend in part on one's conception of barter.

For most laymen and professional economists the prototype of a barter situation is a *direct* exchange of goods or services for goods or services when the parties to the exchange are the ultimate consumers of the goods and services involved.[28] When persons accept goods or services in trade not because they want to use (consume) them but because they can exchange them later for other goods or services they do want to use, indirect exchange has begun and pure barter has ceased.[29] Thus barter situations are matters of degree, depending upon the extent to which the parties involved perceive the objects being exchanged as symbols of the ability to exercise purchasing power. To the degree that an item being exchanged is viewed as such a symbol it has become money. "Moneyness" is also a matter of degree rather than of kind. Thus, in so far as we are considering only the medium-of-exchange

[27] Chandler, *Money and Banking*, p. 15.
[28] Cf. Boulding, *Economic Analysis*, vol. 1, p. 18.
[29] Cf. Blau, *Exchange and Power*, p. 268; and Max Weber, *The Theory of Social and Economic Organization*, trans. by A. M. Henderson and Talcott Parsons, and edited with an introduction by Talcott Parsons (New York: Free Press, 1964), pp. 177, 179, 202–3.

function of money, it is the degree to which an exchange is direct or indirect that determines whether we classify it as barter or as a monetary transaction.

If there is agreement among laymen and economists as to what constitutes barter, why belabor the point? Reiteration of the common conception of barter is necessary if we are to appreciate the extraordinary nature of the conception of barter in the writings of Deutsch and Parsons. For Deutsch and Parsons power at first appears to mediate political exchange, thus differentiating it from political barter, just as money mediates economic exchange, thus differentiating it from economic barter. The importance of this phenomenon is indicated by Parsons' observation that "a complex polity could not operate on a basis of political barter."[30] What is remarkable about their conception of barter is that it is defined not so much in terms of direct versus indirect exchange as in terms of *what* is being exchanged.

> As regards the political system, households may be considered in the most simple case as making *specific* demands upon the political system. They offer *specific* support to rulers who in turn use this support to make and enforce binding decisions of the kind desired by their supporters. Thus, in effect, *specific* support appears exchanged for dependable *specific* decisions, responsive to *specific* demands, in a political analogy to economic barter.
>
> In a slightly more extended case, however, the government may assume a *generalized* leadership role – it assumes *responsibility* – far beyond this or that particular decision; and the population may give it *general* political *loyalty* – that is, *generalized* political support and trust – to some extent regardless of the greater or lesser popularity of any one of the government's policies. For beyond the former political logrolling, or trading of favors, *generalized* support is asked for and given in terms of an only partly quantifiable "currency" of responsibility and loyalty.[31]

---

[30] Parsons, "Political Aspect," p. 90.

[31] Deutsch, *Nerves of Government*, pp. 118–19. (Italics added.) See Parsons, "Concept of Political Power," pp. 254–5; "Political Aspect," pp. 87, 90, 93, 98, 100. At times Parsons appears to see barter as direct exchange; see "Concept of Political Power," p. 256 and "Concept of Influence," pp. 40–2. One must distinguish, however, between the conception of barter that Parsons identifies and the one that he uses. Although he has defined barter as the direct exchange of one item of commodity or service for another

The crucial distinction here between barter and non-barter transactions is the specificity of the items being exchanged. If specific support is exchanged for specific policy decisions, political barter is occurring. If general support is exchanged for general responsibility for policy decisions, political monetization is occurring. The economic analogy would be to regard the exchange of one apple for one orange as barter but to regard the exchange of a truckload of assorted fruit for a boatload of miscellaneous items as a monetary transaction. According to the common conception, what Parsons and Deutsch call a monetary transaction would be nothing more than a "package deal" based on barter. Although few would deny the need in complex polities to have generalized support exchanged for generalized policy-making responsibility, it is not apparent whether such exchanges are or must be mediated by a political equivalent of money. Deutsch confuses the issue when he describes loyalty as a "currency." Loyalty *is* political support, not a symbol thereof. The crucial question, for most people, is whether the generalized support is exchanged *directly* for generalized policy-making responsibility or whether the exchange occurs *indirectly* through a symbolic medium akin to money.

Symbols of power   The moment item X is accepted in exchange not because of its "use value" but because of its "exchange value" item X has become to some degree a symbol, i.e., a thing that represents something else. Since every medium of exchange is symbolic in this sense, it is probably redundant to describe money as a symbolic medium of exchange. When something (shark's teeth, colored beads, dollar bills, bank checks, or whatever) comes to be widely accepted as a symbol of the ability to exercise generalized purchasing power, we call it money. To compare power with money is thus to suggest that power is a symbol just as money is a symbol. Here we confront a basic dilemma in the power–money analogy: are we to regard power as a symbol or as something to be symbolized?

["Concept of Political Power," p. 237], his usage of the term elsewhere implies that a direct exchange of a package of vaguely defined goods or services for another similar package would not be barter. It is the specificity of the items being exchanged that seems to matter for Parsons, not the directness of the exchange.

Parsons and Deutsch treat power as a symbol. For Parsons it symbolizes the capacity for effective collective action;[32] for Deutsch it symbolizes "the ability to change the distribution of results, and particularly the results of people's behavior."[33] Many political scientists may find this confusing. For them power is not a symbol of the ability to change the results; it *is* the ability to change results. It is not a symbol of A's ability to affect B's behavior; it *is* A's ability to do so.

There is a further source of confusion in Deutsch's treatment of the symbolic nature of power and money. This becomes apparent as soon as one introduces the distinction between symbols functioning in social processes and symbols used in inquiry into such processes.[34] We use the word "money" in inquiring into the role of those things (dollars, pounds, lira, woodpecker scalps, wampum, etc.) that actually function as symbols of purchasing power. The difference is that one can buy things with dollars, but one can buy nothing with the word "money." When Deutsch suggests that it is the word "power" that symbolizes the ability to change the distribution of results, he is unlikely to be disputed, since all words are symbols.[35] This suggestion, however, is not very helpful in understanding the power–money analogy. Are we to compare the word "power" with the word "money" or with those concrete symbols that actually function as money in the economic system? Like the word "money," the word "power" cannot be used to exercise power; it does not function in political processes; it is merely a symbol used in analyzing such processes. Although such semantic comparison may be useful, it is not the kind of comparison that is usually implied by the power–money analogy.

Ordinarily, those who suggest the analogy are interested in stimulating a search for symbols that perform functions in political exchange similar to those performed by (things called) money in economic exchanges. Those who undertake this search will find that the literature on political power has focused much attention on political symbols. The influential study by Lasswell

---

[32] Parsons, "Concept of Influence," p. 48.
[33] Deutsch, *International Relations*, p. 47.
[34] On this distinction, see Lasswell and Kaplan, *Power and Society*, pp. xviii–xix.
[35] Deutsch, *International Relations*, pp. 46–7.

and Kaplan viewed political interactions as "constituted by patterns of *influence* and *power*, manifested in and affected by *symbols*. . . ."[36] This does not mean, however, that such symbols resemble money.

In the process of using money to exercise purchasing power, the symbol of ability to exercise purchasing power changes hands. The person who has received money in an economic exchange can in turn use it to exercise purchasing power. Are there symbols of political power that can be similarly used as media of exchange to transfer political power from one person (or group) to another? I suggest that the nearest political counterpart of money is found in those symbols of legitimate political power, the possession and use of which allows one to exercise legitimate political power. Why *legitimate* political power? Because it is in this realm that widely accepted symbols are most often found. Indeed, the concept of "legitimacy" of the symbols of political power corresponds closely to the concept of "acceptability" (or liquidity) of the symbols of purchasing power.[37] The symbols of legitimate political power might include such things as titles (judge, senator, president, etc.), uniforms, badges, identification cards, official cars, votes, office space in public buildings, crowns, thrones, etc. Note that not all political symbols are included. Possession of an American flag may not allow one to exercise much political power. Possession of a police uniform, however, may well allow one to exercise political power even if one is not a policeman – at least for a while.

Although we are accustomed to thinking of money in terms of an exchange process, there is something disconcerting about viewing political symbols in a similar way. In what ways do these symbols function as media of exchange? One example would be the town representative who pins a sheriff's badge on John Wayne in a western movie, thus allowing Wayne to exercise legitimate political power. Similarly, the Amerian people, as the joint owners of all the official badges, buildings, vehicles, and titles, can be seen as giving these things to certain people as symbols of their support. The people to whom such symbolic support has been given can then use it to exercise legitimate political power. It is easier to think of

[36] Lasswell and Kaplan, *Power and Society*, p. 53.
[37] Cf. Parsons, "Concept of Political Power," p. 238; and Coleman, "Political Money," p. 1081.

voting as an exchange process, since we are accustomed to thinking of ourselves as "having a vote" and as "giving it to someone."
We are not, however, accustomed to thinking of ourselves as
owners of the White House who permit selected persons to live
there in exchange for the performance of certain services. The
process by which the people exchange symbols of legitimate
political power for performance of governmental functions has
become so bureaucratized that it is easy to lose sight of it. Evidence
of a basic residue of understanding of this exchange process,
though, is found in the irate driver caught speeding who reminds
the policeman who has stopped him that as a taxpayer he is in
some sense the policeman's employer.

In summary: (1) there is nothing revolutionary in the concept of
political exchange; (2) it is probably more useful to consider
power as a kind of exchange than to consider it as a medium of
exchange; (3) the conception of barter most likely to be helpful in
analyzing political exchange is that defined in terms of the
directness of exchange; (4) it is probably more useful to regard
power as a relation to be symbolized than to regard it as a symbol;
and (5) the nearest political equivalent of money is a set of symbols
of legitimate political power, the possession and use of which
facilitates the exercise of political power. To say that certain
symbols of legitimate political power are the closest political
counterparts to money is not to say that the similarities are great.
It may well be that the differences between these two kinds of
symbolic media are more interesting than the similarities. Let us
take a closer look at the degree to which the symbols of purchasing
power resemble those of political power.

HOW MUCH ISOMORPHISM?

Thus far we have been discussing money in terms of its role as a
medium of economic exchange. This neglect of the other functions
often attributed to money is typical of discussions based on the
power–money analogy. These other functions are: (1) measure of
value, (2) standard of deferred payments, and (3) store of value.
Since the last two are often treated as secondary functions of

money, their neglect is perhaps not so important.[38] To ignore the standard-of-value function of money, however, is to risk a gross misunderstanding of the basic nature of money. Almost everyone who has discussed the power–money analogy has alluded in one way or another to the difficulty of extending it to include the measure-of-value function of money. Some have regarded this difficulty as significant, while others have viewed it as a relatively minor discrepancy between power and money.

Measuring power

Although there is widespread agreement that purchasing power is easier to measure than political power, there is less agreement as to why this is true and what the implications are for the power–money analogy. Thus, Parsons argues that power is "directly parallel in logical structure" to money in its ability to function as both a medium of exchange and a measure of value.[39] A few pages later in the same article he notes that a "crucial difference" between money and power is that money can be measured in linear terms; whereas power measurement involves a quite different dimension which makes power harder to measure than money.[40] Deutsch tends to minimize the difference in the measurability of power and money by focusing attention on the fact that "like other currencies, power can be quantified, although far more imperfectly so."[41] The question that goes unanswered here is whether there is more significance for political scientists in the fact that power and money can both be quantified or in the fact that quantification is easier for money than for power. To clarify this question let us examine the origins of money, not in historical terms but in terms of the logic of the situation.

If there were no money, there would still be a number of resources (base values or power bases) that could be used to exercise purchasing power in direct exchange. These would include every commodity or service for which there is any demand.

---

[38] Cf. Chandler, *Money and Banking*, p. 5; and T. E. Gregory, "Money," *Encyclopedia of the Social Sciences*, vol. 9 (New York: Macmillan, 1937), p. 601.

[39] Parsons, "Concept of Political Power," p. 234.

[40] Ibid., p. 242.

[41] Deutsch, *Nerves of Government*, p. 120. See also, *International Relations*, p. 48.

Since there is no generally agreed upon standard of value, the price of every resource would theoretically have to be stated in terms of every other resource. Thus, if there were 500,000 resources, each one would have 499,999 different prices. Since this is extremely inconvenient, the invention of money is almost inevitable if exchange is to occur. One power base will be chosen to serve as a standard by which to measure the value of the other power bases. Their value will henceforth be treated as derivative rather than primary; and all power bases will be priced in terms of the primary power base, e.g., gold, beads, rice, or whatever. Once a standard of value has been established, a medium of exchange can emerge. The power resource selected as a medium of exchange need not be the same as that selected as a standard of value, but it must be measurable in terms of a power resource that is a standard of value.[42] Viewed from this perspective, the standard-of-value function of money is not just another function of money; it is a prerequisite to performance of the medium-of-exchange function. The implications for the power–money analogy are significant. To say that power is like money except for the lack of standardized measuring rod for power is to put oneself in a rather awkward position: if the two characteristics in terms of which money is defined are its ability to function first as a medium of exchange, and second as a standard of value, and if these functions are highly interdependent, it is difficult to see how power can be regarded as similar to money if it is severely deficient in its ability to perform one of these functions.[43] Deutsch's treatment of the measurement problem is illustrative:

[42] Cf. Talcott Parsons and Neil J. Smelser, *Economy and Society* (London: Routledge & Kegan Paul, 1956), pp. 140–1; Roy Harrod, *Money* (London: Macmillan, 1969), p. 4; D. H. Robertson, *Money*, 4th edn (Cambridge: Cambridge University Press, 1948), p. 3; Weber, *Social and Economic Organization*, p. 179; Gregory, "Money," pp. 601–3; and Boulding, *Economic Analysis*, vol. 2, pp. 68–9.

[43] Parsons's analogy between language and money can also be used to illustrate the high degree of interdependence between these two functions of money. He compares the medium-of-exchange function with message transmission and the measure-of-value function with the code used to give meaning to the message. Both are obviously necessary for communication. See "Concept of Influence," pp. 38–9. Although Ilchman and Uphoff recognize the absence of a common denominator of political value, they underestimate the far-reaching implications of this lack for their analysis. See Warren F. Ilchman and Norman Thomas Uphoff, *The Political Economy of Change* (Berkeley and Los Angeles: University of California Press, 1969), pp. 54–5.

Like other currencies, power can be quantified, although far more
imperfectly so. Power cannot be counted exactly, but it can be
estimated in proportion to the power resources or capabilities that
are visibly available, such as the numbers of countable supporters,
voters, or soldiers available or required in a particular political
context.[44]

Likewise, one could say that prior to the invention of money,
purchasing power could not be measured exactly, but could be
estimated in terms of a variety of power resources. This was
precisely the situation that the invention of money was designed to
eliminate. The point of inventing money is to make measurement
of purchasing power easy by eliminating the need to express
purchasing power in terms of 499,999 resources. *To say that
power is like money except for the lack of a standardized measure
of power is to say that the problem of measuring political power is
very much like the problem of measuring purchasing power in an
economy without money.*

If political scientists are to benefit from comparing the measurement of purchasing power with the measurement of political
power, we must understand *why* one is easier to count than the
other. To attribute this to some "peculiar property"[45] of political
power is not very helpful. Parsons explains the relative difficulty of
measuring political power in terms of an inherent quality that he
calls "the hierarchical aspect of power systems."[46] This line of
argument leads us to think that purchasing power has always been
easier to measure than political power because the peculiar nature
of political power makes it inherently harder to quantify.
Purchasing power, however, has not always been easier to
measure than political power. The Almighty did not create a
standardized measuring rod for purchasing power at the time He
or she created life. People had to invent their own measure of value.
Prehistoric people may even have found political power easier to

[44] Deutsch, *Nerves of Government*, p. 120. Although Deutsch makes a similar point in
International Relations (p. 48), he seems more cautious about stressing the similarities
between money and power in this book.

[45] Mitchell, *Sociological Analysis*, p. 90.

[46] See Parsons, "Concept of Political Power," pp. 242–8; "Political Aspect," p. 79; and
Mitchell, *Sociological Analysis*, p. 90.

measure, i.e., widespread agreement on physical strength as the measure of political power but relatively little agreement on a standard by which to measure purchasing power. The base values of political power are no harder to count than the base values of purchasing power. It is just as easy to count soldiers, tanks, votes, and official badges as it is to count pigs, dollars, woodpecker scalps, and gold. What differentiates money from the other resources of purchasing power is not its countability but rather the widespread *consensus* that the value of other resources should be expressed in terms of this particular resource. Purchasing power is easy to measure because men have agreed upon a standardized measuring rod; political power is difficult to measure because men have not so agreed. In short, the difficulty of measuring political power is due to the absence of something that fulfills the measure-of-value function of money.

One may agree that there is no standard unit of account similar to money in the political realm but deny that it matters. Does recognition of the absence of a generally accepted measure of political value draw attention to aspects of politics that are worth looking into? This recogntion can be valuable in at least three ways:

1 Those who would study the media of political exchange cannot afford to ignore the measure-of-value function of money. Peter Blau describes the development of a generally valid measure of comparative value as "the crucial problem of indirect exchange."[47] Anything that cannot easily be expressed in terms of a standardized unit of account is likely to be severely limited in the extent to which it can serve as a medium of exchange.

2 Awareness of the lack of a standard of political value can help us to understand the state of the discipline of political science. It was not without reason that Catlin singled out the absence of

---

[47] "The crucial problem of indirect exchange is that of a generally valid measure of comparative value. The cost a man is willing to incur for an object he wants to use in trade depends on his estimate of what it is worth to others, not on its subjective worth to himself, as would be the case were he only interested in using it himself. For men to make such estimates realistically, there must be universal agreement in a community on a standard of value in terms of which diverse products and services can be compared. A universalistic standard of value, into which the worth of the different products of labor can be translated, serves as a medium of exchange" (Blau, *Exchange and Power*, p. 268). See also, Weber, *Social and Economic Organization*, pp. 179, 202–11.

such a measuring rod as "the supreme difficulty of a science of politics."[48] When Parsons invites us to view political analysis as parallel to economic analysis in the sense that "a central place in it is occupied by a generalized medium involved in the political interaction process, which is also a 'measure' of the relevant values,"[49] he is obscuring one of the most important differences between economics and political science. One of the fundamental reasons why political analysis is so enormously difficult is the *absence* of a "generalized medium involved in the political interaction process, which is also a 'measure' of the relevant values."[50] Lasswell and Kaplan were especially concerned about the consequences of a failure to realize that political power was tied to particular power bases and could not be expressed in terms of a "unitary conception of power."[51] They warned: "Failure to recognize that power may rest on various bases, each with a varying scope, has confused and distorted the conception of power itself, and retarded inquiry into the conditions and consequences of its exercise in various ways."[52] Purchasing power also rests on various bases, but it does not matter so much, since economists can convert the potential purchasing power of each base into a common denominator. The power–money analogy can be helpful if it stimulates awareness of the similarities between barter and political exchange, but the analogy can be harmful if it tempts us to single out a particular base value in terms of which to express the value of the others. If there is no general agreement on a measure of political value, it would be folly to pretend that there is.

3   Recognition that political exchange occurs under conditions that are more akin to barter than to the sophisticated markets of a

[48] Catlin, *Science*, p. 251.

[49] Parsons, "Concept of Political Power," p. 234.

[50] William Mitchell seems to agree that it is useful to focus attention on the difference between money and its political analogues. Contrary to the above interpretation, however, he sees Parsons' approach as helping to produce this focus. See Mitchell, *Sociological Analysis*, pp. 87–93.

[51] Lasswell and Kaplan, *Power and Society*, p. 92.

[52] Ibid., p. 85. On the difficulty of analyzing power without a satisfactory common denominator to which different forms of power can be reduced, see also Robert A. Dahl and Charles E. Lindblom, *Politics, Economics, and Welfare* (New York: Harper & Row, 1953), pp. 228–9.

modern money economy can lead us to ask a number of theoretically provocative questions. Why are the media of political exchange not more like money? Under what conditions might one expect generalized media of political exchange to emerge? Would it be desirable to have media of political exchange that were more like money? What are the consequences of using relatively primitive media of political exchange?[53] These questions and others like them are unlikely to be asked by those who focus only on the similarities between the media of political and economic exchange and neglect the differences.

Scope and domain

One important consequence of a standardized measure of economic value is that economists need not be so careful as political scientists must be in specifying the scope and domain of power relations. Whereas economists rarely bother to specify the scope and domain of purchasing power, Dahl and Lasswell both have warned that it is practically meaningless for a political scientist to discuss power without reference to these two dimensions of power.[54] Economists can compare the purchasing power of diverse goods and services simply by converting them into the common denominator of money. Money may be thought of as different from other resources primarily in its higher degree of liquidity.[55] This "liquidity" is a function of (1) time, (2) scope, and (3) domain. In other words, the difference between money and other resources is that with money one can buy a greater variety of things from more people more quickly. Because money is so generalized in scope and domain and because the value of most goods and services can be expressed in monetary terms, economists can ignore scope and domain and get away with it – at least most of the time.[56]

[53] Mitchell's *Sociological Analysis* (pp. 87–93) contains some very interesting speculation on the implications of the absence of a political analogue to money. He suggests that there is a significant degree of uncertainty in political calculation that is due to the absence of a standardized measure of political values.

[54] Dahl, "Power," p. 408; Lasswell and Kaplan, *Power and Society*, p. 76.

[55] Cf. Blau, *Exchange and Power*, p. 269; and Boulding, *Economic Analysis*, vol. 2, pp. 70–2.

[56] For an example of a case in which failure to specify the scope and domain of the

The media of political exchange, however, seem to be much more limited in scope and domain than the media of economic exchange. The authority of policemen is usually quite narrow in terms of scope and domain. Even the chief executive's powers are relatively circumscribed in Western democracies. There is no "general purpose" currency that can be used to exercise political power of generalized scope and domain. In economic exchange one man's money is as good as the next man's, but in politics the symbols of power are more closely tied to particular contexts.

Parsons' contention that complex polities cannot operate without generalized media of political exchange may be similar to the pessimistic theorizing on the flight capabilities of the bumblebee. Media as generalized as money may be neither necessary nor desirable in complex polities. One suspects that relatively narrow limits on the scope and domain of the symbols of legitimate political power may be important safeguards of limited government. In a totalitarian political system the right political symbol – say, membership in the ruling party – will allow one to exercise generalized political power in a vast number of situations – in homes, at parties, in stores, and on the street. But in constitutional political systems the symbols of legitimate political power are not generalized; instead they permit the exercise of power only within narrowly specified limits. Let us not be hasty in describing this "inefficiency" in the political exchange process as undesirable; perhaps we would not want a political equivalent to money even if we could get it.[57]

Gold and force

Both Deutsch and Parsons have suggested that the power–money analogy be expanded to include the proposition that physical force is to power as gold is to paper money. This is a dangerous undertaking, since it involves singling out one of the most frequent sources of confusion in political analysis (the role of force) for

purchasing power of money had serious consequences for public policy, see my discussion of soft loans and American foreign policy: David A. Baldwin, *Economic Development and American Foreign Policy: 1943–1962* (Chicago: University of Chicago Press, 1966).

[57] For a study that treats the lack of a political analogue for money as a "defect" in the political exchange system, see Coleman, "Political Money."

comparison with a recurrent source of confusion in monetary analysis (the role of gold). The basic rationale of an analogy is to clarify the unfamiliar by comparing it with that which is clearly understood. Comparison of one popular fallacy with another may only compound confusion.

There are two analytical pitfalls that are particularly dangerous when comparing gold with force. One is to treat them as the ultimate measuring rods of economic and political value; and the other is to assume a fixed systemic role for each. Just as popular political discussion often assumes that political power ultimately comes from a gun barrel, so popular economic discussion is prone to assume that the purchasing power of money is ultimately based on gold. Such reasoning usually grows out of a belief that force is the most intrinsically effective political power base and that gold is the most intrinsically effective purchasing power base. This kind of argument is anathema to most economists. For example:

> Popular economic discussion often assumes that things have an intrinsic worth. As soon as we perceive the truth of . . . [the "law of diminishing marginal utility"], however, it becomes clear that what a thing is worth to us depends on how much of it we have, and that therefore the worth is not anything *in* a commodity. It is not a physical property of an object like weight or volume, but is simply how we feel about it. Things are valuable because somebody thinks they are, and for no other reason whatever. This is true, as we shall see, even of gold – a commodity which people are inclined to think has an *intrinsic value*. Gold, like everything else, is valuable only because people think it is.[58]

It is the attitudes of people, not the intrinsic properties of gold and force, that determine their social role. In some societies, gold and force are very liquid assets, i.e., they are readily convertible into other assets; in other societies they are less liquid. There is nothing intrinsically valuable about gold – as King Midas learned.

Parsons' discussions of gold and force are likely to encourage thinking in terms of intrinsic worth. When he speaks of the value

---

[58] Boulding, *Economic Analysis*, vol. 1, p. 23. Cf. Thomas C. Schelling, *The Strategy of Conflict* (Cambridge, Mass.: Harvard University Press, 1960), pp. 92–4.

of money as grounded in the value of gold,[59] of gold as the "rock bottom" of economic security,[60] and of gold and force as the ultimate symbolic bases of security of the value of money and power, respectively,[61] Parsons risks seriously confusing his readers. He goes on, moreover, to compare the grounding of the value of money in gold with the grounding of the value of power in physical force, which he regards as the "most intrinsically effective of all means of coercion."[62] Regardless of Parsons's intended meaning, his readers may be forgiven if they understand him to be saying that gold is the most intrinsically effective means of exercising purchasing power, just as force is the most intrinsically effective means of exercising political power.

Although Parsons at times rejects the idea that gold is the ultimate determinant of the value of money (and correspondingly that force is the ultimate determinant of power), at other times he seems to embrace it. This ambivalence is illustrated by his suggestion that there are two directions in which one can pursue the answer to the question: "On what basis does the 'value of money' rest?"[63] These two directions lead to the conclusion that the value of money is determined, in the first case, by the value of the monetary metal backing it up and, in the second case, by the general confidence in the productivity of the economic system.[64] Parsons' treatment of these two kinds of explanation implies that both are intellectually respectable, even though the monetary metal version "does not tell quite the whole story."[65] He implies that the portion of the story it does tell is correct but incomplete. Most economists, however, would regard explanations of the

[59] Parsons, "Concept of Political Power," pp. 237, 240. Max Weber's discussions of money and monetary metals are also likely to bewilder a contemporary reader. See Weber, *Social and Economic Organization*, pp. 173–81, 280–309.

[60] Parsons, "Concept of Influence," p. 46.

[61] Parsons, "Reflections on the Place of Force," p. 69.

[62] Parsons, "Concept of Political Power," pp. 238, 240. See also Parsons's discussion of the intrinsic qualities of gold and force in "Concept of Influence," pp. 48–9. Parsons usually places the word "intrinsic" in quotation marks, leaving the reader to wonder whether he really means it. On Parsons's habit of using quotation marks in this way, see Coleman, "Comment," p. 81.

[63] Parsons, "Reflections on the Place of Force," pp. 43–4.

[64] Ibid., pp. 43–8. A similar difficulty is found in Coleman, "Political Money," pp. 1074–6, 1080–1.

[65] Parsons, "Reflections on the Place of Force," p. 44.

value of money in terms of the value of gold not merely as incomplete, but as incorrect. When economists refer to the belief that gold determines the value of money, they usually depict it as one of several discredited or erroneous beliefs on this subject.[66] On the basis of his dual explanation of the value of money, Parsons observes that "the question of whether it [force] is or is not the 'basis' of power is ambiguous in a sense exactly parallel to that of the question of 'basing' the value of money on command of gold reserves."[67] In the eyes of most economists, however, it is not ambiguous to say that monetary value is based on gold; rather, it is wrong. Although Parsons may not intend to argue that gold and force are the ultimate determinants of economic and political power, he is certainly ambivalent on the issue. Given the widespread misunderstanding of both gold and force, such ambivalence is likely to do more harm than good.

The second pitfall to be avoided in comparing gold with force is the assumption of a fixed social role for each. Although Deutsch and Parsons frequently say that the role of force on political systems is parallel to the role of gold in economic systems, it is not clear what this means. It is obvious that they view force as occupying a special place in political systems comparable to the special place that they think gold occupies in economic systems; but precisely what is this special place, and why is it occupied by gold and force?[68] Apparently, they see gold and force as the most intrinsically effective bases of purchasing and political power. As such, they are usually held in reserve and used only in "showdown" situations. In such situations the ultimate weapons of gold and force are brought into action as "damage-control mechanisms."[69] Just as governments will often use force to bolster confidence in their political power, so they will also use gold to bolster confidence in the purchasing power of money.

Although one could dispute the particular social roles attributed by Deutsch and Parsons to gold and force – e.g., Parsons'

---

[66] See, for example, Chandler, *Money and Banking*, p. 24; and Hart, "Money," p. 431.

[67] Parsons, "Reflections on the Place of Force," p. 47.

[68] See Parsons, "Concept of Political Power," pp. 237–40; "Reflections on the Place of Force," p. 48; and "Concept of Influence," p. 47. Parsons usually thanks Deutsch for having called his attention to the similarities between gold and force.

[69] Deutsch, *Nerves of Government*, pp. 122–3.

contention that gold provides the base upon which a complex credit structure is erected[70] – such disputes would matter less than the overall assumption that the social roles of gold and force are unchanging. From the writings of Deutsch and Parsons one gets the impression that there is some generally shared conception of "the role of gold in economic systems" and "the role of force in political systems." When Parsons talks about the role of gold in "the 'normal' circumstances of monetary transactions,"[71] we are apparently expected to know what he means. In discussing gold, Deutsch and Parsons seem to have in mind one of the roles played by gold in certain economic systems for a few years before the Second World War. Gold has played several roles in economic systems, and these roles have never been fixed.[72] Contemporary students will find it hard to reconcile the discussion of gold and force by Deutsch and Parsons with Samuelson's observations that metallic backing for money has no real meaning any more, that gold ceased to be legal tender in America in 1933, that it would be illegal for an American to use gold to pay a debt even if he wanted to, and that gold is not even one of the components of the US money supply, let alone the most effective component.[73] When Parsons and Deutsch tell us that the role of force in political systems is parallel to the role of gold in monetary systems, we are entitled to ask: Which role of gold? In which monetary systems? During which period of history? Similar questions could also be asked concerning force. The social roles of gold and force do not grow out of their intrinsic nature; they grow out of social attitudes toward gold and force, attitudes that vary in space and time.

Whether or not Deutsch and Parsons have avoided falling into the analytical pitfalls described above, it is difficult to deny that they have led others dangerously near the edge. The gold-and-

[70] Parsons, "Reflections on the Place of Force," p. 44.

[71] Ibid.

[72] On the evolutionary nature of the role of gold in monetary systems, see Robert Triffin, *Our International Monetary System: Yesterday, Today, and Tomorrow* (New York: Random House, 1968); and Gregory, "Money," pp. 605–8.

[73] Paul A. Samuelson, *Economics*, 8th edn (New York: McGraw-Hill, 1969), pp. 259–61. Compare Deutsch's claim that gold is "the power to purchase in its most tangible form" (*International Relations*, p. 48) with Boulding's observation that most people "would never think of going down to the store with a bag of gold dust, and it would be most doubtful whether they could buy anything with it if they did" (*Economic Analysis*, vol. 2, p. 72).

force analogy, as presented by Deutsch and Parsons, is a step backward in the analysis of power. One of the most important contributions of Lasswell and Kaplan was to impress upon political scientists the crucial importance of recognizing that power may rest on various bases and that there is no primary power base from which all the others can be achieved.[74] The gold-and-force analogy tempts us to become preoccupied with a single power base, to treat it as pre-eminent, and to treat others as derived from it. This temptation, together with the widespread popular misunderstanding of both force and gold, suggests the need to search for more fruitful ways to develop the power–money analogy.

Does isomorphism matter?

Although isomorphism does matter, it is a mistake to attribute the value of the power–money analogy to the similarities between money and the symbols of power. In science the value of an analogy depends on the extent of "actual structural correspondence between the two systems from which the analogy is drawn."[75] It is thus the isomorphism between political and economic systems that matters, not that between money and power. To focus on money is to focus on the single most important *difference* between political and economic systems, i.e., the fact that only the latter has a generalized medium of exchange that also serves as a standardized measure of value. One of the most valuable services the analogy between politics and economics can render to political scientists is clear identification of this difference. In comparing political with economic processes we may find the differences as interesting as the similarities.

THE "ZERO-SUM PROBLEM"

In developing his version of the power–money analogy Parsons claims to have solved something he calls "the famous zero-sum

[74] Lasswell and Kaplan, *Power and Society*, esp. pp. 83–94.
[75] Deutsch, *Nerves of Government*, p. 78.

problem."[76] In evaluating the significance of Parsons' work for political scientists William Mitchell sees revolutionary implications in his treatment of this problem.[77] The "zero-sum problem" stems from an alleged tendency in the literature on power to assume that "there is a fixed 'quantity' of power in any relational system and hence any gain of power on the part of A must by definition occur by diminishing the power at the disposal of other units, B, C, D. . . ."[78] Whereas the dominant tendency in the literature on power has been to treat it as a fixed quantity to be divided up, Parsons has challenged this unquestioned assumption about the nature of power.[79] This "orthodox" view of power as a zero-sum phenomenon is attributed to Dahl, Lasswell, and Kaplan.[80] There are, of course, many political scientists who have treated power as a quantifiable mass to be divided among rival claimants; but it is surprising to find Dahl, Lasswell, and Kaplan among them. In the struggle to replace the conception of power as a quantifiable mass with the conception of power as a relation they are usually considered leaders.

If Parsons' version of the power–money analogy is incompatible with the basic concept of power developed by Dahl, Lasswell, and Kaplan, the implications could indeed be revolutionary. Before storming the barricades, however, let us ask whether Dahl, Lasswell, and Kaplan really do have a zero-sum conception of the nature of power.[81] For them power relations refer to situations in which one person or group affects a specified aspect of the behavior of another person or group. One has not defined a power relation until one has specified both scope and domain.[82] Thus, as long as Robinson Crusoe and Friday have separate islands, neither

---

[76] Parsons, "Concept of Political Power," p. 258.

[77] Mitchell, *Sociological Analysis*, pp. 89–90.

[78] Parsons, "Concept of Political Power," pp. 232–3.

[79] Mitchell, *Sociological Analysis*, pp. 89–90.

[80] Parsons, "Concept of Influence," p. 60; "Concept of Political Power," pp. 232–3, 250–1; "Political Aspect," pp. 99–100. Parsons also attributes the zero-sum assumption to V. O. Key and C. Wright Mills. I have not examined their writings to determine the accuracy of this claim.

[81] Parsons refers to the works of Dahl, Lasswell, and Kaplan, but never identifies specific pages or passages. The sole exception is his reference to chapter 5 of the first edition of Dahl's *Modern Political Analysis*.

[82] Lasswell and Kaplan, *Power and Society*, pp. 75–6; and Dahl, *Modern Political Analysis*, p. 27.

has any political power. When Friday comes to live on Robinson Crusoe's island, either or both may gain political power, but neither can lose what he does not have. Since Dahl, Lasswell, and Kaplan could describe such situations as increases in the power of either (or both), their conception of power cannot be said to involve the assumption that one person's gain in power is always offset by another person's loss. Parsons seems to have overlooked the fact that Dahl, Lasswell, and Kaplan do not consider control over one's own behavior as political power; thus, a loss of individual autonomy is not tantamount to a loss of political power. The Dahl–Lasswell–Kaplan conception of power also permits us to describe situations in which A's ability to get B to do X increases *simultaneously* with B's ability to get A to do X. If Robinson Crusoe handcuffs himself to Friday, he may increase his ability to affect Friday's movements; but he also increases Friday's ability to affect his (Crusoe's) movements. Similarly, the United States military involvement in Vietnam increased not only American ability to affect Vietnamese policy but also Vietnamese ability to affect American policy. The assumption that an increase in one person's political power is always offset by a decrease in another person's political power is not inherent in the conception of power put forth by Dahl, Lasswell, and Kaplan. The claim that Parsons' solution of the zero-sum problem heralds a revolution in political science appears exaggerated, for Parsons has "solved" a problem that does not exist.

DEVELOPING THE ANALOGY: SPECULATION

Although the power–money analogy is not new, systematic development of it has not proceeded very far. A few of the more promising lines of development may now be surveyed in the hope of stimulating further investigation.[83]

---

[83] Useful suggestions for developing the analogy are found in Coleman, "Comment," pp. 77–80; Coleman, "Political Money," pp. 1082–7; Deutsch, *Nerves of Government*, pp. 125–7; Mitchell, *Sociological Analysis*, pp. 95–7; and Ilchman and Uphoff, *Political Economy*.

1   *Political banking.* Perhaps the most provocative suggestion for expanding the analogy is Parsons' comparison of the process by which banks create money with the process by which power is generated in a polity.[84] He compares lending support to a political group (e.g., by joining it or voting for it) to depositing money in a bank. Just as banks can safely lend out part of the money deposited with them without specific authorization from depositors, so political groups can lend out part of the power deposited with them without specific authorization. Political leaders can thus increase the amount of power in a polity just as bankers can increase the amount of money in an economy. One consequence of this power creation, however, is that, like bankers, politicians will be unable to meet all their obligations instantaneously. This illiquidity presents no problem for either politicians or bankers as long as the psychological atmosphere within which transactions occur remains relatively stable. If it is disturbed, however, there may be a confidence crisis that will start a rush to withdraw deposits of money and/or power.

The politics–banking analogy must be developed with extreme care. Describing the process by which banks create money is not easy, as anyone who has ever tried to explain it to undergraduates will testify. Both Coleman and Deutsch have damaged the analogy while attempting to improve it. They have fallen victim to the common fallacy of assuming that banks lend more money than has been deposited with them.[85] In fact, no bank could or would allow its outstanding loans to exceed its total deposits. Banks can create money only if the money they lend is redeposited in the banking system. Thus, assuming a 20 percent reserve requirement, an initial deposit of $10 million can lead to $40 million in new loans *only* if each loan is redeposited in a bank. At the end of the money-creation process the banking system will show total loans outstanding of $40 million, but it will also show total deposits of $50 million. This is not a trivial point. Just as banks cannot lend money that has not been deposited with them, so political groups

[84] Parsons, "Concept of Influence," pp. 59–62; "Concept of Political Power," pp. 250–7; "Political Aspect," pp. 90–104. See also, Deutsch, *Nerves of Government*, pp. 120–1; and *International Relations*, pp. 43–4.
[85] Coleman, "Comment," p. 72; Deutsch, *Nerves of Government*, p. 121; and *International Relations*, p. 49.

cannot lend support they do not have. Just as loan recipients must have enough confidence in the banking system to redeposit their loan funds, so recipients of political support must have enough confidence in the system to redeposit it; otherwise, the process of creating political or financial credit comes to a halt. The expansion of such credit depends on the existence of an atmosphere of mutual trust and confidence. Parsons has performed a valuable service in calling our attention to the importance of expectations and the linkages between them and the political process.

2 *Inflation and deflation.* The phenomena of inflation and deflation should not be confused with the related but analytically distinguishable phenomena of credit expansion and contraction. Creating money is inflationary only if it changes the purchasing power of money. If the goods and services on the market expand simultaneously with the increase in money, there will be no inflation (*ceteris paribus*). Similarly, an increase in the number of symbols of legitimate political power results in political inflation only if it decreases the amount of power that each symbol allows one to exercise; e.g., if everyone walked around dressed in a policeman's uniform, real policemen would find themselves the victims of political inflation; but if the increase in the number of people wearing police uniforms increased at the same rate as the population, the power of each policeman might remain stable.

Investigation of the analogies between political and economic inflation and deflation is hampered by the fact that we have so many definitions of the terms. The *International Encyclopedia of the Social Sciences*, for example, defines inflation as a fall and deflation as a rise in the purchasing power of money, but it then proceeds to offer four additional definitions.[86] The existence of several definitions makes more precise definitions imperative in the search for political counterparts to inflation and deflation. In particular, it is important to distinguish between definitions and empirical observations. In Parsons' writings, for example, it is clear that economic and political deflation are likely to culminate in the use of gold and force, respectively, but it is not clear whether

[86] M. Bronfenbrenner, "Inflation and Deflation," *International Encyclopedia of the Social Sciences*, vol. 7 (New York: Free Press, 1968), pp. 289–90. The definition of inflation as a fall in purchasing power of money is employed in the previous paragraph.

40   *Money and Power*

this is true by definition or by observation.[87] Also, the distinction between power (purchasing or political) and the symbols thereof must be especially clear in analyses of inflation or deflation, since most definitions agree that these terms are supposed to focus attention on the relation between purchasing power and its symbols.

Another definition of inflation/deflation which may be useful to political scientists is as follows: Inflation is a condition in which too much money chases too few goods; and, conversely, deflation is a condition in which too many goods chase too little money.[88] Rather than focusing on whether the purchasing power of money has gone up or down, this definition focuses on whether the amount of purchasing power of money is adequate in terms of a postulated standard of social desirability. One could use this conception of deflation to describe such situations as: (a) Scarcity of generalized media of economic exchange (money). This might be applied to situations in which lack of money necessitated reliance on barter, thus slowing the transaction flow to an undesirable degree. (b) Scarcity of generalized media of political exchange (symbols of legitimate political power). This might be used to explain either why revolutions[89] occur or why world government does not. In both cases political exchange is hampered by the lack of agreement on a common standard of political value that can be used as a medium of exchange. As long as people disagree as to whether legitimacy should be accorded to the wealthy, the clever, the strong, the ideologically correct, or the side with the most votes, no generally acceptable medium of exchange is likely to emerge; and the rate at which political transactions flow is likely to be undesirably slow.

The inflation/deflation comparison could also be extended to sub-types of these phenomena. Creeping and runaway inflation are radically different phenomena, as are recessions and depressions. It is sometimes suggested that the extremes of hyper-inflation and deep depression resemble each other in some ways. It might be

---

[87] This definitional difficulty is also reflected in Chalmers Johnson, *Revolutionary Change* (Boston: Little-Brown, 1966), pp. 28–30, 69, 91.

[88] This is one of the additional definitions offered by Bronfenbrenner, "Inflation and Deflation," p. 290.

[89] See Johnson's *Revolutionary Change* for an imaginative exploration along these lines.

worthwhile to ask whether this applies to the political counterparts of these phenomena.[90]

3 *Employment levels.* Another direction in which to develop the analogy is to search for political equivalents of the degree to which economic resources are productively employed in an economy. Mitchell has contributed a number of suggestions looking toward this end including the possibility of a political counterpart to business cycles.[91]

Questions concerning the optimum level of political employment could be especially interesting. Although the prevailing view is that full employment is desirable in the economy, it is not at all clear that this would apply to the polity. Perhaps such a focus could lead to new ways of looking at such problems as limited government and totalitarianism. One hypothesis to be considered, for example, is that constitutional government requires maintenance of equilibrium at levels of political resource use that are well below full employment.

4 *Investment and saving.* Deutsch has suggested that, like money, power can be saved, spent on consumption, or invested.[92] Two focuses for research on this topic are: (a) Under what conditions do people choose to spend power resources on consumption instead of saving them? (b) Under what conditions are people willing to tie up their savings of power resources in long-term investment instead of keeping them in liquid form? The concept of "liquidity" in economics bears some similarity to that of "power potential" in political science. A liquid power resource would be one that could readily be used to exercise power, whereas it would be more difficult to realize the power potential of an illiquid power resource. Power potential, like liquidity, is a matter of degree. Economists have identified three primary motives for holding money: the transactions motive refers to the need to smooth out irregularities in the conduct of day-to-day business; the speculative motive refers to benefits of "being ready when the time is right"; and the precautionary motive refers to a

---

[90] On this point see Ilchman and Uphoff, *Political Economy*, pp. 136–59.

[91] Mitchell, *Sociological Analysis*, pp. 81, 86, 95, 133–6.

[92] Deutsch, *International Relations*, pp. 50–2.

desire to mitigate uncertainty.[93] Discovery of political counterparts for these motives could be very interesting.

5 *Uncertainty and risk.* In one sense money is a device for reducing uncertainty in an economic system. Barter exchange necessitates a "double coincidence of wants." This is basically an information scarcity problem in the sense that it arises from the difficulty ·of answering the question, "How do I identify the persons who want what I have and who have what I want?" Money makes it possible to concentrate on finding those who have what one wants and allows one to assume with confidence that they will accept money in payment. Just as money helps us identify those who have purchasing power, so uniforms, titles, and identification cards help us to identify those who have political power. There is, after all, a certain utility in being able to reduce uncertainty as to whether the man standing in an intersection waving his arms is a policeman or a drunk.

Little attention has been devoted to the role of uncertainty in political systems. Mitchell suggests that the absence of a close political counterpart to money means that the level of uncertainty in the polity will be significantly higher than in the economy.[94] Does this matter? How can uncertainty be reduced? Would its reduction be desirable? How is uncertainty distributed in the political system? Answers to these and other questions could be generated by comparing economic and political exchange processes.

6 *Byways of economics.* Political scientists may be well advised to avoid the main road of sophisticated econometrics and advanced economic theory and to concentrate instead on some less traveled roads to economic understanding. Two areas that are of relatively little interest to contemporary economists but that should be of interest to political scientists are the non-market economies and the history of economic thought. If it is true, as was suggested above, that political exchange resembles barter, then we may want to focus attention on the transition from barter exchange to monetary exchange. The process of monetization of

---

[93] Hart, "Money," p. 428.
[94] *Sociological Analysis*, pp. 86, 92–3. See also Frank H. Knight, *Risk, Uncertainty and Profit* (New York: Harper, 1921).

economic symbols is comparable to the process of legitimation of political symbols. Economic anthropology is likely to be at least as useful in understanding this problem as is formal economics.[95]

The works written by economists when their discipline was in its early stages of development should not be overlooked. They may well be more appropriate to the present stage of political science than the sophisticated models of contemporary economics. Among works that should be useful are those by Adam Smith, John Stuart Mill, Alfred Marshall, Frank H. Knight, Clarence Ayres, John Maynard Keynes, Joseph Schumpeter, and Jacob Viner, to name but a few. The point is that the most up-to-date ideas in economics may not be the most useful to political scientists at this time.

CONCLUSION

Dissatisfaction with particular formulations of the power–money analogy should not blind us to the value of the underlying assumption that it is useful to compare political and economic processes. The analogy encourages us to consider politics and economics as subsets of a family of social processes. One can accept the contention of Catlin or Parsons that there are important parallels between the conceptual schemes appropriate for the analysis of economic and political aspects of society without necessarily accepting the conclusions they draw from this parallelism. If power relations pervade human relations as much as Dahl claims, we should not be surprised to find that other social sciences have something to say about them. Coleman's claim that the theory of money "comes closer than any other to a theory of influence systems"[96] may not be true, but it should at least provoke an interest in further investigation. The economists' good fortune in having money to study is our good fortune also. They have been able to erect a formidable body of theory. Although we may never be able to emulate them, we can at least understand our

[95] See, for example, George Dalton (ed.), *Primitive, Archaic, and Modern Economies: Essays of Karl Polanyi* (Garden City, N.Y.: Doubleday, 1968).
[96] Coleman, "Comment," p. 77.

own discipline better if we understand how they did it and why they have succeeded in doing what we have been unable to do.

There is, however, no automatic or intrinsic heuristic value in comparing economic and political processes. The basic rationale of analogy is to improve understanding of the unfamiliar by comparing it with the familiar. The analogy can be a useful device for political scientists to the extent that they are familiar with such matters as the functions of money, the process of credit creation, theories of the value of money, monetary history, and the role precious metals have played in monetary systems. Without such familiarity the heuristic value of the comparison may be negative. Although we are accustomed to envying the economists because they have money, we should not forget that this is not an unmitigated blessing for them. It is only too easy to confuse monetary aspects of economic affairs with what is happening in terms of real goods and services. When economists speak of the need to "pierce the veil of money" in order to see what is really happening in the economy,[97] we should take it as a warning that the power–money analogy can conceal as much or more than it reveals.

In evaluating the power–money analogy a willingness to try new ways of thinking must be balanced by healthy skepticism. Perhaps Deutsch set the proper tone for a balanced approach when he said: "Political science cannot and will not become simply the 'economics of power,' but it can benefit from the limited similarities between money and [the symbols of?] power by using them as guides to the deeper similarities and differences behind them. For these similarities, though limited, are by no means trivial."[98] There may be no revolutionary implications in the analogy, but we may at least get a reshuffling of the Cabinet.

[97] Robertson, *Money*, pp. 1, 9–10; and Boulding, *Economic Analysis*, vol. 1, p. 20.
[98] Deutsch, *International Relations*, p. 48.

3

Thinking about Threats

The development of a science of threat systems is a desirable but slow – dangerously slow – process.[1] The uneven evolution of this science has given it several characteristics of doubtful value. In the first place, "strategic thinking" has acquired military connotations. When students of international politics refer to "the strategists," they usually have in mind those who are primarily concerned with military policy – and they expect other students of international politics to know that this is what they have in mind. Although there are many nonmilitary situations in international politics in which the ability of one nation to gain its ends depends to an important degree on what other nations do,[2] such situations are rarely viewed as "strategic."

Even within the field of military affairs, the term "strategic thinking" usually connotes a concern with nuclear deterrence policies. Although the valuable contributions to theorizing about threats by students of nuclear strategy must be acknowledged, it would be undesirable to treat such theories as the exclusive province of such scholars.

In addition to its military connotations, the concept of strategic thought has become associated with game theory. Thinking about threats, however, is too important to be left to the game theorists. For example, after a highly stimulating discussion of "fractional

[1] Cf. Kenneth E. Boulding, "Towards a Pure Theory of Threat Systems," *American Economic Review*, 53 (1963), pp. 424–34.
[2] Cf. Thomas C. Schelling, *The Strategy of Conflict* (Cambridge: Harvard University Press, 1960), p. 5.

threats," Schelling talks about them as if the importance of his discussion lay in having found a rationale for such tactics in game-theory terms.[3] But what if Schelling had failed to find a niche in game theory for fractional threats? Should we then forget about them? Such tactics are clearly phenomena of the real world. Many students of international politics can benefit from Schelling's imaginative discussions regardless of their implications for game theory. This might be called the problem of "how to steal without getting caught" – that is, how can the student of international politics "steal" Schelling's ideas without getting caught by Schelling's game-theory orientation? For many students of international politics, the primary significance of Schelling's work lies in improved understanding of the real world, not in his contributions to game theory.

Threats pervade human relations and should not be discussed solely in terms of nuclear deterrence or game theory. The purpose of this chapter is to broaden the context within which threats are discussed by looking at selected aspects of recent thinking about threats from a more general perspective than that of either game theory of nuclear strategy. The discussion will focus on: (1) the basic concept of threat, (2) the relationship between threats and promises, (3) the coerciveness of threats, (4) the costs of threats, (5) the role of ambiguity in threat systems, and (6) the relationship between threats and the concept of deterrence.

THE THREAT: UNDERTAKING, OUTCOME, OR RELATIONSHIP?

Precisely what is the statement "A threatens B" supposed to tell us? Three different meanings are often conveyed. For game theorists a threat is a strategic move available to game participants.[4] As such, threats are defined in terms of A's activities. Threat, in other words, is an *undertaking* by A intended to change B's future behavior.

Social psychologists, on the other hand, are likely to define threats in terms of B's psychological condition. For them threats are defined not in terms of A's activities but in terms of B's

[3] Ibid., p. 184.
[4] Ibid., pp. 123, 150, 160.

attitudes – "*threat* refers to the anticipation of harm. . . . Threat is thus a purely psychological concept, an interpretation of a situation by the individual."[5] Thus, B may be threatened by A regardless of what A is doing; B may even be threatened by A when A does not exist.[6] In the psychologists' definition, threat is the *outcome* of A's (intended future) activities as perceived (or imagined) by B. It is thus futile for Schelling to complain about the tendency of psychologists to associate certain psychological consequences for B with threats.[7] It is precisely these psychological consequences that define threats for many psychologists. The typical game theorist and the typical social psychologist are simply not referring to the same thing when they say, "A threatens B."

A third meaning of "A threatens B" is that there is a relationship between A and B such that A is attempting to make B feel threatened and succeeding. Although one reads much about the desirability of defining power in relational terms, one almost never encounters a similar call for a relational concept of threats. Yet the same arguments advanced in favor of the first concept could also be used in favor of the second. Each of these three definitions of threat can be useful to the student of international politics, but only if they are clearly distinguished one from the other.

THREATS VERSUS PROMISES

Although students of international politics have accustomed themselves to such phrases as "the theory of threat systems," "the threat that leaves something to chance," "the deterrent threat," and so on, such students are not used to phrases such as "the theory of promise systems," "the promise that leaves something to chance," or "the deterrent promise." Although Boulding implies

---

[5] Richard S. Lazarus, "Stress," *International Encyclopedia of the Social Sciences*, vol. 15 (New York: Free Press, 1968), p. 340.

[6] Cf. Dorwin Cartwright, "Influence, Leadership, Control," in *Handbook of Organizations*, ed. James G. March (Chicago: Rand McNally, 1965), p. 36; Jack H. Nagel, "Some Questions About the Concept of Power," *Behavioral Science*, 13 (1968), pp. 129–37; and Peter Bachrach and Morton S. Baratz, "Decisions and Nondecisions: An Analytical Framework," *American Political Science Review*, 57 (1963), pp. 632–42.

[7] Thomas C. Schelling, "War Without Pain and Other Models," *World Politics*, 15 (1963), pp. 486–7.

that promise systems have already been thoroughly discussed by economists, there is very little evidence that such discussions have been applied to politics. Indeed, the role of positive sanctions (actual or promised rewards) in politics has received very little attention relative to that lavished on negative sanctions (actual or threatened punishments).[8] The typical student of politics either fails to distinguish positive from negative sanctions or ignores positive sanctions. The need for thinking about promises in politics is at least as great as the need for thinking about threats – perhaps greater.

If the difference between positive and negative sanctions is trivial, of course, the failure to discuss promises matters less. It is sometimes implied that the difference is merely technical or semantic: "Since threats are merely negative promises, everything I say about one can easily be applied to the other, *mutatis mutandis.* It would be repetitious for me to discuss both promises and threats. Thus, I shall leave it to the reader to figure out what *mutatis mutandis* means in this context." Unfortunately, the assumptions that must be made in order to make generalizations about threats applicable to promises are far from obvious. The behavioral implications for both A and B of using positive rather than negative sanctions concern such matters as: A's planning processes, the role of costs, the prospects of success, the after and side effects on B, difficulty of legitimation, symbolic importance, A's view of human nature, efficacy, systemic stability, surveillance difficulties, vulnerability to blackmail, and many other things as well.[9] The differences between positive and negative sanctions are neither obvious nor trivial.

The distinction between these sanctions usually implies a psychological definition of threats and promises. In this definition, threats are distinguished from promises in terms of whether B anticipates a punishment or a reward. From this viewpoint, any attempt to differentiate threats from promises in terms of the

---

[8] Robert A. Dahl, *Modern Political Analysis* (Englewood Cliffs, N.J.: Prentice-Hall, 1963), p. 51; Johan Galtung, "On the Meaning of Nonviolence," *Journal of Peace Research*, 3 (1965), pp. 228–57; and Johan Galtung, "On the Effects of International Economic Sanctions, with Examples from the Case of Rhodesia," *World Politics*, 19 (1967), pp. 378–416.

[9] See the discussion of positive sanctions in the following chapter.

formal structure of A's conditional commitment is bound to fail.[10] One cannot tell whether "If you do X, I will give you $10" is a promise or a threat *without referring to B's expectations.* If B expected a $10 reward regardless of whether he did X, he may well regard the statement as a conditional commitment to withdraw an expected reward rather than a conditional commitment to give an unexpected reward. Thus, what looks like a promise may really be a threat – if the threats and promises are distinguished in terms of B's perceptions of them. This psychological concept of threats and promises corresponds closely to intuitive notions about these terms.

Defining threats in terms of A's moves in a game, rather than in terms of B's attitudes, is likely to lead to some intuitively offensive observations about threats and promises. Schelling, for example, first tries to distinguish between threats and promises in terms of the party to whom A makes his conditional commitment.[11] Later, he claims that the "distinctive character of a threat is that one asserts that he will do, in a contingency, what he would manifestly prefer not to do if the contingency occurred, the contingency being governed by the second party's behavior"[12] – a distinctive character that is no help at all in differentiating threats from promises. Still later, he acknowledges the difficulty he has in distinguishing threats from promises and finally concludes that they are merely names for different aspects of the "same tactic of selective and conditional self-commitment."[13] The most disconcerting manifestation of Schelling's unusual conception of the difference between a threat and a promise is his treatment of "compellent threats."[14] The threat that compels, he says, often takes the form of administering the punishment *until* B acts rather than *if* B acts. Schelling thus reverses the time sequence usually associated with threats so that a conditional commitment to

[10] Peter M. Blau, *Exchange and Power in Social Life* (New York: Wiley, 1964), p. 116; William A. Gamson, *Power and Discontent* (Homewood, Ill.: Dorsey, 1968), pp. 75–6; and John R. P. French and Bertram Raven, "The Bases of Social Power," in *Studies in Social Power,* ed. Dorwin Cartwright (Ann Arbor: University of Michigan Press, 1959), p. 158.

[11] Schelling, *Strategy of Conflict*, pp. 35–46, 123–4.

[12] Ibid., p. 123.

[13] Ibid., pp. 133–4.

[14] Ibid., pp. 195–9; and Thomas C. Schelling, *Arms and Influence* (New Haven, Conn.: Yale University Press, 1966), pp. 69–91.

punish and a conditional commitment to stop punishing are both regarded as threats. This is not to suggest that Schelling is either right or wrong. The point to be noted is that Schelling's initial conception of a threat as a strategic move is difficult to reconcile with generally accepted intuitive notions as to the difference between a threat and a promise.

ON COERCIVENESS

It is generally agreed that threats (and promises) vary in degree of coerciveness and that this degree is determined by B's perceptions of the capabilities and intentions of A.[15] If threats are being discussed in the context of A's influence attempt on B, however, A's intentions are contingent on B's compliance or noncompliance with A's demands. A may cause B to feel "threatened" by announcing his intention to hurt B; but if A is not trying to change B's behavior, he is not making an influence attempt. We must distinguish between the "threats" of a sadist and those of a would-be influencer of B's future behavior.

Most people perceive their governments as credibly committed to punishing murderers and as capable of carrying out this threat; yet very few people feel coerced or threatened by this perception. Many people would feel more threatened by a law against consumption of alcoholic beverages that carried a maximum penalty of one year in prison than by a law against murder carrying a mandatory death penalty. Although large rewards are often said to be coercive, few people would feel coerced by a promise to pay one billion dollars to the man who discovers a cure for cancer. Apparently B's estimates of A's capabilities and intentions do not suffice to explain the coercion of B. If B has no intention of committing murder, he will not feel coerced by his government's threat to hang murderers. In order to explain the coerciveness of a threat, one must look not only at B's estimates of A's capabilities and intentions but also at B's estimates of his own capabilities and intentions. The degree to which B feels coerced by

[15] J. David Singer, "Threat-Perception and the Armament-Tension Dilemma," *Journal of Conflict Resolution*, 2 (1958), p. 94; and Richard Brody, "Deterrence," *International Encyclopedia of the Social Sciences*, vol. 4 (New York: Free Press, 1968), p. 131.

A's *threat* will vary directly with B's estimate of the probability that he will disobey A; the degree to which B is coerced by A's promise, however, will vary inversely with B's estimate of the probability that he will disobey A.

THREATS AND COSTS

It costs more to make some threats credible than it does to make other threats credible. It is easy and relatively cheap to threaten to fight if attacked, but it is harder and more costly to threaten to do what one would obviously prefer not to do, such as destroying all life on earth. Schelling and other deterrence strategists seem to be fascinated by threats of the latter type.[16] This is a legitimate and useful analytical focus and should not be disparaged. The danger arises when those who study such threats begin to suggest that the term "threat" should be applied *only* to this category.[17] It is one thing to offer the *empirical observation* that threats often take the form of a conditional commitment to mutual harm, but it is another to say that all threats take this form by *definition*. It is one thing to hypothesize that sadists will find it difficult to use threats, but it is another to make it *definitionally* impossible for them to do so. Threats of mutual harm should be viewed as one important kind of threat – *not the only kind.*

The cost factor also serves to remind us of the differences between threats and promises. The costs of threats and of promises are asymmetrically related to the probability of success.[18] The asymmetry can be summarized as follows: the bigger the threat, the higher the probability of success; the higher the probability of success, the less the probability of having to implement the threat; the less the probability of having to implement the threat, the cheaper it is to make big threats. And also, the bigger the promise, the higher the probability of success;

---

[16] Cf. Schelling, *Strategy of Conflict*, pp. 35–6, 123–4; and his *Arms and Influence*, pp. 35–6.

[17] Cf. Schelling, *Strategy of Conflict*, pp. 123–4; and Jack Sawyer and Harold Guetzkow, "Bargaining and Negotiation in International Relations," in *International Behavior*, ed. Herbert C. Kelman (New York: Holt, Rinehart, and Winston, 1965), p. 483.

[18] Cf. Schelling, *Strategy of Conflict*, pp. 177–8.

the higher the probability of success, the higher the probability of having to implement the promise; the higher the probability of having to implement the promise, the more costly it is to make big promises (other things being equal). Given this asymmetry any observation about the relative costs of promises and threats must imply an assumption about the probability of making a successful influence attempt. When Deutsch claims that threats are cheaper than promises, he supports the claim by pointing out how costly it would be to reward those who obey the law in a society in which most people are law-abiding citizens.[19] Is Deutsch suggesting that the probability of making a successful influence attempt is the same in the international and domestic political arenas? The frequent references to the contrast between domestic harmony and international anarchy suggest caution in accepting Deutsch's implied assumption. In discussing the costs of influence attempts based on conditional commitments, one must always remember that threats cost more when they fail; while promises cost more when they succeed.

CLARITY AND VAGUENESS

When we say that A is influencing B with a threat or a promise, we imply that B is modifying his behavior because of his estimates of A's capabilities, intentions, and preferences. If A wants to use threats or promises to get B to do X, he must ensure that B has answers to three questions:[20] (1) what does A want B to do, (2) what will A do if B does not comply, and (3) what will A do if B does comply? To say that B must have these three kinds of information is to say nothing about the clarity of such information. One must not confuse the minimum, the optimum, and the maximum degrees of clarity.

The role of ambiguity in threat relationships has received far less attention than it deserves.[21] Although it is often recognized that

---

[19] Karl W. Deutsch, *The Analysis of International Relations*, 3rd edn (Englewood Cliffs, N.J.: Prentice-Hall, 1988), p. 16.

[20] This information need not be *provided* by A. It is only necessary that B have it, not that A provide it.

[21] For an important exception, see Robert Jervis, *The Logic of Images in International Relations* (Princeton: Princeton University Press, 1970), pp. 113–38.

ambiguity regarding the promised reward or the threatened penalty is possible and perhaps desirable, the importance of this is usually underestimated.[22] Clear threats tend to be important in nuclear deterrence policies; therefore, it is understandable that students of nuclear strategy have emphasized this type of threat. Those who study Canadian–American relations, however, must focus on a more subtle phenomenon – the vaguely hinted threat. The typical threat for day-to-day use in international politics is implicit rather than explicit.

What about ambiguity regarding the kind of response A desires B to make? It is often implied that ambiguity has no place here; it is either conceptually or empirically undesirable. Bachrach and Baratz seem to make *clear* communication of A's desires a definitional requirement of a power relationship: "In a power situation there must be clear communication between the person who initiates policy and the person who must comply."[23] Although it seems obvious that B must have some clue as to A's preferences, there is no reason to assume that he must understand them *clearly*. Singer's objection to ambiguous demands by A is based more on empirical than conceptual grounds. He claims that unless B understands "the precise nature" of the action which A prefers B to take, B cannot respond in a mutually advantageous fashion.[24] This statement is obviously false, since there is always the possibility that B will respond in a mutually advantageous fashion by pure chance. Even ignoring this possibility, it seems unwise to make *precise* understanding by B a requisite for a successful influence attempt by A. Clarity is a matter of degree, and it is quite probable that A can influence B by communicating his preferences with something less than maximum clarity. Most people, after all, do not understand the precise nature of the legal definition of murder; but this does not greatly impair the utility of laws that

---

[22] Dean G. Pruitt, "National Power and International Responsiveness," *Background*, 7 (1964), pp. 165–78; Dean G. Pruitt, "Definition of the Situation as a Determinant of International Action," in Kelman (ed.), *International Behavior*, pp. 393–432; J. David Singer, "Inter-Nation Influence: A Formal Model," *American Political Science Review*, 57 (1963), p. 430; Schelling, *Strategy of Conflict*, pp. 38–9, 119–61, 187–203; and Schelling, *Arms and Influence*, pp. 3–4, 35–91.

[23] Bachrach and Baratz, "Decisions and Nondecisions," pp. 633–4.

[24] Singer, "Inter-Nation Influence," p. 430.

threaten to punish murderers. Most people have a *clear enough* understanding of murder to make the threat quite effective.

In choosing the degree of clarity with which to communicate a threat to B, A has a number of options, as table 1 indicates. Thus an influence attempt might take the following form: a vague promise of a reward for compliance, a clear threat to punish for noncompliance, and a vague specification of the nature of compliance. The *minimum* requirements for a threat (or promise) relationship are: (1) B must have some idea as to what A wants him to do; and (2) B must perceive a difference between the way A will respond if B complies and the way A will respond if B fails to comply.

TABLE 1   *Information components of a threat relationship*

What A will do if B complies	What A will do if B fails to comply	What constitutes compliance
Clear promise of reward	Clear threat to punish	Clear specification
Vague promise of reward	Vague threat to punish	
Clear commitment not to punish	Clear commitment not to reward	
Vague commitment not to punish	Vague commitment not to reward	Vague specification

Are there circumstances in which A might actually prefer to make vague demands on B? Such circumstances are well illustrated by the disturbances in American universities in the 1960s. The university administrators were interested in ensuring that protests did not get out of hand. When potential protesters asked the administrators for a precise definition of unacceptable protest, the administrators were faced with a strategic dilemma. On the one hand, one cannot deter unacceptable forms of protest unless one gives would-be protesters at least a vague idea as to the nature of unacceptable protest. On the other hand, a precise definition of unacceptable protest would also clarify loopholes. Since the administrators were unable to anticipate all the ideas that might occur to the protesters – a group that had shown fantastic imagination – they were reluctant to give a precise definition of unacceptable protest in advance. Many administrations thus confined their demands to forbidding "disruptive behavior," "interference with the orderly processes of the college," or "infringement of the spirit of free inquiry." When A is quite sure that he knows precisely what he wants B to do, it is probably advantageous for him to state his demands clearly. But when A is uncertain as to what he wants B to do in the future, he may want to be less precise in communicating his demands to B. Thus, the parent who wants to deter a child from playing in the street may be quite specific: "If you play in the street I will spank you." But the parent who merely wants to influence the child's general behavior may be less precise: "If you misbehave, I will spank you." In view of the high degree of uncertainty in the international system and the often stated desire of foreign policy-makers to "preserve their options," we should not be surprised to find that vague demands are common in international politics. The use of a vague demand in making an influence attempt does not necessarily indicate that A is either foolish or ignorant.[25]

THREATS AND DETERRENCE POLICIES

Students of international politics often make a great fuss over the distinction between deterrence and compellence, dissuasion and persuasion. However depending on one's definition of X (the desired behavior), any influence attempt can be described in terms of A's ability to get B to do X. America's nuclear deterrence policy, for example, can be described as an attempt by A (America) to get B (Soviet Union) to do X (refrain from launching a nuclear attack). The reasons for distinguishing between persuasion and dissuasion are usually treated as self-evident. When they are explained, the justification usually focuses on the relative ease of deterring as opposed to compelling. As Deutsch has pointed out, the autonomous probability that B will do X when X is defined as anything except the narrowly specific act Y is usually high relative to the

---

[25] Cf. Schelling, *Arms and Influence*, pp. 84–5; and Jervis, *Logic of Images*, pp. 123–30.

autonomous probability that B will do X when X is defined as a narrowly specific act.[26]

To demand that the Soviets do anything except launch a nuclear attack on a given day is to promote an outcome that was highly probable in the first place, but to demand that the Soviets actually launch a nuclear attack on a given day is to take on the much harder task of promoting an outcome with a very low autonomous probability of occurrence. In short, deterrence is usually a matter of trying to get B to do something that B was quite likely to do anyway – e.g., refrain from murder, rape, or nuclear attack.

It is useful to distinguish between A's attempts to promote probable outcomes and his attempts to promote improbable outcomes for two reasons: (1) Attempts to promote probable outcomes tend to make A appear more powerful than he is, while attempts to promote improbable outcomes give the opposite impression. (2) Since promises and threats are asymmetrically related to the probability of success, they will play different roles when A is promoting probable outcomes than they do when A is promoting improbable outcomes. An explicit distinction between attempts to promote probable outcomes and attempts to promote improbable outcomes is likely to be more useful to students of international politics than the distinction between deterrence and compellence.

The concept of deterrence can even be detrimental to clear thinking about threats and promises. In policy analysis it is useful to distinguish ends from means. Only then can one proceed to discuss the alternative ways in which a given foreign policy goal may be pursued. The concept of deterrence, however, fuses ends and means. Deterrence both connotes and denotes an attempt to reduce the probability that B will do X *by means of threats.*[27] Thus, the following question is loaded in favor of negative sanctions: by what means can the United States *deter* the Soviet Union from nuclear attack? The question rules out consideration of positive sanctions to reduce the likelihood of Soviet attack.

[26] Deutsch, *Analysis of International Relations*, pp. 28–30.
[27] Cf. any standard dictionary; Brody, "Deterrence"; Schelling, *Arms and Influence*, pp. 70–1; and Glenn H. Snyder, "Deterrence and Power," *Journal of Conflict Resolution*, 4 (1960), p. 163.

Regardless of what one thinks of the utility of positive sanctions in inter-nation influence attempts, they should not be ruled out before the discussion even begins. If we are to think clearly about the public policy alternatives, we must be aware of the concept of deterrence, since it has an inherent bias in favor of negative sanctions.[28]

CONCLUSION

Bargaining theory can be a useful tool in international political analysis. Nations send and perceive threats in many ways and in all issue-areas. The above discussion suggests that bargaining theory could be more useful to students of international politics if several weak points in current thinking were eliminated. Among the more important topics that need attention are the following: (1) Clearer distinctions must be made between the concepts of threat as a strategic move, as a psychological condition, and as a social relationship. (2) More emphasis should be placed on promises and on the relationships between threats and promises. A threat is far more than a negative promise. (3) In discussing the coerciveness of threats, B's estimates of his own capabilities and intentions should be included. (4) The asymmetrical way in which threats and promises are related to costs has many implications for international political analysis. To date, these implications have not received much attention. (5) The role of ambiguity in threat relations has been greatly underestimated, especially with regard to the demands A makes on B. (6) The concept of deterrence has an inherent bias in favor of negative sanctions that raises serious questions about its utility as a tool of foreign policy analysis. The lack of a science of threat systems is both intellectually undesirable and politically dangerous. A severely distorted or inadequate science of threat systems, however, could be even more undesirable and more dangerous to world peace. We have already begun to sip from this Pierian Spring; we now must be prepared to drink deeply or suffer the consequences.

---

[28] These issues are discussed further in chapter 8.

4

The Power of Positive Sanctions

Political science has made valuable contributions to the progressive clarification of the concept of power since the Second World War. In view of the attention political scientists have traditionally lavished on the concept of power, it seems fitting that they should help clarify it. Thanks to the efforts of such scholars as Harold Lasswell and Robert Dahl, many political scientists today are keenly aware of the need to define power in relational terms, to distinguish power relations from power resources, to specify scope, weight, domain, and so on.[2] There is, however, one distinction that is rarely considered by political scientists – that between positive and negative sanctions. The purpose of this chapter is to clarify this distinction and show how and why it matters.

It is not that political scientists have said wrong things about the role of positive sanctions in power relations; it is just that they

---

[1] The term "positive sanctions" has elicited critical comment from some political scientists, who have suggested that this is yet another example of unnecessary social science jargon polluting the English language. The idea that "sanctions" could include rewards, however, can be traced at least to the seventeenth century according to the *Oxford English Dictionary*. The entry for "Sanction, Social" in the *Encyclopaedia of the Social Sciences* published in 1937 also lends authority to this usage.

[2] Harold D. Lasswell and Abraham Kaplan, *Power and Society* (New Haven: Yale University Press, 1950); Robert A. Dahl, "The Concept of Power," *Behavioral Science*, 2 (1957), pp. 201–15; and Robert A. Dahl, "Power," *International Encyclopedia of the Social Sciences*, vol. 12 (New York: Free Press, 1968), pp. 414–15.

have said little.[3] Most of their discussions of power have focused on severe negative sanctions. Can one influence more flies with honey than with vinegar? Can one influence more Vietnamese with economic aid than with napalm? The literature of political science not only gives few clues to the answers, it often implies that such questions are not even worth asking. Dahl recognizes but understates the problem: "The existence of both negative and positive coercion is sometimes a source of confusion in political analysis, since writers often either confound the two or ignore positive coercion."[4]

Although it is not the purpose of this chapter to survey the literature, a brief look at the various ways of handling positive sanctions is in order. Among the more common approaches are the following:

1 *Explicit rejection.* Most political scientists pay so little attention to the distinction between positive and negative sanctions that their exclusion of positive sanctions from the concept of power is implicit rather than explicit. A few, however, have explicitly rejected positive sanctions in defining power.[5]

Two sociologists who have influenced political science have also excluded positive sanctions from their concept of power. Both Talcott Parsons[6] and Peter M. Blau[7] have carefully distinguished positive from negative sanctions and have explicitly defined power in terms of negative sanctions. Blau suggests that Max Weber also excluded positive sanctions from his concept of power.[8] Although

---

[3] Although the primary focus of this discussion is political science, other social science disciplines have also underemphasized positive sanctions. The *International Encyclopedia of the Social Sciences*, for example, contains an index entry for "threat" but none for "promise" and an article on "punishment" but none on "reward." See also James T. Tedeschi, "Threats and Promises," in Paul Swingle (ed.), *The Structure of Conflict* (New York: Academic Press, 1970), pp. 155–91.

[4] Robert A. Dahl, *Modern Political Analysis* (Englewood, Cliffs, N.J.: Prentice-Hall, 1963), p. 51.

[5] This group includes David Easton, *The Political System* (New York: Alfred A. Knopf, 1953), pp. 143–4; and Gerald Garvey, "The Domain of Politics," *Western Political Quarterly*, 23 (March 1970), pp. 120–37. In the second edition of *Modern Political Analysis*, Dahl joins this group: Robert A. Dahl, *Modern Political Analysis*, 2nd edn (Englewood Cliffs, N.J.: Prentice-Hall, 1970), pp. 32–3.

[6] Talcott Parsons, "On the Concept of Political Power," *Proceedings of the American Philosophical Society*, 107 (1963), pp. 232–62.

[7] Peter M. Blau, *Exchange and Power in Social Life* (New York: Wiley, 1964).

[8] Ibid., p. 115.

Weber's concept of power seems to include both positive and negative sanctions, his concept of *political* power emphasizes the actual or threatened use of force.[9] Such emphasis tends to focus attention on negative rather than positive sanctions in power relations.

2 *Conversion.* Positive sanctions can be conceptually converted into negative ones. Thus Dahl offers a definition of power in terms of severe penalties and then observes that large rewards "can be made to operate" rather like severe penalties.[10] Similarly, the concept of B's opportunity costs of noncompliance with A's demands blurs the distinction between rewards and penalties.[11] Regardless of whether A promises B a reward of $100 for compliance or threatens B with a penalty of $100 for failure to comply, the opportunity costs to B of noncompliance are the same.

3 *Mutatis mutandis.* Perhaps the lack of attention to positive sanctions is partially explained by an implicit assumption that the distinction between positive and negative sanctions is not worth making. Even those who include both positive and negative sanctions in their concepts of power may believe that all or most generalizations about one are applicable to the other − if the proper assumptions are made.[12] Since the relevance of generalizations about sticks to generalizations about carrots is so easy to see, why belabor the obvious?

4 *Inconsistency.* One may explicitly include both positive and negative sanctions in a definition of power and then proceed to ignore the positive and accentuate the negative. References to power that are not applicable to positive sanctions are then likely to be passed off as mere "slips of the pen." When Dahl identifies several dimensions useful in measuring A's power, we hardly notice that he includes the degree of B's threatened deprivation

[9] Max Weber, *The Theory of Social and Economic Organization*, trans. A. M. Henderson and Talcott Parsons, and edited with an introduction by Talcott Parsons (New York: Free Press, 1947), pp. 152−7.

[10] Dahl, *Modern Political Analysis*, pp. 50−1.

[11] John C. Harsanyi, "Measurement of Social Power, Opportunity Costs, and the Theory of Two-Person Bargaining Games," *Behavioral Science*, 7 (1962), pp. 67−80. Throughout this book, A refers to the actor exerting or attempting to exert power, and B refers to the actor over whom A is exerting or attempting to exert power.

[12] Kenneth E. Boulding appears to take this position in *Conflict and Defense* (New York: Harper & Row, 1962), pp. 253−8.

and ignores the degree of B's promised reward.[13] When Karl Deutsch defines power in terms of "expected capability to *inflict* sanctions,"[14] no harm is done. After all, one could talk of A inflicting rewards on B – although one never does. When Felix Oppenheim virtually ignores positive sanctions in his book-length study of power, it is all right because he includes a footnote which mentions "just in passing the promise of reward as another type of influence."[15] When Bachrach and Baratz say that a necessary condition of a power relationship is B's perception of the threatened sanction as a deprivation,[16] or when they observe that the actual application of sanctions is an admission of defeat by A[17] (a statement applicable only to negative sanctions), there is no reason for concern, because they have specifically included both rewards and penalties in their definition of sanctions.[18] Any – but not all – of these examples can easily be dismissed as nothing more than unfortunate diction, a mere "slip of the pen." Scholarship pays little attention to "slips of the pen" on the assumption that they are random and tend to cancel out. When pens slip consistently in one direction, however, the effect is cumulative; the scholarly implications are different. In discussing the role of sanctions in power relations, the pens of political scientists often slip toward negative sanctions and almost never slip toward positive sanctions.

No work published since 1945 has had a greater impact on the way political scientists think about power than Lasswell and Kaplan's *Power and Society*. Here too one finds a tendency to emphasize negative sanctions. Consider the following points:

1 A decision is defined as "policy involving severe sanctions (deprivations)" (p. 74).

[13] Dahl, "Power," p. 414.

[14] Karl W. Deutsch, *The Nerves of Government* (New York: Free Press, 1963), pp. 120–1; italics added.

[15] Felix E. Oppenheim, *Dimensions of Freedom* (New York: St Martin's Press, 1961), p. 45.

[16] Peter Bachrach and Morton S. Baratz, "Decisions and Nondecisions: An Analytical Framework," *American Political Science Review*, 57 (1963), p. 634.

[17] Ibid., p. 636.

[18] Ibid., p. 634.

2   Power is defined as "participation in the making of decisions" (p. 75).

3   In differentiating power from influence in general, they focus on the "availability of sanctions when the intended effects are not forthcoming." "Power is a special case of the exercise of influence: it is the process of affecting policies of others with the help of (actual or threatened) severe deprivations for nonconformity with the policies intended" (p. 76). Since only negative sanctions are implemented (or threatened) for nonconformity, it appears that Lasswell and Kaplan are not referring to positive sanctions.

4   The word "deprivations" is often used as a synonym for "sanctions" (pp. 76, 84, 86). It is difficult to believe that they intend to include both positive and negative sanctions in the term "deprivations," since they define a sanction as positive "when it *enhances* values for the actor to whom it is applied," and as negative "when it *deprives* him of values" (pp. 48–9, italics added).

5   Lasswell and Kaplan list control over B's "well-being," i.e., physical health and safety, as a power base for A. Although this would seem to imply A's ability to add to B's well-being as well as to subtract from it, the forms of power based on control of well-being are decidedly negative – violence, terror, discipline, rape, brute force, brigandage, forced labor, and inquisition (p. 87).

The discussion of power by Lasswell and Kaplan is clearly and consistently cast in terms of negative sanctions, that is, until one considers the last section of the chapter on power, the section labeled "Choice and Coercion" (pp. 97–102). This section explicitly incorporates both positive and negative sanctions into the concept of power. There seems to be no way to reconcile this section with the rest of the chapter on power. The value of this immensely useful book would be enhanced more by a frank recognition of this inconsistency than by pretending that it does not exist. Although Dahl[19] at one time viewed Lasswell and Kaplan's concept of

[19] Robert A. Dahl and Charles E. Lindblom, *Politics, Economics, and Welfare* (New York: Harper & Row, 1953), p. 106.

power as limited to negative sanctions, he later contended that a "close reading" of *Power and Society* "indicates that they include both negative and positive coercion in their definition of power, though the inclusion of positive coercion is not obvious."[20] I shall leave it to the reader to decide whether close reading of *Power and Society* reveals obscure inclusion of positive sanctions or outright contradiction; either way it seems that the handling of positive sanctions in this influential book leaves much to be desired.

The two most important tasks of this chapter lie ahead. First, a clear distinction between positive and negative sanctions must be drawn; and, second, the relevance of this distinction to political analysis must be shown.

THE CONCEPT OF POSITIVE SANCTIONS

Positive sanctions are defined as actual or promised rewards to B; negative sanctions are defined as actual or threatened punishments to B. Although these definitions appear simple enough, there are both conceptual and empirical difficulties in distinguishing between positive and negative sanctions. Some things take the form of positive sanctions, but actually are not: e.g., giving a bonus of $100 to a person who expected a bonus of $200, or promising not to kill a person who never expected to be killed in the first place. Likewise, some things take the form of negative sanctions, but actually are not: e.g., a threat to cut by $100 the salary of a person who expected his salary to be cut by $200, a threat to punch in the nose, next week, a person who knows he will be hanged at sunrise, or the beating of a masochist. Is withholding a reward ever a punishment? Always a punishment? Is withholding a punishment

---

[20] Dahl, *Modern Political Analysis*, p. 51. In the 2nd edition of *Modern Political Analysis* (p. 32), Dahl abandons this interpretation and returns to his previous position. No explanation is offered; nor is there any indication that Dahl recognizes the contradictory nature of Lasswell and Kaplan's discussion. The 2nd edition of *Modern Political Analysis* gives even less attention to positive sanctions than the first edition – a seeming impossibility. Compare *Modern Political Analysis* (1963), pp. 50–1, with *Modern Political Analysis* (1970), pp. 32–3. The 4th edition of this book, published in 1984, contains a separate chapter on the "Forms of Influence," which devotes significant attention to positive sanctions.

ever a reward? Always a reward? The answers depend on B's perception of the situation.[21]

In order to distinguish rewards from punishments one must establish B's baseline of expectations at the moment A's influence attempt begins.[22] This baseline is defined in terms of B's expected future value position, i.e., expectations about B's future position relative to the things B values. Positive sanctions, then, are actual or promised improvements in B's value position relative to B's baseline of expectations. Negative sanctions are actual or threatened deprivations relative to the same baseline. Whereas conceptual establishment of B's baseline is vital but not difficult, empirical establishment of the baseline is both vital and difficult.

Three pitfalls await those who would distinguish the concept of positive from that of negative sanctions. The pitfalls concern B's perceptions, time, and conditional influence attempts. As Bachrach and Baratz have reminded us, explanations of power relations should specify from whose point of view the situation is being viewed.[23] In any given power relationship, A may perceive himself as employing carrots, while B may perceive A as using sticks. Although many Americans perceive their foreign aid program in terms of positive sanctions, many recipients perceive it differently. There is also a danger that the outside observer, i.e, the political scientist, will substitute his or her own baseline for that of B, e.g., "if someone gave me a million dollars, I would regard it as a reward."

The second pitfall concerns time and is illustrated by Dahl's discussion of positive coercion. After defining power in terms of negative sanctions, he observes that substantial rewards can be made to operate in the same way: "For if . . . [B] is offered a very large reward for compliance, *then once his expectations are adjusted to this large reward*, he suffers a prospective loss if he does not comply."[24] The italicized words indicate that time is not being held constant. Only *after* B's expectations are adjusted, does he perceive withholding the reward as coercive. What Dahl has done

[21] Cf. John R. P. French, Jr and Bertram Raven, "The Bases of Social Power," in Dorwin Cartwright (ed.), *Studies in Social Power* (Ann Arbor: University of Michigan Press, 1959), p. 158.
[22] The concept of the baseline is drawn from Blau, *Exchange and Power*, p. 116.
[23] Bachrach and Baratz, "Decisions and Nondecisions," pp. 640–1.
[24] Dahl, *Modern Political Analysis* (1963), pp. 50–1; italics added.

here is to use two different baselines. In referring to negative sanctions, he uses the baseline existing at the moment of A's influence attempt, while his references to positive sanctions use the new baseline after B has taken account of A's influence attempt. Since the purpose of A's influence attempt is to shift B's baseline, i.e., to cause B to change the expected values associated with doing X, Dahl's treatment tends to conceal the dynamics of the influence process. In distinguishing carrots from sticks one must be careful to specify not only B's baseline of expectations, but also the point in time at which that baseline was established.

It is important, however, to recognize that the baseline changes over time. Today's reward may lay the groundwork for tomorrow's threat, and tomorrow's threat may lay the groundwork for a promise on the day after tomorrow. Thomas Schelling's[25] discussions of "compellent threats" could be improved by recognition of this fact. The threat that compels, he says, often takes the form of administering the punishment *until* B acts, rather than *if* B acts.[26] To call such a conditional commitment to withdraw punishment a "threat" is counter to both common usage and the analysis presented above. Such situations could be more usefully described as ones in which A uses a negative sanction (the punishment) to lay the groundwork for the subsequent use of positive sanctions (the promise to withdraw the punishment if B complies). What A is doing in such situations is using the stick to shift B's baseline so as to make the subsequent promise of a carrot more attractive. A's offer to stop tipping the boat if B will row is unlikely to be perceived by B as a carrot unless A is actually tipping the boat at the time the offer is made. A tips the boat in order to shift B's expectations baseline, so that B will perceive the offer to stop tipping the boat as a reward. In his discussions of compellent threats Schelling blurs the distinction between positive and negative sanctions. Indeed, he turns the time sequence usually associated with threats around, so that a conditional commitment to punish and a conditional commitment to stop punishing are both called threats. Common usage, however, suggests a difference

[25] Thomas C. Schelling, *The Strategy of Conflict* (Cambridge, Mass.: Harvard University Press, 1960), pp. 195–9; and Thomas C. Schelling, *Arms and Influence* (New Haven: Yale University Press, 1966), pp. 69–91.
[26] Schelling, *Strategy of Conflict*, p. 196; and his *Arms and Influence*, p. 70.

between offering to pull a thorn out of B's foot and a threat to stick a thorn in.

The third pitfall is associated with conditional influence attempts, i.e., those in which A conditionally commits himself to reward or punish B for compliance or noncompliance.[27] The problem is that it seems to be easier to distinguish rewards from punishments than to distinguish promises from threats. The possibility that withholding a reward may be regarded by B as a punishment tempts one to regard threats and promises as two sides of one coin. The argument runs as follows: "An unconditional commitment by A to reward (or punish) B regardless of whether he does X or not is not a promise (or threat). Thus, a promise to reward if B complies *must* imply a threat not to reward if B fails to comply. Likewise, a threat to punish B for noncompliance *must* imply a promise not to punish for compliance. Thus, all threats imply promises and all promises imply threats; they are simply different ways of describing the same conditional influence attempt." An implicit assumption along these lines may explain why so few political scientists bother to distinguish between threats and promises. An explicit example of such reasoning is found in Schelling's *Strategy of Conflict*. After considering several definitions and after admitting that the distinction between a threat and a promise is not obvious, he finally concludes that threats and promises are merely "names for different aspects of the same tactic of selective and conditional self-commitment" (pp. 131–4).

The fallacy in this line of reasoning lies in the assumption that withholding a reward is *always* a punishment and withholding a punishment is *always* a reward. If rewards and punishment (and, correspondingly, promises and threats) are defined in terms of B's expectations at the moment A begins the influence attempt, it is clear that a conditional commitment not to reward if B fails to comply is not *necessarily* a threat. "If you do not do X, I shall not reward you" is a threat to punish if – and only if – B had a prior expectation of receiving the reward. "No bonus for you tomorrow unless you work hard today" means one thing on the day before

---

[27] Following Harsanyi, we leave open the possibility that influence attempts may take other forms, including unconditional rewards or punishments (see "Measurement of Social Power," p. 71).

Christmas bonuses are traditionally handed out and quite another on the day after such bonuses have been distributed.

In order to distinguish threats from promises so that A may promise without *necessarily* threatening, one must identify three kinds of conditional commitments available to A: (1) conditional commitment to reward (promise), (2) conditional commitment to punish (threat), and (3) conditional commitment neither to reward nor punish (assurance).[28] The "assurance" would make it conceptually possible for A to promise a reward to B for compliance without simultaneously threatening to punish B for noncompliance. Instead of threatening B, A may "assure" B (explicitly or implicitly) that B will not be rewarded for noncompliance.

Two advantages of conceptually isolating threats from promises should be mentioned. First, one may thereby distinguish between conditional commitments to deprive B of something she expects to have and conditional commitments to deprive her of something she does not expect to have. People respond differently to such situations.[29] Second, it permits a more comprehensive description of the full range of policy options open to A in making an influence attempt. This, as Harsanyi has noted, is one of the main purposes for which social scientists use the concept of A's power over B.[30] The following table indicates some of these possibilities. Note that the table allows for variations in A's behavior along the following dimensions: (1) type of sanction (positive or negative), (2) degree of probability that the sanction will be implemented, and (3) degree to which A is explicit in specifying his commitment. Although A must at least imply that he will behave differently if B complies than he would if B fails to comply, A may choose from a number of possible combinations. For example, A may say to B: "If you comply, I guarantee not to punish you and I may even reward you; but if you do not comply, I guarantee not to reward you and I may even punish you." The table makes sense, however,

---

[28] In *Arms and Influence* (p. 74) Schelling apparently uses the term "assurance" in this way.

[29] Cf. Elton B. McNeil, "Psychology and Aggression," *Journal of Conflict Resolution*, 3 (1959), p. 203; and Kenneth E. Boulding, "Towards a Pure Theory of Threat Systems," *American Economic Review*, 53 (1963), p. 426.

[30] Harsanyi, "Measurement of Social Power," p. 69.

TABLE 2   *A's options when making conditional influence attempt on B*

If B complies	If B does not comply
No indication (you guess)	No indication (you guess)
May reward	May not reward
Probably reward	Probably not reward
Guarantee reward	Guarantee not to reward
May not punish	May punish
Probably not punish	Probably punish
Guarantee not to punish	Guarantee to punish

only if one distinguishes clearly between withholding a reward and punishing.

A clear distinction between the concepts of positive and negative sanctions can be drawn in terms of B's expectations about B's future value position. The possibility of making such a distinction, however, is not sufficient to justify doing so. As Cartwright points out, the study of power relations is already riddled with interminable theoretical distinctions.[31] The remainder of this chapter will therefore be devoted to two propositions: (1) that positive and negative sanctions have different behavioral implications; and (2) that the difference is significant from the standpoint of political science.

POSITIVE VERSUS NEGATIVE SANCTIONS: THE DIFFERENCE IT MAKES

The differences between positive and negative sanction situations are neither trivial nor obvious. Even though some of these not-so-obvious and not-so-trivial differences can be deduced from the logical opposition of positive and negative sanctions, this is rarely done. Deductions, however, can only clarify some of the differences. Although positive and negative sanctions are opposites in logic, they are not opposites in their behavioral consequences.[32] Both A

[31] Dorwin Cartwright, "Influence, Leadership, Control," in James March (ed.), *Handbook of Organizations* (Chicago: Rand McNally, 1965), p. 4.
[32] Cf. Thomas W. Milburn, "What Constitutes Effective Deterrence?" *Journal of Conflict Resolution*, 3 (1959), p. 139; and B. F. Skinner, *Science and Human Behavior* (New York: Free Press, 1953), pp. 182–93.

and B behave differently in positive sanction situations than they do in negative sanction situations. What follows is a survey of the more important hypothesized differences between such situations.

1 *A's burden of response.* When A's influence attempt is based on a promise, B's compliance obligates A to respond with a reward; whereas B's failure to comply calls for no further response from A.[33] Thus, a nation using threats will invest time and effort in planning its response to B's noncompliance. Such a nation has little incentive to ponder what it will do if B complies, since compliance requires no response from A. In other words, threats provide an incentive for A to base its planning processes on the assumption that B will not cooperate. To the extent that nations (or other political groups) behave as other nations assume (or expect) they will behave, threats would seem to make compliance less likely. This is not a logical necessity, just a psychological probability. A nation using promises need not expect compliance, but it has an incentive to do so. The point is that A's responsibilities and planning processes are different when A uses promises rather than threats.

2 *The role of costs.* One important consequence of the asymmetry between positive and negative sanctions is that promises tend to cost more when they succeed, while threats tend to cost more when they fail.[34] Thus, threats and promises are related to the probability of success in different ways. The difference can be summarized as follows: The bigger the threat, the higher the probability of success; the higher the probability of success, the less the probability of having to implement the threat; the less the probability of having to implement the threat, the cheaper it is to make big threats. The bigger the promise, the higher the probability of success; the higher the probability of success, the higher the probability of having to implement the promise; the higher the probability of having to implement the promise, the more expensive it is to make big promises.[35] If A has doubts about his ability to

---

[33] The asymmetry between positive and negative sanctions has been noted by Boulding, "Threat Systems," p. 428; and Parsons, "Concept of Political Power," p. 239.

[34] Schelling, *Strategy of Conflict*, p. 177.

[35] This assumes that other things remain equal. Two especially important assumptions

calculate the probability of success accurately, A may want to hedge. Whereas, with promises, hedging is likely to take the form of scaling down the promise, with threats, hedging is likely to take the form of building up the threat: too big a threat is likely to be superfluous rather than costly.[36]

3   *Propensity to use and prospects of success.* Since A's incentive to use promises instead of threats tends to increase as the probability of success decreases, one may hypothesize that A is more likely to use positive sanctions when A thinks the prospects of success are poor (*ceteris paribus*).[37] This hypothesis suggests the need to re-examine some widely held opinions about the relationship between positive sanctions and political integration. Whereas the international political arena tends to be associated with anarchy and negative sanctions, the domestic political arena tends to be associated with integration and positive sanctions. Whereas the underworld tends to be associated with mutual distrust and negative sanctions, the overworld (?) tends to be associated with trust, good faith, and positive sanctions. Advocates of increased use of positive sanctions in international politics are often pictured as unrealistic dreamers who want to use influence techniques that are obviously unsuitable in the international arena. The above hypothesis, however, suggests that positive sanctions are more relevant to international than to domestic politics, to the underworld than to the overworld. Since the prospects for success are lower in the international and underworld arenas, the incentive to use positive sanctions instead of negative ones should be greater (assuming, of course, that other things are equal). In a well-integrated domestic polity, however, negative sanctions are more useful. It is only because of the high probability that most people will obey the law that governments can afford to enforce laws with

are that cost varies directly with the risk of implementation and that the credibility of a threat or promise is not affected by its size. Although either of these assumptions is questionable in other contexts, they do not seem to be directly related to differentiating between positive and negative sanctions.

[36] Schelling, *Strategy of Conflict*, p. 177.

[37] It is important to note that the point being made here turns on the difference between threats and promises rather than actual rewards and punishments. Evidently overlooking this point, one author attributes to me the view that "managers would reward employees doing unsatisfactory work." See David Kipnis, *The Powerholders* (Chicago: University of Chicago Press, 1976), pp. 60, 69.

threats. It is much cheaper to punish the few who disobey than to reward the many who obey.[38]

Negative sanctions are often associated with situations in which A's influence attempt, if it succeeds, leaves A better off and B worse off than they otherwise would have been.[39] The above hypothesis suggests a re-examination. Other things being equal, A's prospects of success are worse when she tries to promote improbable outcomes than when she tries to promote probable ones.[40] One may also assume that there is a low autonomous probability that B will do things that are bad for her and a high autonomous probability that B will do things that are good for her. Thus, one may formulate the following syllogism: "The lower the probability that X is bad for B, the higher the autonomous probability that B will do X; the higher the autonomous probability that B will do X, the higher the probability that A's attempt to get B to do X will succeed; the higher the probability of success, the more likely A is to use threats." Threats are most likely to be used in situations in which A is trying to make sure that B does something that B is quite likely to do anyway, e.g., refrain from murder, rape, larceny, or nuclear attack. It is not unlikely that B would agree that it is good for him to be deterred from such actions.

In practice there may be a difference between the actual probability that A will succeed and the probability perceived by A. There is some evidence that A will tend to overestimate the probability that her influence attempt will succeed.[41] This would partially explain what appears to be a bias toward using negative sanctions in actual practice.

4 *Indicators of success.* Empirical observation of influence attempts based on threats and promises is tricky, since the indicators of success for each differ. Whereas a successful threat requires no action by A, a successful promise obligates him to

---

[38] Cf. Karl W. Deutsch, *The Analysis of International Relations*, 3rd edn (Englewood Cliffs, N.J.: Prentice-Hall, 1988), pp. 16–17.

[39] See, for example, Boulding, "Threat Systems," p. 426.

[40] Cf. Deutsch, *International Relations*, pp. 28–31.

[41] Cf. Deutsch, *Nerves of Government*, pp. 212–13; Ward Edwards, "Utility, Subjective Probability, Their Interaction and Variance Preferences," *Journal of Conflict Resolution*, 6 (1962), pp. 42–51; Robert Jervis, "Hypotheses on Misperception," *World Politics*, 20 (1968), pp. 454–79; and J. David Singer, "Inter-Nation Influence: A Formal Model," *American Political Science Review*, 57 (1963), p. 426.

implement that sanction. In a well-integrated social system, where the probability that B will comply with A's wishes is relatively high, promises will be more visible than threats. In fact, it is precisely because threats are so successful in domestic politics that they are so difficult to detect.[42] One suspects that a lower rate of success makes threats more salient in international than in domestic politics. Let us assume that an equal number of threats and promises are made in the domestic and international political arenas (an unrealistic assumption). Let us further assume that the probability of success is lower in the international than the domestic realm (a realistic assumption). What will the empirical observer see? Whereas domestic life will appear harmonious and tranquil, international life will appear to be a war of all against all. The low rate of international compliance will activate negative sanctions and obviate positive ones, while the high rate of domestic compliance will activate positive sanctions and obviate negative ones. Thus, one may formulate the following hypothesis: "Empirical observers will tend to overestimate the role of threats relative to promises in international politics and to underestimate the role of threats relative to promises in domestic politics."[43]

5 *Deterrence.* The asymmetrical way in which threats and promises are related to success helps to explain the tendency to associate negative sanctions with policies of deterrence. Logically, of course, one could just as well speak of deterring B (that is, reducing the probability that B will do X) with promises as with threats; for example, "I will give you a reward if you will refrain from doing X." Time and again, however, writers imply that deterrence is a matter of threats alone, or perhaps threats combined with promises, but never a matter of promises alone.[44]

---

[42] This point has been noted by Talcott Parsons, "Some Reflections on the Place of Force in Social Process," in Harry Eckstein (ed.), *Internal War* (New York: Free Press, 1964), pp. 51–3.

[43] There is probably a tendency to overestimate the importance of threats relative to promises in underworld politics also.

[44] For an example of explicit association of negative sanctions and deterrence, see Talcott Parsons, "Concept of Political Power," pp. 239–40. Less explicit examples are Blau, *Exchange and Power*, pp. 116–17; Glenn H. Snyder, "Deterrence and Power," *Journal of Conflict Resolution*, 4 (1960), pp. 163–78; Richard A. Brody, "Deterrence," *International Encyclopedia of the Social Sciences*, vol. 4 (New York: Free Press, 1968), pp. 130–2; and Schelling, *Strategy of Conflict* and *Arms and Influence*. Schelling implies

The connection between threats and deterrence is rarely explained, merely implied as a matter of truth – either intuitively obvious or definitional.

How does one explain this propensity to imply a special relationship between deterrence policies and negative sanctions? Consider three possible explanations:

1   Dictionary definitions of "deterrence" usually depict it as discouragement through fear. Such definitions make the concept of a deterrent promise a contradiction in terms. It is difficult to believe, however, that semantics can account for the United States government's reliance on threats rather than promises in order to lower the probability of Soviet attack.

2   Talcott Parsons has suggested that negative sanctions have more intrinsic effectiveness than positive sanctions in deterrence situations.[45] Parsons produces no evidence and very little argument to support this contention, however.

3   The asymmetrical way in which threats and promises are related to success offers another explanation. As Deutsch has pointed out, the autonomous probability of B's doing X when X is defined as anything but Y is usually high relative to the autonomous probability of B's doing X when X is defined as a narrowly specific act.[46] In other

the association between threats and deterrence by the scant attention he gives to promises relative to threats. The association is also implied in observations such as the following: "It is a paradox of deterrence that in threatening to hurt somebody if he misbehaves, it need not make a critical difference how much it would hurt you too – *if* you can make him believe the threat" (*Arms and Influence*, p. 36.) This is *not* true of attempts to deter that are based on positive sanctions. It *is* true of all influence attempts based on conditional use of negative sanctions – regardless of whether such attempts seek to deter or compel. Thus the paradox should be called a paradox of negative sanctions, not a paradox of deterrence. A few writers have attempted to link positive sanctions with deterrence policies: see Milburn, "What Constitutes Effective Deterrence?" pp. 138–45; E. James Lieberman, "Threat and Assurance in the Conduct of Conflict," in *International Conflict and Behavioral Science*, ed. Roger Fisher (New York: Basic Books, 1964), pp. 110–22; and Jerome D. Frank, *Sanity and Survival* (New York: Vintage, 1967), pp. 162–3. See also, Alexander L. George and Richard Smoke, *Deterrence in American Foreign Policy: Theory and Practice* (New York: Columbia University Press, 1974), pp. 588–615.

[45] Parsons, "Concept of Political Power," pp. 239–40.
[46] Deutsch, *International Relations*, pp. 28–31.

words, deterrence is usually a matter of promoting a highly probable outcome. As noted above, there is a special relationship between threats and situations in which A's influence attempt is likely to succeed. Thus the association of threats with policies of deterrence can be partially explained in terms of the broader special connection between threats and attempts by A to promote probable outcomes. A is likely to use threats rather than promises in attempting to deter B from doing X because the probability of success tends to be relatively high.

6 *B's immediate response.* B's immediate reaction to sticks usually differs from B's immediate reaction to carrots. Whereas fear, anxiety, and resistance are typical responses to threats, the typical responses to promises are hope, reassurance, and attraction. Three important examples of the difference this can make are as follows: (a) Threats cause B to feel stress, which is likely to affect (that is, enhance or impair) B's problem-solving capacity, i.e., B's rationality.[47] (b) Threats tend to generate resistance by B. Cartwright, and French and Raven, have suggested that it is useful to distinguish between opposition to an influence attempt and resistance generated by the influence attempt itself.[48] (c) Whereas positive sanctions tend to convey an impression of sympathy and concern for B's needs, negative ones tend to convey an impression of indifference or actual hostility toward B. Cartwright argues that such impressions have a profound effect upon the outcome of any particular influence attempt.[49]

7 *After-effects and side-effects.* Positive sanctions differ from negative ones not only in their immediate effect on B, but in their after- and side-effects as well. An important side-effect is the "spillover effect" on B's relations with A with respect to other

---

[47] Singer, "Inter-Nation Influence," p. 429.

[48] Cartwright, "Influence, Leadership, Control," pp. 33–4; French and Raven, "Bases of Social Power," pp. 156–7.

[49] Cartwright, "Influence, Leadership, Control," p. 15. On the importance of B's perceptions of A's motives see also Tedeschi, "Threats and Promises"; and H. H. Kelley, "Attribution Theory in Social Psychology," in *Nebraska Symposium on Motivation*, ed. D. Levine (Lincoln: University of Nebraska, 1967), pp. 192–238.

issues. While positive sanctions tend to enhance B's willingness to cooperate with A on other issues, negative sanctions tend to impede such cooperation. For example, America's use of negative sanctions to fight communism increases the difficulty of simultaneous cooperation with Communist nations on cultural exchanges, international trade, and air pollution. Whereas the "spillover effect" refers to the effect on A's *concurrent* relations with B, the "scar effect" refers to the effect on A's *future* relations with B. If A uses positive sanctions today, B will tend to be more willing to cooperate with A in the future, but if A uses negative sanctions today, B will tend to be less willing to cooperate with A in the future.[50] Today's choice by A between positive and negative sanctions affects not only today's response by B, but tomorrow's as well. Just as the memory of America's past interventions colors today's relations between Latin America and the United States, so the memory of Russia's intervention will color relations between Czechoslovakia and the USSR for years to come. Likewise, the memory of American influence attempts in Vietnam will play an important part in international politics long after the shooting has stopped.

8 *Legitimation.* It is usually easier to legitimize demands based on positive sanctions than demands based on negative ones.[51] An example is provided by one of the most important social institutions in the world – the institution of private property. Most societies have one set of rules specifying the conditions under which a person may be deprived of property and quite a different set of rules specifying conditions under which a person's property may be augmented. In general, these rules make it much easier for A to add to B's property than to subtract from it. The person who threatens to deprive B forcibly of $10 if he fails to do X is likely to

[50] On the "scar effect" see Cartwright, "Influence, Leadership, Control," pp. 35–6; French and Raven, "Bases of Social Power," pp. 156–8; Morton Deutsch, "Trust and Suspicion," *Journal of Conflict Resolution*, 2 (1958), pp. 265–79; John R. Raser, "Learning and Affect in International Politics," *Journal of Peace Research*, 3 (1965): 216–26; and Bertram H. Raven and Arie H. Kruglanski, "Conflict and Power," in *The Structure of Conflict*, ed. Paul Swingle (New York: Academic Press, 1970), pp. 69–109.

[51] French and Raven, "Bases of Social Power," pp. 156–60; Dahl and Lindblom, *Politics, Economics, and Welfare*, pp. 107–8.

wind up in jail. The person who offers B $10 to do X may not succeed, but is less likely to be jailed.

The international political arena may be an exception to the general rule on legitimation. It is true, of course, that aggressive warfare is illegal while foreign aid is not. But it is also true that many people would view deterring nuclear attack by a threat to retaliate in kind as more moral than deterring nuclear attack by offering a bribe to the potential attacker. Likewise, the contemporary mores of statecraft seem to make it more moral to drop napalm on a man to prevent him from becoming a Communist than to bribe him to do the same thing. A useful research project could focus on comparing the relative ease of legitimating demands based on positive sanctions in the domestic arena with the legitimation of such demands in the international arena.

9 *Symbolic importance.* Negative sanctions have become psychologically linked with such characteristics as courage, honor, and masculinity. Soldiers, not diplomats, symbolize masculine virtues. In international politics these psychological links are especially pronounced. The statesman who would use positive sanctions risks being perceived by both foreigners and his domestic public as soft, weak, or lacking in toughness. When the North Koreans seized the *Pueblo*, it was "unthinkable" that President Johnson would offer to buy it back. National honor was at stake. It is "honorable" to fight but "dishonorable" to try to buy one's way out of a fight. My purpose here is neither to condemn nor to condone the symbolic functions of positive and negative sanctions; it is merely to note that there is a difference between their psychological functions in politics.

10 *Human nature.* The propensity to use either positive or negative sanctions is partially determined by A's view of human nature. It has been hypothesized that those who view people as basically lazy, wishing to avoid responsibility and desirous of security above all else are more likely to emphasize negative sanctions than are those with a more optimistic view of human nature.[52] Regardless of the viability of this particular hypothesis, it

---

[52] Cartwright, "Influence, Leadership, Control," pp. 13–15.

seems worthwhile to explore the correlation between views of human nature and propensities to use positive or negative sanctions.

11 *Efficacy.* The relative effectiveness of positive and negative sanctions in getting B to do X has been the focus of much research in psychology.[53] Although the precise conditions under which one type of sanction is more effective than the other have yet to be spelled out, it is quite unlikely that positive and negative sanctions will be equally effective in any given influence attempt. The tendency of political scientists to assume *a priori* that negative sanctions work better than positive ones is not justified.

A more obvious difference between the efficacy of positive and negative sanctions concerns specific types of goals that are attainable by one means but not by the other. A sadist will find it difficult to attain his goals with positive sanctions. Those who seek love, affection, respect, friendship, dignity, or solidarity may find them impossible to attain through negative sanctions. Many kinds of human relationships can be destroyed but not created by negative sanctions.[54]

12 *Systemic stability.* If A rewards B, then B is more likely to reward A when he gets the chance (*ceteris paribus*). He who uses negative sanctions is more likely to have negative sanctions used on him. He who lives by negative sanctions is likely to die by them. George Homans has suggested that the tendency of rewards to

[53] No attempt to cite this vast literature will be made here. For interesting starting points and further references see Blau, *Exchange and Power*, pp. 224–7; Lewis A. Froman, Jr and Michael D. Cohen, "Threats and Bargaining Efficiency," *Behavioral Science*, 14 (1969), pp. 147–53; Skinner, *Science and Human Behavior*, pp. 182–93; Tedeschi, "Threats and Promises," pp. 162–91; Herbert C. Kelman, "Compliance, Identification, and Internalization: Three Processes of Attitude Change," *Journal of Conflict Resolution*, 2 (1958), pp. 51–60; and Kenneth Ring and Harold H. Kelley, "A Comparison of Augmentation and Reduction as Modes of Influence," *Journal of Abnormal and Social Psychology*, 66 (1963), pp. 95–102. For one of the few attempts by a political scientist to comment on the asymmetrical effectiveness of positive and negative sanctions, see Denis G. Sullivan, "Towards an Inventory of Major Propositions Contained in Contemporary Textbooks in International Relations" (unpub. Ph.D. dissertation, Northwestern University, 1963), pp. 127–40.

[54] This paragraph draws on Dahl and Lindblom, *Politics, Economics, and Welfare*, p. 108.

spawn more rewards, and of punishment to spawn more punishment, affects systemic stability: "While the exchange of rewards tends toward stability and continued interaction, the exchange of punishments tends toward instability and the eventual failure of interaction in escape and avoidance. . . ."[55] Kenneth Boulding suggests that another reason for the relative instability of systems based on negative sanctions is that harm can be done much faster than good. He adds as a corollary that, over the long run, more good can be done than harm. There is a limit of total deprivation on the extent to which negative sanctions can be employed. After all, A cannot deprive B of what B does not have. Positive sanctions, however, are different since there is no upper limit on the amount by which A may reward B.[56]

13 *Surveillance.* Influence attempts based solely on negative sanctions provide B with no incentive to comply with A's demands if B can find a way to avoid detection. This fact, together with the relative difficulty of legitimizing influence attempts based on negative sanctions, means that A must spend more on specialized machinery for monitoring B's activities when A uses negative instead of positive sanctions.[57]

14 *Blackmail.* Habitual use of positive sanctions is more likely to encourage blackmail attempts than is habitual use of negative

[55] George C. Homans, *Social Behavior: Its Elementary Forms* (New York: Harcourt, Brace, Jovanovich, 1961), p. 57. Cf. Sullivan, "Towards an Inventory," p. 267–71.

[56] Boulding, "Threat Systems," p. 432.

[57] Dahl and Lindblom, *Politics, Economics, and Welfare*, pp. 107–8; Ring and Kelley, "Comparison," pp. 95–102; John W. Thibaut and Harold H. Kelley, *The Social Psychology of Groups* (New York: John Wiley 1959), pp. 105, 242–4. Thibaut and Kelley argue that A need not monitor B's activities at all when using positive sanctions, since B can be counted on to present evidence of compliance to A if A is using promises and not threats. This is carrying the argument too far. Consider first the possibility that B may comply with A's demands, yet fail to present A with evidence of compliance for any or all of the following reasons: (1) incompetence; (2) misperception of A's intentions and/or of the degree of his own compliance; (3) reluctance to incur the costs of gathering such evidence. Since the credibility of his future promises to C, D, E, and F is affected by the way A *appears* to treat B, A may not want to allow B's compliance to go unrewarded no matter how incompetent or reluctant B is to present evidence of compliance. Consider also the possibility that B may present A with falsified evidence of compliance. Without a surveillance system of his own, A will have no way of checking up on B's honesty. Although positive sanctions present A with less difficult surveillance problems, they do not do away with such problems altogether.

sanctions.[58] If a person has a reputation for buying off those who oppose him, other people have an incentive to place themselves in conflict with him in order that they may benefit by being bought off. It is the belief that positive sanctions are possible and the hope that they will be forthcoming that motivates blackmailers. It is sometimes suggested, perhaps in jest, that poor nations have an incentive to create or maintain an internal Communist threat in order to qualify for foreign aid from the United States. However that may be, there appears to be little or no incentive to try to blackmail someone who has demonstrated convincingly that he is either unable or unwilling to reward the blackmailer. Poor people don't get blackmailed; rich people do.

The purpose of the foregoing discussion has been to show that there are a number of differences between positive and negative sanction situations. One can better predict, explain, prescribe, and describe the behavior of A and B if one is aware of these differences.

CONCLUSION

The most important question of all remains to be answered: "So what?" Before taking up this question, however, it would be well to clarify what I have *not* attempted to do in this chapter. First, I have made no attempt to "prove" that the literature of political science tends to ignore positive sanctions. Although I cited a few examples from important works, these were illustrations rather than proof. For the most part, the bias against positive sanctions in the literature of political science has been assumed. Second, I have offered little in the way of an explanation as to why such a bias exists. Is it due to the influence of Weber, or Lasswell and Kaplan, to a desire to be considered "realistic" enough to look the unpleasant fact of negative sanctions in the eye, to a fascination with violence, or to something else? No answer is suggested here. Third, I have not presented systematically gathered empirical findings about the behavioral consequences of using positive or

[58] Cf. Johan Galtung, "On the Effects of International Economic Sanctions: With Examples from the Case of Rhodesia," *World Politics*, 19 (1967), p. 380.

negative sanctions in politics. Indeed, one of the main goals of this chapter is to stimulate precisely this kind of empirical research.[59] In the absence of such findings, I have suggested the behavioral differences between carrots and sticks hypothesized above by deduction, by borrowing the findings about non-political spheres of social life from other disciplines, and by intuitive observation. Although the fourteen behavioral differences presented above are often phrased as factual assertions, they should be treated as tentative hypotheses to be tested for their applicability to politics.

Why does it matter whether political scientists neglect positive sanctions or not? After all, we could distinguish between blonde and brunette political actors, but we do not. Additional distinctions mean additional variables, and we already have more variables than we know what to do with. If we treat both rewards and punishments as opportunity costs to B, then we have reduced two variables to one, thus providing a more "economical explanation." The problem is that the concept of opportunity costs economizes without explaining. When B reacts one way to a promise of $100 if he will do X, and another way to a threat to deprive him of $100 if he fails to do X, the concept of opportunity costs makes it difficult to explain why. The most important reason why the distinction between positive and negative sanctions ought to matter to political scientists is that it matters to both A and B. Because both A and B are likely to behave differently toward positive sanctions than toward negative ones, those who purport to describe, explain, and predict political behavior cannot afford to ignore the distinction between the two kinds of sanctions.

Granted that political scientists ought to consider positive sanctions, why insist that the concept of "power" be broad enough to include them? Why not use the label "power" to refer to influence attempts based on negative sanctions and invent another label for influence attempts based on positive sanctions? Blau and Parsons, after all, do not ignore positive sanctions; they simply exclude them from their definition of power. The problem is that,

---

[59] For a concurring opinion that social scientists have said little about the role of positive sanctions in politics, see ibid., p. 414; and Galtung, "On the Meaning of Non-violence," *Journal of Peace Research*, 3 (1965), pp. 239–42. An example of the type of research needed is Fred H. Lawson, "Using Positive Sanctions to End International Conflicts: Iran and the Arab Gulf Countries," *Journal of Peace Research*, 20 (1983), pp. 311–28.

for political scientists, "power" is not just another term to be defined; it is a term that – whether we like it or not – occupies a unique place in political analysis. For many political scientists, the concept of power is the most fundamental in the whole of the discipline.[60] Even those who would do away with the term "power" altogether are willing to admit that it is too deeply embedded in the vocabulary of politics for this to happen.[61] Because political scientists do not and will not regard power as "just another word," it is desirable to define power broadly enough to include positive sanctions. Positive sanctions cannot get separate but equal treatment from political scientists; positive sanctions must therefore be integrated with the concept of power.

The neglect of positive sanctions in political analysis has consequences for public policy as well as for political theory. As Harsanyi has pointed out, "one of the main purposes for which social scientists use the concept of A's power over B is for the description of the policy possibilities open to A."[62] Today, more than ever before, it is essential that we be able to describe the full range of A's options, not just those options based on negative sanctions, for today the unwise use of negative sanctions may put an end to all life, political or otherwise. The nuclear age has not brought an end to influence attempts; indeed, it appears that human survival will require more and more social control. In such a world there will be an increasing need for "imagination when it comes to inventing positive sanctions."[63] The discipline of political science (but not necessarily each member of that discipline) has a duty to make it clear – to make it unmistakably clear – to policy-makers that A can often get B to do X with positive sanctions as well as with negative ones. On this issue the requirements of sound theory appear to coincide with those of sound policy.

[60] Lasswell and Kaplan, *Power and Society*, p. 75.
[61] See, for example, Harold and Margaret Sprout, *Toward a Politics of the Planet Earth* (New York: Van Nostrand Reinhold, 1971), p. 168.
[62] Harsanyi, "Measurement of Social Power," p. 69.
[63] Galtung, "Non-violence," p. 242. Cf. Skinner, *Science and Human Behavior*, pp. 345–6; and Roger Fisher, *International Conflict for Beginners* (New York: Harper & Row, 1969).

5

The Costs of Power

Nearly forty years have passed since the publication of the path-breaking study *Power and Society* by Lasswell and Kaplan.[1] It in no way belittles the contribution of subsequent analysts of power to describe much of their work as footnotes to *Power and Society*. In the best traditions of science, scholars have stood on the shoulders of Lasswell and Kaplan in order to see further.

One of the most important shortcomings of the concept of power presented by Lasswell and Kaplan was its failure to discuss the costs of exercising power. During the 1950s various writers[2] touched on this aspect of power relations, but no frontal attack was mounted. In summarizing the literature on power in the *International Encyclopedia of the Social Sciences*, Dahl[3] credits Harsanyi[4] with having introduced the concept of costs into the analysis of power. Harsanyi argued that characterizations of power relations should include both the opportunity costs to A of attempting to influence B and the opportunity costs to B of refusing to comply with A's demands.

The long delay in focusing attention on the costs of power

---

[1] Harold D. Lasswell and Abraham Kaplan, *Power and Society* (New Haven, Conn.: Yale University Press, 1950).

[2] E.g., Karl W. Deutsch, *Nationalism and Social Communication* (Cambridge, Mass.: MIT Press, 1953); and John W. Thibaut and Harold H. Kelley, *The Social Psychology of Groups* (New York: Wiley, 1959).

[3] Robert A. Dahl, "Power," *International Encyclopedia of the Social Sciences*, vol. 12 (New York: Free Press, 1968), p. 409.

[4] John C. Harsanyi, "Measurement of Social Power, Opportunity Costs, and the Theory of Two-Person Bargaining Games," *Behavioral Science*, 7 (1962), pp. 67–80.

partially accounts for Cartwright's observation that very little research has been done on this topic.[5] Still, the complacent assumption that this is "just a matter of time" is not in order. Harsanyi's study should be the beginning, not the end, of research on the costs of power. It may be that Harsanyi's discussion is pitched at such an abstract level as to be of little help to empirical researchers. The main purpose of this chapter is to discuss the costs of power at a lower level of abstraction than does Harsanyi and thus to give more specific guidance to empirical researchers as to what to look for and where to look for it.

CHOICE AND COSTS

Since the concept of "cost" is almost as slippery as the concept of "power," we must use it with equal care. There are several concepts of "cost" that may be useful to the student of power. One may, for example, wish to subdivide costs into such categories as fixed or variable, long-term or short-term, average or marginal, implicit or explicit. The utility of such categories, of course, depends on what one wants to explain. For the purposes of this chapter we are interested mainly in the general conception of costs that underlies such categories.

The generally accepted concept of costs refers to the opportunities foregone in making a choice. More specifically, the cost of a given course of action is equal to the highest valued alternative (or opportunity) that must be forsaken in choosing the course of action.[6] Because resources are scarce, people cannot have every-

[5] Dorwin Cartwright, "Influence, Leadership, Control," in *Handbook of Organizations*, ed. James March (Chicago: Rand McNally, 1965), p. 8. Although Cartwright was writing in 1965, his observation is still pertinent.

[6] Robert A. Dahl and Charles E. Lindblom, *Politics, Economics, and Welfare* (New York: Harper & Row, 1953), p. 164; George J. Stigler, *The Theory of Price*, rev. edn (New York: Macmillan, 1952), pp. 96–110; Armen A. Alchian, "Cost," *International Encyclopedia of the Social Sciences*, vol. 3 (New York: Free Press, 1968), pp. 404–14; Kenneth E. Boulding, *Economic Analysis*, 4th edn (New York: Harper & Row, 1966), vol. 1, pp. 76–7; Frank H. Knight, *Risk, Uncertainty and Profit* (New York: Harper & Row, 1921), pp. 51–93; Frank H. Knight, "Some Fallacies in the Interpretation of Social Cost," *Quarterly Journal of Economics*, 38 (1924), pp. 592–3; and James M. Buchanan, *Cost and Choice* (Chicago: Markham, 1969).

thing they want. They must therefore choose among alternative uses of such resources. In doing so they give up some valued alternatives in order to gain others. All concepts of cost, regardless of their differences, refer to this basic choice situation. In a world in which everyone could "have his cake and eat it too," neither the concept of cost nor the concept of choice would have any meaning. The same would hold for a world in which "everyone could have his cake but no one could eat it." If resources are either unlimited (free) or have no alternative use, it makes no sense to talk about choice or costs. From this perspective, all costs are opportunity costs.

Gamson's discussion of power costs is based on the contrary – and, I believe, fallacious – assumption that not all costs are opportunity costs. Although he acknowledges the possibility of using the concept of opportunity costs, he explicitly rejects it in favor of a concept "which focuses on the resources consumed in the influence transaction."[7] The difficulty with such a concept is: How are we to measure the value of the resources consumed in the influence transaction? If such resources have no alternative uses, are we to attribute value to them? We do not usually treat the consumption of free resources as a cost. The air consumed in human breathing, after all, is not usually added into the cost of living. There is no way to measure the value of the resources consumed in the influence transaction except in terms of alternative uses of those resources. The fallacy of assuming that resource consumption involves a concept of costs that differs from the concept of opportunity costs was pointed out by Frank Knight more than fifty years ago:

> Fundamentally, then, the cost of any value is simply the value that is given up when it is chosen; it is just the reaction or resistance to choice which makes it a choice. Ordinarily we speak of cost as a consumption of "resources" of some kind, but everyone recognizes that resources have no value in themselves; that they simply represent the products which could have been had by their use in some other direction than the one chosen.[8]

---

[7] William A. Gamson, *Power and Discontent* (Homewood, Ill.: Dorsey, 1968), pp. 83–91.

[8] Knight, "Fallacies," pp. 592–3.

The student of power can use the concept of opportunity cost in a number of ways, but he cannot avoid it by focusing on the resources consumed in the influence transaction.

DIRECT COSTS TO A

The technique A uses to make an influence attempt is an important determinant of the kinds of costs he incurs. Harsanyi identifies four main types of influence techniques available to A.[9] We shall examine each in turn and comment on their cost accounting problems.

1   A may provide B with unconditional rewards and/or deprivations in an attempt to affect B's calculations of the opportunity costs of various alternative courses of action. In this case A's costs are relatively simple to determine. The costs of rewarding or depriving B are the costs of the influence attempt.

2   A may supply B with information (or misinformation) on the real or alleged opportunity costs of alternative courses of action. A's costs are those of gathering and communicating the information to B. If A already possesses the required information, his only costs are those of communication.

3   A may rely on legitimate authority over B. Although it might seem that A only incurs communication costs in this case, this should not be assumed *a priori*. Some people are born with legitimate authority, i.e., they acquire it with little or no cost to themselves, while others must work for it. Given the immense costs of becoming President of the United States, for example, it would be unwise to say that Presidential attempts to wield authoritative power never involve any costs other than those of communication. Still, it is possible that A has incurred the costs of acquiring legitimacy for reasons other than the desire to influence B. In such cases the researcher will have to make a rather arbitrary allocation of costs on the basis of a judgment of A's motives for acquiring legitimacy.[10]

4   A may supply B with contingent rewards and/or punishments. This type of influence technique presents the most difficult

[9] Harsanyi, "Measurement of Social Power," p. 71.
[10] Cf. Alchian, "Costs," p. 411.

problems of cost determination. In order to clarify some of these problems, let us identify some alternative approaches to cost accounting in conditional influence attempts. First is the "actual expenditure" approach. According to this line of reasoning the costs of an influence attempt are those A "actually" pays. Thus, a successful threat to implement an expensive punishment and an unsuccessful promise of an expensive reward may both be described as virtually costless influence attempts.

There are two difficulties associated with the "actual expenditure" approach. The first difficulty is that it fails to consider the reduction in A's resources that occurs at the moment A makes a conditional commitment to use some of them either to punish B for non-compliance or to reward B for compliance. This conditional commitment lowers the probability that A will have these resources at some future time. We would regard a person with a million dollars today and a probability of 0.8 of having a million dollars next week as richer than the person with a million dollars today and a probability of 0.4 of having a million dollars next week. Likewise, the person who has no conditional commitments to use his power resources is "richer" than the one who owns an equal amount of power resources but has conditionally committed some of them to reward or punish B. The second difficulty with the "actual expenditure" approach is that it fails to distinguish between lucky people and powerful ones. If two people each place one bullet in an empty six-shooter and then threaten to shoot themselves unless B complies with their demands, each runs the same risks of getting shot. Suppose B defies them both and both pull the trigger. If one gets shot and the other does not, the "actual expenditure" approach would say that one paid an extremely high cost for the influence attempt while the other paid almost nothing.[11]

A second approach is Harsanyi's definition of A's costs in terms of the *expected value* of the costs of the attempt.[12] According to

[11] It may seem that the question of lucky vs. powerful people is a question of *effectiveness* rather than *cost*. The main point of including costs in the concept of power, however, is to deny that power is solely a matter of effectiveness. The point is to assert that power should be conceived and measured in terms of *both* cost and effectiveness. See Harsanyi on this point.

[12] Harsanyi, "Measurement of Social Power," p. 68.

this approach the person who shot himself (the unlucky one) and the person who did not (the lucky one) incurred equal costs in their influence attempts. For Harsanyi, A's costs depend on the risks A runs rather than on the price A winds up paying.

Nagel has suggested modifications in Harsanyi's approach to costs. He points out that although Harsanyi defines the costs of A's power over B in terms of expected value, subjective probabilities tend to be ignored in his subsequent formulations. Nagel further suggests that Harsanyi's formulations leave out an important type of costs that A incurs regardless of whether his influence attempt succeeds or fails.[13] These are the costs of monitoring B's activities and of preparing and maintaining incentives for B to comply. The costs of threatening B are not confined merely to the costs of punishing him in the event that he fails to comply.

Whereas Nagel suggests that Harsanyi has *underestimated* A's costs, there is another aspect of Harsanyi's treatment that tends to *overestimate* A's costs. Harsanyi represents the cost of threatening B as the cost of punishing B weighted for the probability that B will defy the threat, the assumption being that B's failure to comply with A's demands obligates A to punish B. In the real world this is unlikely – and what is more important – both A and B are likely to know it. In most threat situations both A and B will have to consider the probability that A is bluffing or that A will change his mind when the time comes to carry out the threat. The probability that A will carry out his threat is not the same as the probability that B will refuse to comply..

A comprehensive estimate of A's costs in making a conditional influence attempt would include the following elements: (1) costs of communicating the threat and/or promise; (2) costs of making the threat and/or promise credible; (3) costs of monitoring B's activities; and (4) costs of carrying out the threat and/or promise. The price of any given degree of credibility varies from one threat (or promise) to another. Whereas some threats are inherently credible, others are inherently incredible.[14] The reason it is useful to distinguish between the costs of communicating a threat and the

[13] Jack H. Nagel, "Some Questions About the Concept of Power," *Behavioral Science*, 13 (1968), pp. 132, 135–6.

[14] Thomas C. Schelling, *Arms and Influence* (New Haven, Conn.: Yale University Press, 1966), pp. 35–6.

costs of making it credible is to clarify the policy possibilities open to A, which, as Harsanyi notes is "one of the main purposes for which social scientists use the concept of A's power over B."[15] Thus, A has a number of options ranging from an empty threat (or promise) on the one hand to a fully credible one on the other. Schelling's assertion, that in order to communicate a threat or promise "one has to communicate the commitment that goes with it,"[16] obscures these policy options open to A. The empty threat cannot and should not be defined out of existence.

Costs (1), (2), and (3) are incurred by A regardless of B's compliance.[17] The costs of actually rewarding or punishing B (4), however, are contingent on B's response to the influence attempt. Thus, they must be weighted for the probability that A will incur them. This probability can be subdivided into three important kinds of probability: (a) the probability that B will comply (or not comply); (b) the probability that A will carry out the threat (or promise) if B does not (does) comply; and (c) the probability that A will inadvertently carry out the threat regardless of what B does. This is not a matter of making endless distinctions for no purpose. Estimating these three probabilities requires different things of A, and A may not be equally adept at each of them. In order to illustrate the importance of subdividing the probability of implementing a threat, let us consider two situations. A *bluff* situation occurs when A estimates the probability that B will comply at 0.1; the probability that he will carry out the threat if B fails to comply at 0.1, and the probability of accident at 0.1. A *confidence* situation occurs when A estimates the probability that B will comply at 0.9, the probability that he will carry out the threat if B fails to comply at 0.9, and the probability of accident at 0.1.

In each situation the probability that A will actually carry out the threat is the same; yet in one A is bluffing and in the other he is not.[18] In neither case is A likely to incur the costs of punishing B, but in one case this is because of what B is likely to do and in the other it is because of what A is likely to do. Because these two

[15] Harsanyi, "Measurement of Social Power," p. 69.

[16] Thomas C. Schelling, *The Strategy of Conflict* (Cambridge, Mass.: Harvard University Press, 1960), p. 147.

[17] Cf. Gamson, *Power and Discontent*, pp. 84–7.

[18] Cf. ibid., p. 87.

situations pose different policy problems for A (and B, for that matter), it is useful for analysts of power (not to mention A and B) to distinguish between them. For example, if A wants to lower the probability of incurring the costs of punishing B, he can: (a) try to increase the probability of B's compliance by making the threat more credible; (b) change the degree of his commitment to implement the threat in the event of noncompliance; and/or (c) try to lower the probability of accidents. If one agrees with Harsanyi that "one of the main purposes for which social scientists use the concept of A's power over B is for the description of the policy possibilities open to A,"[19] it would seem desirable to subdivide the probability of incurring the costs of contingent rewards and/or punishments as suggested above.

In allocating the costs of conditional influence attempts it matters whether A is using threats or promises.[20] There is an asymmetry between threats and promises in that promises usually cost more when they succeed while threats usually cost more when they fail.[21] Thus, increasing the size of a promised reward is likely to increase the probability of incurring the costs of the reward, while increasing the size of a threatened punishment is likely to decrease the probability of incurring the costs of the punishment. Very little research has been done on the behavioral implications of this asymmetry between threats and promises.

The analysis of Thibaut and Kelley, suggests that the costs of monitoring B's activities are affected by A's choice of threats or promises. Indeed, they argue that A need not monitor B's activities at all when using positive sanctions. They reason that B can be counted on to present evidence of compliance to A if A is using only promises.[22] Although one can agree that the costs of monitoring B's activities are likely to be greater in the case of threats than in the case of promises, it is difficult to justify the

---

[19] Harsanyi, "Measurement of Social Power," p. 69.

[20] We are concerned here only with direct costs. The difference between the indirect costs of promises and threats will be considered later.

[21] Cf. Schelling, *Strategy of Conflict*, pp. 36, 177; Kenneth E. Boulding, "Towards a Pure Theory of Threat Systems," *American Economic Review*, 53 (1963), p. 428; and Talcott Parsons, "On the Concept of Political Power," *Proceedings of the American Philosophical Society*, 107 (1963), p. 239.

[22] Thibaut and Kelley, *Social Psychology*, pp. 105, 242–4. See also, Gamson, *Power and Discontent*, pp. 74–5.

extreme position taken by Thibaut and Kelley. Consider first the possibility that B may comply with A's demands yet fail to present A with evidence of compliance for any or all of the following reasons: (1) incompetence; (2) misperception of A's intentions or of the degree of his own compliance; (3) reluctance to incur the costs of gathering such evidence. An especially onerous cost of supplying evidence of compliance might be the humiliation associated with having to ask for the reward. B may reason as follows: "It's bad enough that I had to comply; I shouldn't have to beg for the reward also." One could argue, of course, that B's failure to offer evidence of compliance to A is either of no concern to A or a cause for rejoicing at not having to reward B. However, A may not want B to go unrewarded no matter how incompetent or reluctant B is to present evidence of compliance. The credibility of A's future promises to C, D, E, and F are affected by the way A *appears* to treat B. For the sake of "appearances" A may want to ensure that B's compliance is rewarded.[23]

A more compelling reason for A to monitor B's activities when using promises is that B may present falsified evidence of compliance. Without a surveillance system, A will have no way of checking up on B. In a world where deceit, incompetence, misperception, and reputations play an important role, A has an incentive to incur the costs of monitoring B's behavior when using promises, as well as when using threats.

INDIRECT COSTS TO A

In discussions of the cost of power the indirect costs to A usually receive scant attention. One such indirect cost is the effect on future influence attempts. There is some evidence that influence attempts based on threats and/or punishments generate feelings of hostility in B that increase A's costs of securing B's compliance in subsequent influence attempts.[24] To the extent that this is true,

---

[23] Nagel, "Some Questions," (p. 136) states that if B's action is nonrepetitive, it makes no difference whether A monitors or rewards him. According to the above reasoning, however, if A's influence attempts are repetitive, it may make a big difference to A.

[24] See Cartwright "Influence, Leadership, Control"; John R. P. French and Bertram Raven, "The Bases of Social Power," in *Studies in Social Power*, ed. Dorwin Cartwright

such increased costs are properly attributable to A's influence attempt.

There are also a number of indirect benefits of influence attempts that are often overlooked. Nagel, for example, notes that A must perform some activities that he would not otherwise perform in order to get B to do X. He indicates that these behaviors are caused by B's reluctance to do X, that they are likely to involve opportunity costs, and that they therefore indicate the scope of B's power over A.[25] It is possible, however, that A's behavior is not entirely attributable to B's reluctance to do X.[26] Let us consider three situations in which A's influence attempt may have indirect benefits.

First, the use of positive sanctions (promises and/or rewards) is likely to lower the future costs to A of influencing B by generating in B feelings of attraction for A. These long-run, indirect benefits may more than offset the immediate direct costs of the influence attempt. In such cases some (or all) of A's influence attempt behavior may be "caused" not by B's current reluctance to do X but by A's anticipation of B's future reluctance to do W, Y, and Z.

Second, A may *learn* enough in his attempt to influence B to offset the costs of the attempt. A may acquire information about B's responses to A's influence attempts, i.e., his methods of defending himself, his capabilities for defense, and so on. A may also acquire information about his own capabilities and responses. During the early stages of the Vietnam War (1960–3), it was sometimes suggested that the United States viewed Vietnam as an opportunity to train men and try out new equipment and ideas. Regardless of whether that was true, it was not absurd to consider

(Ann Arbor: University of Michigan Press, 1959), pp. 150–67; Bertram H. Raven and A. W. Kruglanski, "Conflict and Power," in *The Structure of Conflict*, ed. Paul Swingle (New York: Academic Press, 1970), pp. 69–109; George C. Homans, *Social Behavior: Its Elementary Forms* (London: Routledge & Kegan Paul, 1961); and John R. Raser, "Learning and Affect in International Politics," *Journal of Peace Research*, 2 (1965), pp. 216–26.

[25] Nagel, "Some Questions," pp. 135–6. In a later study Nagel revises his position, arguing that "the effects a weaker actor may have upon a stronger cannot generally be construed as power, because they are not necessarily the consequence of the weaker actor's preferences" Jack H. Nagel, *The Descriptive Analysis of Power* (New Haven, Conn.: Yale University Press, 1975), p. 141n).

[26] Cf. Alchian, "Costs," p. 411.

this possibility. A is not the only one who learns from influence attempts, however. One must also consider the possibility that B (and perhaps C, D, and E) will learn about A's methods and capabilities.[27] The point is, however, that the experience A gains in attempting to influence B today may help to lower the costs of influencing B, C, D, and E tomorrow. A's influence attempt behaviour may be "caused" more by this prospect than by B's reluctance to do X today.

And third, A may derive direct psychological satisfaction from attempting to influence B. By making an influence attempt, A at least achieves the satisfaction of knowing that he has "given it the old college try." The direct enjoyment of influence attempts is by no means a rare occurrence. As Dahl and Lindblom note: "One of the most formidable problems of politics arises because with many people power is so easily converted from a goal that is mostly instrumental to one that provides enormous direct satisfactions."[28] A may use a lot of "muscle" in his influence attempt not because this is necessary to overcome B's reluctance to do X but simply because A enjoys pushing B around. In such situations it is misleading to describe A's behavior as "caused" by B's reluctance to do X.

It is tempting to add prestige as a fourth benefit of making influence attempts. There is, however, an important difference between prestige and the benefits described above. Whereas the benefits described in the three situations above accrue to A regardless of whether he succeeds or fails, the benefits of prestige do not. The benefits of prestige must be weighted for the probability of success. It is useful to distinguish between those benefits or costs that are functions of the undertaking and those that are functions of the outcome.

PERCEPTIONS AND COSTS

The most important relationship between perceptions and costs was identified by Harsanyi in "Measurement of Social Power" (p. 71). He argued that for the purpose of a formal definition of a

---

[27] Cf. Schelling, *Strategy of Conflict*, p. 176.
[28] Dahl and Lindblom, *Politics, Economics, and Welfare*, p. 27.

power relation the costs to A should be stated in objective terms while the costs to B should be stated in terms of B's perceptions. According to Harsanyi, B's perceived costs of noncompliance provide a measure of B's incentives for doing X, a measure that Harsanyi calls "the strength of A's power over B." Unfortunately, Harsanyi's algebraic treatment of the strength of A's power over B is inconsistent with his verbal treatment. Whereas verbally (pp. 68–71) he treats the strength of A's power over B as equivalent to the total incentives B has to do X, algebraically (p. 72) he treats it as the *difference* between B's incentives to do X *before* A's influence attempt and B's incentives to do X *after* A's influence attempt.[29]

Consider the following points:

1 In introducing his discussion, Harsanyi indicates his desire to include in the concept of power "the opportunity costs to B of refusing to do what A wants him to do, i.e., of refusing to yield to A's attempt to influence his behavior. As these opportunity costs measure the strength of B's incentives for yielding to A's influence, we shall call them the *strength* of A's power over B" (p. 68). Although it is true that such a concept would provide a measure of B's total incentive to do X, it would not tell us the extent to which this incentive is attributable to A's influence attempt.

2 In developing his ideas in a section subtitled "The Strength of Power" Harsanyi continues to refer to "the opportunity costs to B of noncompliance, which measure the strength of B's incentives to compliance and which we have called the strength of A's power over B" (pp. 69–71). The only time that this section of the paper gives any hint that Harsanyi may have in mind the *amount of change* in B's perceived costs that A is able to bring about rather than B's total perceived costs is when a specific example of a presidential influence attempt is being explicated.

[29] Harsanyi, "Measurement of Social Power," pp. 68–72.

3 Later in the same section, Harsanyi suggests that "the strength of A's power serves to explain B's subjective motivation for compliant behavior" (p. 71). This is true if, and only if, the strength of A's power is defined in terms of B's total incentive to do X.

4 In discussing the relationship between his concept of the strength of power and Dahl's[30] concept of the amount of power, Harsanyi (p. 72) expresses the strength of power algebraically as the *difference* between B's perceived opportunity costs of doing X prior to A's influence attempt and B's perceived opportunity costs of doing X after A's influence attempt. In short, he defines it as the difference that A's influence attempt makes in B's cost calculations.

5 In the latter part of the paper, Harsanyi observes that "the sum (r+t) is the sum of the *reward* B would obtain for compliance, and of the *penalty* he would suffer for noncompliance, both expressed in utility terms. The sum measures the *difference it would make* for B to have A as his enemy instead of having him as his friend. It represents the total opportunity cost to B of choosing noncompliance leading to the conflict situation instead of choosing compliance" (p. 77).

In Harsanyi's formulations, however, the sum (r+t) refers only to the incentives furnished by A, *not* to B's total incentives. The proposition that the sum (r+t) measures the difference it would make to B to have A as his enemy rather than his friend is almost certain to be false. In order to measure the difference noncompliance makes to B one must consider B's total estimate of the opportunity costs of doing X, not merely that portion of the total estimate that was affected by A's influence attempt. The sum (r+t) will measure the difference noncompliance makes to B if, and only if, B estimated the opportunity costs of doing X prior to A's influence attempt as zero. In the real world this assumption will almost never hold.

In measuring the *amount* of A's power over B we do not consider the total probability that B will do X but only that

[30] Robert A. Dahl, "The Concept of Power," *Behavioral Science*, 2 (1957), pp. 201–15.

portion of the total probability attributable to A's influence attempt. Likewise, in measuring the *strength* of A's power over B we should not consider B's total incentives to do X but only that portion of the total attributable to A's influence attempt. B may have reasons for wanting to do X other than those furnished by A. The Soviets, after all, may have reasons for wanting to avoid nuclear war other than those provided by the American deterrent threat.

Harsanyi's inconsistent treatment of B's costs matters for two reasons. First, inconsistency impedes evaluation, since it is difficult to refute an unclear argument. In science it is better to be right than wrong, but it is better to be wrong than to be unclear. Second, the fact that the inconsistency takes the form of saying one thing with algebra and another with words is especially unfortunate. At this particular stage in the development of social science, fluency in English and algebra is not evenly distributed among social scientists. It is desirable to narrow rather than widen the communication gap between those who express themselves primarily with words and those who use the language of algebra.

Three aspects of B's perceived costs present especially difficult problems for both theory and empirical research. The first concerns the costs generated by the influence attempt itself.[31] B's estimate of the costs of doing X may change when he learns of A's influence attempt. Although B may have been indifferent to doing X before, he may be very reluctant to do X while under pressure from A. On the other hand, B may be more willing to do X after learning of A's desires than he was before, not because of A's rewards or punishments but simply because B likes A. In any case, both researcher and theorist must be aware that B's cost estimates may not remain stable during an influence attempt.

A second difficulty, also related to time, stems from the possible effects of cognitive dissonance on B's cost calculations. The process of choosing to comply with A's demands may be a rather painful one for B in terms of value foregone. The fact that he chooses to comply, of course, implies that the costs of non-compliance would be even greater. Blau has suggested that B's

[31] See Cartwright, "Influence, Leadership, Control," pp. 33–4; and Raven and Kruglanski, "Conflict and Power," pp. 69–109.

---

effort to reduce cognitive dissonance in such situations is likely to take the form of depreciàting the costs of compliance *after B has decided to comply.*[32] The behavioral implications of this post-commitment cost depreciation have received little attention. Decisions that require an initial commitment from B with subsequent steps in commitment to follow are not uncommon in politics, the American decision to build an anti-ballistic missile system being a case in point.[33]

A third difficulty in relating the costs to perceptions grows out of the failure of mathematical treatments of utility to distinguish between privation and deprivation.[34] For B, opportunity costs of $100 for noncompliance may be incurred either by a threat by A to deprive B of $100 if he fails to comply or by a promise by A to give B $100 if he does comply.[35] Although the behavioral implications of these two situations might be quite different, Harsanyi's formulation does not allow us to distinguish between them. Focusing on opportunity costs can easily lead us to forget that people react differently to threats than they do to promises.

AUTONOMY AND COSTS

Although Dahl[36] credits Harsanyi with having introduced the concept of costs into power analysis, Deutsch[37] claims to have suggested this concept in 1953.[38] The dispute is of more than historical interest since it raises important questions about the concept of the costs of power.

[32] Peter M. Blau, *Exchange and Power in Social Life* (New York: Wiley, 1964), pp. 207–8.

[33] This phenomenon should also be applicable to A's estimate of the costs of his influence attempt.

[34] Elizabeth Converse, "The War of All Against All," *Journal of Conflict Resolution*, 12 (1968), p. 502.

[35] This also applies to A's cost estimates. In deciding whether to make an influence attempt A may face either a situation in which a successful influence attempt gains him $100 while no attempt costs him nothing, or a situation in which doing nothing costs him $100 while a successful influence attempt allows him to avoid this loss.

[36] Dahl, "Power," p. 409.

[37] Karl W. Deutsch, *The Nerves of Government* (New York: Free Press, 1963), p. 282.

[38] Deutsch, *Nationalism*, pp. 46–59.

Although Deutsch does discuss the *effects* on A of exercising power over B, he does not refer to these effects as costs. In setting forth a "provisional view of power" Deutsch defines power as acceptance of the "least amount of non-autonomous change in one system [A] while producing the largest amount of non-autonomous change in another [B]." In broadening this provisional view he develops the concept of "strength," which he defines as "the ability of a system to preserve only a few essentials of its structure while being capable of change in a wide variety of other aspects."[39] Later, Deutsch defined "net power" as the difference between the amounts of changes imposed by A and changes accepted by A.[40] All of these definitions focus on A's ability to exercise power while either minimizing the effects on himself or preserving his essential structure.

Harsanyi was interested in the *kinds* of effects on A as well as the *magnitudes* of such effects. For him costs were not defined in terms of total changes but rather in terms of net disadvantages, i.e., value forgone. Presumably, this was derived by subtracting the advantageous changes accepted by A from the disadvantageous changes accepted by A. This concept of costs corresponds closely with popular usage.

Whereas Deutsch's conception of costs emphasizes A's ability to preserve his identity or autonomy, Harsanyi's conception emphasizes A's ability to minimize the value he must forgo in exercising power. The crucial difference between these two views can be summarized thus: for Deutsch, A's power is maximized when his costs are zero; for Harsanyi, A's power is maximized when his costs are negative, i.e., when the net effect of making the influence attempt is beneficial.

This is not a matter of one concept being "better" than the other. The important thing is to realize that the concepts of Deutsch and Harsanyi differ and that each can be useful in answering certain kinds of questions. Since Harsanyi's concept of costs is closest to popular usage, it seems preferable to define the costs of power in his terms. Deutsch's concept will be useful to those interested in social autonomy. It was probably his long-

---

[39] Ibid., pp. 46–59.
[40] Deutsch, *Nerves of Government*, pp. 115–16.

standing interest in sovereignty, autonomy, and social identity that led Deutsch to develop his concept of the costs of power.

FINAL COMMENTS

The chief arguments presented in this chapter are as follows:

1   The costs of power should be conceived in terms of the alternative use of resources that is foregone when a choice is made.

2   The influence techniques employed by A are important determinants of the nature and magnitude of the costs incurred by A.

3   Harsanyi's treatment of conditional influence attempts should be modified so as to clarify some of A's more important policy alternatives.

4   A has an incentive to monitor B's activities when using either positive or negative sanctions.

5   Harsanyi's algebraic treatment of B's opportunity costs is inconsistent with his verbal treatment of these costs.

6   Three difficulties in linking costs to perceptions stem from the resistance generated by the influence attempt itself, cognitive dissonance, and the mathematical handling of costs in utility theory.

7   Deutsch's concept of power costs is useful for analyzing problems of autonomy and identity, but Harsanyi's concept is applicable to a broader range of problems because it corresponds more closely to the common meaning of costs.

An understanding of social power requires the integration of findings and concepts from several social science disciplines. It would be wrong to treat the concept of costs as the exclusive province of the economist. Even those who object to Harsanyi's proposal to incorporate costs into the concept of power must take account of costs in some way. No comprehensive explanation of the nature and significance of social power can ignore costs. This chapter has drawn together for critique and comment a number of ideas from various disciplines in an effort to stimulate further research on this important but often neglected aspect of power.[41]

[41] For an example of an empirical study that attempts to demonstrate the importance of costs in power analysis, see David A. Baldwin, *Economic Statecraft* (Princeton: Princeton University Press, 1985).

6

Power and Social Exchange

Conflict studies, power analysis, and social exchange theory are three overlapping yet distinguishable bodies of social science literature. The purpose of this chapter is to examine some of the areas of overlap in order to determine whether conceptual integration is feasible and/or desirable. I will focus primarily on power and social exchange, but the implications for the study of conflict are significant. One study, for example, criticized conflict analysts for neglecting power and proceeded to combine conflict, power, and social exchange theory into a single model.[1] Also, since most power analyses treat conflict as a necessary condition of power, such studies may be viewed as a special type of conflict research.

Improved understanding of the feasibility and/or desirability of conceptually integrating power analysis and social exchange theory should aid in choosing overall social science research strategies. Dahrendorf has argued that at least two basic social science models are needed because "society has two faces of equal reality: one of stability, harmony, and consensus and one of change, conflict, and constraint."[2] Similarly, Eckstein argues that "there are two fundamental sciences of society: that dealing with symmetrical social relationships and that dealing with asymmetric

---

[1] Walter Korpi, "Conflict, Power and Relative Deprivation," *American Political Science Review*, 68 (1974), pp. 1569–78.

[2] Ralf Dahrendorf, "Out of Utopia: Toward a Reorientation of Sociological Analysis," *American Journal of Sociology*, 64 (1958), p. 127.

ones in social units – 'economics' and 'politics.' "[3] There are two basic models of social interaction, however, that may *combine* cooperative and conflictual approaches.[4] Harsanyi claims that modern game theory has demonstrated that "the same theoretical model can handle both conflict and cooperation without any difficulty."[5] The question here is whether social exchange theory can also be used to explain both faces of social reality. The adequacy of such "explanations" has important implications for deciding how one stands on the questions raised by Eckstein and Dahrendorf.

How useful are exchange models in analyzing power relations? According to Homans,[6] the word "power" does not even appear in the original edition of his landmark study of social exchange, *Social Behavior: Its Elementary Forms*, which appeared in 1961. The title and the contents of Blau's *Exchange and Power in Social Life*[7] clearly imply that exchange and power constitute two different realms of human relations. Curry and Wade have noted that critics of exchange models often claim that power "cannot be conceived of in exchange terms by definition since no exchange occurs in a power relationship – there are only 'winners' (the powerful) and 'losers' (the powerless) and no two-way distribution of rewards and costs."[8] The question of whether and how exchange models can be used to enhance our understanding of power has no generally agreed upon answer.

It will be argued that:

1   all exchange relationships can be described in terms of conventional power concepts without twisting the common-sense notions that underlie such concepts;

---

[3] Harry Eckstein, "Authority Patterns: A Structural Basis for Political Inquiry," *American Political Science Review*, 67 (1973), p. 1161.

[4] Roger Masters has called my attention to ethology as a possible third approach that treats both cooperation and conflict in social interaction.

[5] John C. Harsanyi, "Rational Choice Models of Political Behavior vs. Functionalist and Conformist Theories," *World Politics*, 21 (1969), pp. 513–38.

[6] George C. Homans, *Social Behavior: Its Elementary Forms* rev. edn (New York: Harcourt, Brace, Jovanovich, 1974), p. v.

[7] Peter M. Blau, *Exchange and Power in Social Life* (New York: Wiley, 1964).

[8] Robert L. Curry and Larry L. Wade, *A Theory of Political Exchange: Economic Reasoning in Political Analysis* (Englewood Cliffs, N.J.: Prentice-Hall, 1968), p. 118.

2   most – but not necessarily all – power relationships can
    be described in terms of exchange terminology;
3   there are some advantages to conceiving of power in this
    way; and
4   recent social exchange theorists have neither illuminated
    nor recognized most of these advantages.

After a preliminary examination of the concepts of exchange and
power, the discussion will focus on the analytical and conceptual
problems associated with volition, exchange media, asymmetry,
sanctions, and authority.

EXCHANGE MODELS AND POWER CONCEPTS

Robert Dahl has suggested that "power terms in modern social
science refer to subsets of relations among social units such that
the behaviors of one or more units . . . depend in some
circumstances on the behavior of other units."[9] The intuitive idea
or common-sense notion behind power terminology has been
described by Dahl[10] in terms of A getting B to do something he
would not otherwise have done. Is this notion adequate to describe
an exchange relationship?

Suppose A's goal is to get B to sell a loaf of bread. Walking into
B's store, A has several options in choosing what kind of influence
attempt to make. A can pull out a gun and say, "Sell me the bread
or else." He can get down on his knees and beseech B to sell him
the bread. He can offer B a million dollars if B will sell him the
bread. Each of these strategies has some chance of success, but
each also involves some costs. The best way for A to balance costs
and benefits is probably going to entail checking the price tag and
offering B the amount of money printed on the tag. A walks out of
the store with the bread, having succeeded in getting B to do
something that B would not have done in the absence of A's
influence attempt. An influence attempt has succeeded; an

---

[9]   Robert A. Dahl, "Power," *International Encyclopedia of the Social Sciences*, vol. 12
(New York: Free Press, 1968), p. 407.
[10]   Robert A. Dahl, "The Concept of Power," *Behavioral Science*, 2 (1957), pp. 201–15.

exchange has occurred. Given Dahl's broad concept of power, exchange relations are simply subsets of power relations.

Can power relations be described in terms of exchange concepts? When nation A gives nation B foreign aid in return for support in the United Nations, we may say that nation A has used foreign aid to influence nation B's behavior in the United Nations (assuming that the foreign aid actually made a difference in nation B's behavior, attitudes, and/or propensities to act). It would be just as easy, however, to describe nation A as having *exchanged* foreign aid for support in the United Nations. Thus, at least some power (or influence) relations take the form of exchange.

The difficulty arises when one introduces negative sanctions (threats and/or punishments) or environmental manipulation into the power situation. "Your money or your life" can be converted into exchange terminology as follows: "You give me money, and I will let you keep your life." Some people, however, object to calling such a transaction an "exchange."[11] The phrase "your money or your life" is usually attributed to an unsavory gun-wielding outlaw, which may account for some of its bad press. The phrase is rarely attributed to the physician who has just informed the patient that he will die within a year unless he can afford the expensive operation required to save his life. In such a situation, depicting "your money or your life" as a proposed exchange may not seem quite so objectionable.[12]

Environmental manipulation and brute force are other power situations that are difficult to describe as exchange. If A can secretly control the temperature in B's room, A can get B to take off a sweater without B ever knowing about A's influence attempt.

[11] Blau, *Exchange and Power*, pp. 115–16; and Kenneth E. Boulding, "Towards a Pure Theory of Threat Systems," *American Economic Review*, 53 (1963), pp. 424–34; and Kenneth E. Boulding, "The Economics of Human Conflict," in *The Nature of Human Conflict*, ed. Elton B. McNeil (Englewood Cliffs, N.J.: Prentice-Hall, 1965), pp. 172–91.
[12] Time may also be a critical factor in explaining people's reluctance to view "your money or your life" as an exchange. The typical mugging occurs so quickly that the "muggee" does not have time to adjust his or her value expectation baseline (see Blau, *Exchange and Power*, p. 116) to the new situation. Thus, the mugger's offer of life does not seem especially generous. In airline hijackings or concentration camps, however, there is time for the new probability of losing's one life to be built into one's value expectation baseline. Once this occurs, "your money or your life" is more likely to be viewed as a genuine exchange. It is not uncommon to hear stories of victims thanking guards or hijackers for allowing them to keep their lives.

And country A may change country B's automotive production by bombing its factories. Although Dahl's broad concept of power would consider these as power relationships, most people would be reluctant to call them exchange relationships. There are, then, some power situations that are hard to describe with exchange concepts.

Although exchange relations can be considered a subset of power relations, the social exchange theorists have not provided a satisfactory account of how power relations work. Blau recognizes two concepts of social exchange, one broad, the other narrow. Although the broad one would subsume power, Blau rejects it, first, because he fears his theory will become tautological, and second, because "nothing is gained" by trying to force actions such as power relations into a conceptual framework of exchange.[13] Blau also recognizes two concepts of power, one broad enough to include exchange, the other narrow enough to exclude it.

> Broadly defined, power refers to all kinds of influence between persons or groups, including those exercised in exchange trans-actions, where one induces others to accede to his wishes by rewarding them for doing so . . . Although the customer technically imposes his will upon the jeweler when he makes him surrender a diamond ring by paying for it, this situation clearly should not be confused with that of the gangster who forces the jeweler to hand over the ring at the point of a gun.[14]

Blau thus admits the "technical" possibility of depicting exchange as a power relationship but implies that doing so would confuse the distinction between customers and gangsters. It is quite possible, however, to use a broad concept of social power while preserving the distinction between influence attempts based on positive sanctions and influence attempts based on negative sanctions (see chapter 4 above). Blau opts for a narrow definition of power that

---

[13] Blau, *Exchange and Power*, pp. 4, 6, 88–9. Blau simply asserts that "nothing is gained"; he does not prove it. Likewise, James G. March ("The Power of Power," in *Varieties of Political Theory*, ed. David Easton (Englewood Cliffs, N.J.: Prentice-Hall, 1966), pp. 65–7) acknowledges the possibility of using exchange models to explain power but asserts that we probably would not want to do so.

[14] Blau, *Exchange and Power*, pp. 115–16; see also pp. 115–42.

completely rules out positive sanctions.[15] Thus, instead of synthesizing the concepts of exchange and power, Blau accentuates the cleavage between the two concepts.

In Homans's revised edition of *Social Behavior: Its Elementary Forms*, he devotes a whole chapter to "power and authority" (pp. 70–93). For Homans, power relations are a subset of exchange relations in which one person "gets less" out of the exchange than the other.[16] Homans defines power broadly, however, so as to include both positive and negative sanctions. Thus threats and punishments can be exchanged either for rewards or for other threats and punishments. Homans (pp. 79–81) analyzes the "your money or your life" situation as an exchange and brings out *both* the similarities and differences between coercive exchange and noncoercive exchange. Even though there are drawbacks to Homans' concept of power, which I shall address later, his broad concept of power and his attempt to integrate the concepts of power and exchange are steps toward a synthesis.

To summarize, if one uses the broad concept of power associated with Dahl, exchange relations appear to be subsets of power relations. For Blau, however, exchange and power are separate and distinct realms; neither is a subset of the other. For Homans, power relations are subsets of exchange relations. Obviously, the exchange theorists use a narrower concept of power than Dahl does. It is interesting to note that neither Blau nor Homans cites the work of Dahl or Lasswell and Kaplan.[17] Having introduced the general problem of integrating power concepts into exchange models, I shall next examine several special topics related to such an undertaking.

[15] J. K. Chadwick-Jones (*Social Exchange Theory: Its Structure and Influence in Social Psychology* (London: Academic Press, 1976), pp. 281, 294, 299–300) claims that "reward power" is Blau's main concern. This is a questionable interpretation of Blau, however, since Blau (*Exchange and Power*, p. 117) explicitly defines power in terms of negative sanctions and even says that "inducing a person to render a service by rewarding him for doing so does not involve exercising power over him . . ." (p. 141). Exchange (based on positive sanctions) and power (based on negative sanctions) are separate and distinct realms for Blau.

[16] See pp. 70–93. We shall take up the question of what it means to "get less" from the exchange at a later point.

[17] Harold D. Lasswell and Abraham Kaplan, *Power and Society* (New Haven: Yale University Press, 1950).

VOLITION

"Power," in Max Weber's classic definition, "is the probability that one actor within a social relationship will be in a position to carry out his own will despite resistance, regardless of the basis on which this probability rests."[18] The words "despite resistance" are often interpreted as precluding depiction of power as a kind of exchange. Exchange, it is argued, is voluntary, while power involves A getting B to act "against his [B's] will." Thus, power relations are characterized by conflict, while exchange relations are characterized by cooperation.

Three questions may be asked about dichotomizing power and conflict on the one hand and exchange and cooperation on the other: (1) Is it useful for social analysis? (2) What does it mean? (3) Is conflict present in a routine commercial transaction? If one conceives of most social situations as mixtures of conflict and cooperation, with pure conflict and pure cooperation as polar types rarely found in the real world, then the conflict/cooperation dichotomy is not likely to appeal. Harsanyi and Schelling have argued in favor of models that incorporate both conflictual and cooperative elements.[19] Power without cooperation and exchange without conflict are not prototypical cases, but rather bizarre extremes rarely encountered in real life. In *The Strategy of Conflict*, Schelling showed that even war, often thought to be an example of pure conflict, has significant cooperative dimensions.

We might also ask what it means to describe B either as acting voluntarily or "against his will." If one were to ask whether someone would like to work eight hours a day on an assembly line, it is doubtful that any answer whatsoever would be forthcoming until the reward (wage) was specified or implied. I know very few college professors who would say "yes" if the wages were three dollars per hour, but I know very few who

---

[18] Max Weber, *The Theory of Social and Economic Organization*, trans. A. M. Henderson and Talcott Parsons (New York: Free Press, 1947), p. 152.

[19] Harsanyi, "Rational Choice Models"; and Thomas C. Schelling, *The Strategy of Conflict* (Cambridge, Mass.: Harvard University Press, 1960). When *The Strategy of Conflict* was reprinted in 1980, the author added a preface of particular relevance to the point at hand.

would say "no" if the wages were a million dollars per hour. The point is, of course, that B can make no meaningful assessment of his "will" without taking opportunity costs into account – and neither can the social scientist who wants to explain B's response to A's influence attempt. To describe a power relationship in terms of A getting B to do something against his will is to obscure the heart of the power process, i.e., A's manipulation of the incentives (or opportunity costs) that B associates with various courses of action.[20] It is precisely B's "will" that A is trying to change. The apothegm that "every man has his price" is no doubt false, but it represents an analytical perspective that is more useful to the student of power than the perspective that depicts people as "acting against their wills."[21]

This is not to say that measuring (or estimating) B's willingness to do X (perceived opportunity costs of doing X) is not important in measuring A's power over B; the point is that B's willingness to do X should not be dichotomized so that B is either "willing" or "unwilling" to do X. Parsons and Smelser have pointed out that the same logic that underlies the economists' supply and demand schedules also "applies to the performance–sanction relationship in all social interaction."[22] In other words, the likelihood that B will perform X may depend on the sanction (positive or negative) provided by A. Supply and demand schedules may thus be considered as describing a kind of power relationship. To ask whether B is "willing" to do X is like asking whether General Motors is "willing" to provide you with a car. Neither question can be answered satisfactorily until the price is specified or implied.

Some would deny that a routine commercial exchange involves a significant amount of conflict. The mutual interest of both buyer and seller in reaching agreement and the mechanics of the price system tend to obscure the conflictual aspects of the situation. From the standpoint of the buyer, the lower the price the better.

---

[20] John C. Harsanyi, "Measurement of Social Power, Opportunity Costs, and the Theory of Two-person Bargaining Games," *Behavioral Science*, 7 (1962), pp. 67–80.

[21] Cf. Blau, *Exchange and Power*, pp. 91–2; and Felix E. Oppenheim, *Dimensions of Freedom* (New York: St Martin's Press, 1961).

[22] Talcott Parsons and Neil J. Smelser, *Economy and Society: A Study of the Integration of Economic and Social Theory* (Glencoe, Ill.: Free Press, 1956), pp. 10, 13.

From the standpoint of the seller, the higher the price the better. The exchange will be consummated only if the highest price the buyer is willing to pay overlaps with the lowest price the seller is willing to accept. The price system enables both A and B to cut the costs of acquiring information about each other's bargaining position. The establishment and promulgation of a "going market price" for a loaf of bread provides each with information about what price is likely to be acceptable to the other. Thus, the observer of a routine purchase of a loaf of bread is likely to see very little evidence of conflict, but this is primarily because the price system facilitates rapid resolution of the conflict and agreement on a "fair price."[23] If the same observer were to witness a routine economic exchange in a nonmarket economy, the evidence of conflict between buyer and seller would be more obvious.

In sum, the problem of volition does not provide an insuperable obstacle to conceiving of power as exchange. Both conflict and cooperation are present in most social situations, and the willingness of B to comply with A's demands is a function of the opportunity costs that B associates with compliance. Since the purpose of A's influence attempt is to change B's perceived opportunity costs of compliance (and/or noncompliance), it is not very helpful to describe A as influencing B by getting B to do something "against his will" or "despite his resistance."

MEDIA OF EXCHANGE

Some see power as distinct from exchange; some view power as a kind of exchange; and others treat power as a medium of

---

[23] For an expanded discussion of the role of conflict in economic exchange that also notes the tendency of the market to disguise the dynamics of the situation, see Boulding, "Economics of Human Conflict." Since the market facilitates "anticipated reactions," it is difficult to observe influence relations in routine commercial transactions. Nagel handles this analytical problem very well by pointing out that "in studying influence, attention should not generally focus upon exact sequences of action and response." Such interactions, he notes, are often present but are not a prerequisite for influence to exist. See Jack H. Nagel, *The Descriptive Analysis of Power* (New Haven: Yale University Press, 1975), p. 145.

exchange.[24] Many questions are raised by such viewpoints, but only two will be addressed here. First, what are the implications of considering power as a medium of exchange akin to money? And second, how is economic exchange different from other kinds of exchange? Since I have presented an extended critique of the "power as money" analogy in chapter 2, only brief recapitulation is needed here. The most important point to be made is that the standard social science concept of power[25] as a *relation* is incompatible with the "power as money" analogy. Although purchasing power may be conceived of as a kind of power relation, money is more like a power resource or power base. If one thinks it useful to distinguish between power resources and power relations, one should be wary of attempts to depict power as a medium of exchange. Parsons has explicitly complained that Dahl's concept of power makes it logically impossible to treat power as a "[M]echanism operating to bring about changes in the action of other units."[26] This is true, since Dahl's concept of power refers to a relationship rather than a mechanism. Power defined as a relation refers to the *process* of A getting B to do something B would not otherwise do; but power defined as a

---

[24] Talcott Parsons, "On the Concept of Political Power," *Proceedings of the American Philosophical Society*, 107 (1963), pp. 232–62; and Karl W. Deutsch, *The Nerves of Government* (New York: Free Press, 1963).

[25] Reference to a standard or conventional social science concept of power may strike some readers as presumptuous, since it implies some consensus on power terminology. The frequently heard assertion that there is no such consensus is simply not true. Consensus is a matter of degree and need not imply unanimity. The consensus may be only partial but it certainly does exist. The significant thing is not that Robert Dahl in "Power", and Dorwin Cartwright in "Influence, Leadership, Control," in *Handbook of Organizations*, ed. James March (Chicago: Rand McNally, 1965), pp. 1–47, found it difficult to summarize and integrate the power literature but that they were able to do it so well. The works by Lasswell and Kaplan, Dahl, and Cartwright have many differences, but they have enough in common to justify reference to a "standard" or "conventional" approach to the study of power. For example, all three works conceive of influence as a relation rather than a property; all three stress the need to specify scope; and all three allow for both positive and negative sanctions in discussing influence. References to the conventional social science concept of power in this book refer to the general conceptual outlook of these three works. It should also be noted that in this book the terms "influence," "power," and "control" are used interchangeably. Furthermore, all references to A's effect on B's "behavior" in this book should be interpreted to include changes in B's beliefs, attitudes, opinions, expectation, and/or emotions as well as changes in observable behavior. Cf. Nagel, *Descriptive Analysis of Power*, p. 12.

[26] Parsons, "Political Power," p. 232.

medium of exchange refers to one of several *means* by which A can affect B's behavior.

Much of the confusion about treating approval, status, esteem, compliance, reputation, or power as media of exchange could be eliminated by clarifying the differences between economic exchange and social or political exchange.[27] If one is referring to direct exchange (pure barter) without a common denominator of value,[28] there are not many differences among the following exchange situations:

> One cow for two pigs.
> Two sacks of wheat for five days of work.
> One favor for another.
> Esteem for a favor.
> Love for love.
> Compliance with a request for approval.
> A vote in the United Nations for foreign aid.

In each of these situations the trading partners will have difficulty deciding whether they have made a "fair trade," since they have no standardized measure of value for reference.[29]

In *Exchange and Power* (pp. 8, 93–5) Blau distinguishes social exchange from economic exchange in terms of the specificity of the obligations incurred. When B does A a favor, A incurs an obligation to do B a favor sometime in the future. A's feeling of indebtedness to B, however, lacks specificity because there is no

[27] See Blau, *Exchange and Power*; Homans, *Social Behavior*; Chadwick-Jones, *Social Exchange Theory*; and Sidney R. Waldman, *Foundations of Political Action: An Exchange Theory of Politics* (Boston: Little, Brown, 1972).

[28] Technically, pure barter implies direct exchange, but need not imply the absence of a standardized measure of value. It is thus possible for the measure-of-value function of money to be performed by something other than that which performs the medium-of-exchange function of money. As a practical matter, however, the two functions are so highly interdependent that it is difficult to imagine pure barter in the presence of a common denominator of value (cf. Blau, *Exchange and Power*, pp. 268–9). For purposes of this discussion, therefore, references to barter situations imply the absence of both exchange media and a standardized accounting unit.

[29] Strictly speaking, a standardized measure of value facilitates judgments as to the fairness of an exchange but is not a logical necessity. It is hypothetically possible to imagine a pure barter market in which every item traded has a "going" or conventional exchange rate in terms of every other item. If 1,000 items were traded in the market, each item would have 999 "going market prices." For markets above a certain size, money may be a practical necessity; but it is not a logical necessity.

generally recognized common denominator of value for comparing the worth of various favors. "In contrast to economic commodities, the benefits involved in social exchange do not have an exact price in terms of a single quantitative medium of exchange . . ." (p. 94). It is clear that what Blau has in mind is *not* the general case of economic exchange but rather the special case in which a recognized standard of value is operating as a medium of exchange.

Since barter is so rarely encountered in everyday economic exchange, one might ask why it matters which concept of economic exchange Blau uses. The answer is that only by understanding precisely what difference money makes in economic exchange can one understand the role other media of exchange play in non-economic exchange. The key to understanding social and economic exchange is recognizing that there is one – and only one – important difference between economic exchange in a monetary economy and social or political exchange. That difference is the presence of a generally recognized measure of value that also serves as a highly liquid medium of exchange, i.e., money. It is money that sets economic exchanges apart from other kinds of social interaction.

Blau claims that "social exchange differs in important ways from strictly economic exchange," (pp. 93–5) but all the differences he identifies can be reduced to one – the absence of a counterpart for money. When Blau notes the unspecified obligations arising from social exchange, he is simply pointing out one of the implications of trade without money. When Blau cites the absence of an "exact price in terms of a single quantitative medium of exchange" as "another reason why social obligations are unspecific," the citation is both misleading and redundant. The absence of "an exact price in terms of a single quantitative medium of exchange" is not an additional reason why social obligations lack specificity; it is the *only* reason.

When Blau portrays the "compliance of others" as a "generalized means of social exchange, similar to money in economic exchange (except that it is far less liquid than money)" (p. 170) he implies that money and compliance have a lot in common but differ in degree of liquidity. It is as if he had said, "John is similar to Bill except for his red hair." One would conclude from this that John and Bill share many characteristics other than hair color. The difficulty here is that liquidity is not just one of several characteristics of money; it is the essential defining characteristic. Blau admits as much later in the book (p. 269) when he observes that "money differs from other valuables only in the higher degree of its liquidity, that is, the greater ease with which it can be converted into other commodities." We may now recast Blau's earlier comparison of compliance and money as follows: "Compliance of others is similar to money except with regard to the only characteristic that really matters, the degree of liquidity."

To summarize, the analogy between power and money is rejected as incompatible with the standard social science usage of the term "power." Economic exchange is not much different from social exchange except in a money economy. Although indirect exchange, i.e., exchange via media of exchange, is both conceptually possible and empirically probable in non-economic exchange, no media bearing a significant resemblance to money are likely to be found. Instead of *comparing* the media of non-economic exchange with money – as exchange theorists[30] are prone to do – one should emphasize the *contrast* between economic and non-economic media of exchange. In order to examine the opportunities and limitations of exchange models in the study of power, one must recognize that money is a very unusual (one is tempted to say unique) medium of exchange that also serves as a standardized measure of value. In short, economic exchange (in a money economy) is different because money is special. Attempts to obscure the special qualities of money make it difficult to adapt exchange models to the study of power.

ASYMMETRY IN POWER RELATIONS

The most important obstacle to analyzing power in terms of exchange is the concept of power as an asymmetrical human relationship. As noted at the beginning of this chapter, Eckstein even suggests that the distinction between symmetric and asymmetric social relationships delineates "two fundamental sciences

[30] Chadwick-Jones, *Social Exchange Theory*, p. 20; Blau, *Exchange and Power*, p. 22; and Waldman, *Foundations of Political Action*, p. 77.

of society." Economics, based on exchange and symmetry, and politics, based on power and asymmetry, are thus relegated to fundamentally different categories of social interaction. Such a distinction discourages attempts to synthesize power analysis and exchange analysis.

Exchange theorists might be expected to oppose the conception of power as asymmetrical, emphasizing instead the reciprocal nature of power relations. Not so. Far from rejecting the asymmetrical concept of power, exchange theorists[31] have embraced it and thereby compounded the difficulties of incorporating the standard social science concept of power into exchange models. These difficulties concern the ambiguity of the notion of asymmetrical power, the need to specify scope in defining power, and the treatment of costs.

At least four notions of "asymmetry" can be found in discussions of the inherently asymmetrical nature of power, including asymmetry of causation, imbalance of influence, unequal benefits, and uneven distribution of power. Power may be conceived of as a causal relationship, and all causal relationships are asymmetrical in the sense that if event C causes E, E does not cause C.[32] Both Simon and March suggest that power is also asymmetrical in the sense that if A has power over B, B does not have power over A. March claims that "the statement that A *influences* B excludes the possibility that B *influences* A."[33]

There is a big difference, however, between saying that event E caused event C and saying that person A influenced person B. That difference is implied by the term "scope."[34] Since people perform different activities, it is quite possible – and highly probable – that A's power over B will be limited to certain dimensions of B's behavior. Thus, person A may be influencing person B with respect

[31] Homans, *Social Behavior*, pp. 70–1, 77, 83; Blau, *Exchange and Power*, pp. 117–18, 312–13; Chadwick-Jones, *Social Exchange Theory*, pp. 299–300, 355–7; and Warren F. Ilchman, *Comparative Public Administration and "Conventional Wisdom"* (Beverley Hills, Cal.: Sage, 1971), pp. 18–19.

[32] Cf. Oppenheim, *Dimensions of Freedom*, p. 104; Dahl, "Power," p. 410; Nagel, *Descriptive Analysis of Power*, pp. 35–51, 141–53; and Herbert A. Simon, *Models of Man* (New York: Wiley, 1957), pp. 5, 11–12, 66.

[33] James G. March, "An Introduction to the Theory and Measurement of Influence," *American Political Science Review*, 49 (1955), p. 436.

[34] Lasswell and Kaplan, *Power and Society*, pp. 73, 77.

to X at the same time that person B is influencing person A with respect to Y. It is for this reason that many power theorists consider a statement of an influence relationship that fails to specify scope as virtually meaningless.[35]

It is not the purpose of this discussion to deny either the causal nature of power or the asymmetrical nature of causation. It is to point out that attempts to discuss the implications of causal asymmetry for power analysis often lead to confusion because of failure to give sufficient attention to the specification of scope. Causal asymmetry does not preclude the existence of symmetrical reciprocal influence relationships in the real world. As Nagel has observed, "it is important to distinguish the asymmetry of . . . social relations from the asymmetry of variables in a model. Only the latter is a defining characteristic of power."[36]

A second notion of inherent power asymmetry conceives of power as a situation in which A has more power over B than B has over A.[37] Mutual influence of equal strength, according to Blau in *Exchange and Power* (pp. 117–18), indicates lack of power. This notion of power necessitates comparison between A's power over B and B's power over A, thus implying that the scopes are comparable. Even seemingly comparable scopes, however, are likely to present problems for the power analyst. Soviet–American nuclear deterrence is often thought of as mutual influence. Even granting that these are roughly comparable scopes, there is something anomalous about describing this situation as character-

[35] Lasswell and Kaplan, *Power and Society*, p. 76; Nagel, *Descriptive Analysis of Power*, p. 14; Dahl, "Power," p. 408; and Robert A. Dahl, *Modern Political Analysis*, 4th edn (Englewood Cliffs, N.J.: Prentice-Hall, 1984), p. 27.

[36] Nagel, *Descriptive Analysis of Power*, p. 146. In my opinion, efforts to equate causal asymmetry with power asymmetry have been counterproductive to the extent that they have obscured one of Lasswell and Kaplan's most fundamental points – the need to treat power as a triadic relationship (*Power and Society*, p. 76). In *Models of Man* (p. 63) Simon portrayed his work as "footnotes" to the work of Lasswell and Kaplan and attributed the notion of power asymmetry to them. This was unfortunate, since Lasswell and Kaplan were sensitive to reciprocity and symmetry in power relations and believed that power should not "be conceived as a unilateral relationship" (*Power and Society*, p. 201). Subsequent references to the "asymmetrical notion of power" in this chapter refer to the "imbalance-of-influence" sense of this term unless another meaning is specified. For a thorough discussion of causal asymmetry and power asymmetry, see Nagel, *Descriptive Analysis of Power*.

[37] Eckstein, "Authority Patterns," p. 1146; Blau, *Exchange and Power*, pp. 117–18; and Dennis H. Wrong, "Some Problems in Defining Social Power," *American Journal of Sociology*, 73 (1968), p. 673.

ized by an absence of power. Conventional social science usage would describe Soviet–American nuclear deterrence as two separate and relatively successful influence attempts. Two advantages of conventional usage are, first, that comparing scopes is optional rather than required and, second, that interdependence can be differentiated from independence. Many social scientists find it useful to distinguish between situations characterized by mutual influence among actors (interdependence) and situations characterized by a lack of influence among actors (independence).

Suppose A has the power to get B to play the piano (using positive and/or negative sanctions), while B has the power to get A to rake the yard (using positive and/or negative sanctions). Which one has more power? The notion of power as an imbalance of power between A and B requires an answer, but the conventional concept of power does not. If there were a generally agreed upon common denominator to which forms of power could be reduced, comparing different scopes would be easy – but no such standardized measuring rod for power exists.[38] It is precisely because of the absence of close counterparts to money in non-economic social interaction that scope must be specified in defining influence relationships.

The criticism of the asymmetrical notion of power presented here should be distinguished from that of Wrong. Wrong objects to Blau's contention that power relations are always asymmetrical on the grounds that many power situations are characterized by reciprocal influence with regard to different scopes. Although Wrong admits that "asymmetry exists in each individual act–response sequence," he observes that "the actors continually alternate the roles of power holder and power subject in the total course of their interaction" so that a pattern may emerge in which one actor controls the other with respect to particular spheres of conduct, "while the other actor is regularly dominant in other areas of situated activity."[39] Thus, Wrong posits a social situation in which each individual power relationship is asymmetrical (in that "the power holder exercises greater control over the behavior

---

[38] See the discussion in chapter 2. See also, Dahl, *Modern Political Analysis*, 4th edn, pp. 26–30; and Robert A. Dahl and Charles E. Lindblom, *Politics, Economics, and Welfare* (New York: Harper & Row, 1953), pp. 228–9.

[39] Wrong, "Some Problems in Defining Social Power," pp. 673–4.

of the power subject than the reverse"), but in which A's ability to get B to play the piano is "balanced" by B's ability to get A to rake the yard.[40]

Wrong rightly criticizes Blau's failure to account for different scopes, but he stops short of objecting to the asymmetrical concept of power. In the absence of a common denominator of power values (i.e., a functional equivalent for money) for comparing different scopes, it is difficult to accept the notion of "individual act–response sequences" as asymmetrical. What standardized measuring rod are we to use in comparing A's control over B with B's control over A? When the United States tried to make North Vietnam give up its activities in South Vietnam, how successful was its influence attempt? Although the conventional concept of power permits a straightforward – but not necessarily easy – answer to this question, the "asymmetry imbalance" concept of power requires a comparison between the US attempt to influence North Vietnam and the North Vietnamese attempt to get the Americans to go home. In other words, one is supposed to compare getting a country to give up claims to what it perceives as its own land and people[41] with getting a foreign power to stop intervening in one's country. Although others may describe differently the scopes of the American and North Vietnamese influence attempts, the point is that the two nations were engaged in fundamentally different kinds of influence attempts. Even those

[40] Wrong uses the term "intercursive power" to refer to "relations between persons or groups in which the control of one person or group over the other with reference to a particular scope is balanced by the control of the other in a different scope" ("Some Problems in Defining Social Power," p. 674). Nagel points out that such situations can be analyzed in terms of separate and distinct influence attempts by each party. In such situations A and B control *different* outcomes *vis-à-vis* each other. There are, of course, other situations in which A and B share power over a single outcome (see Nagel, *Descriptive Analysis of Power*, pp. 144–6). Thus, part of the difficulty in conceiving of routine commercial transactions as power relationships stems from the inclusion of both intercursive and shared power over a single outcome in such situations. The price (or exchange rate) is a single outcome over which the buyer and seller share power. Intercursive power, however, is also involved since the buyer is trying to obtain goods and/or services, while the seller is trying to obtain money. A full description of the power dimensions of a commercial transaction would have to include both kinds of power. "Buying a car" and "buying a car at a good price" are not necessarily (or even usually) the same thing – one has to work harder at the second than at the first.

[41] Ralph K. White, *Nobody Wanted War: Misperception in Vietnam and Other Wars* (Garden City, N.Y.: Doubleday, 1970).

who deny the significance of the "territorial imperative" ought to admit the difference between aggression and resistance to aggression, between making an influence attempt and resisting one.[42]

In sum, there are two good reasons for rejecting the notion of power that implies a necessary imbalance of influence between A and B. First, it requires a comparison between influence attempts with different scopes in the absence of a generally agreed upon criterion for making such comparisons. And second, the common-sense intuitive notion of power is captured at least as well by the concept of power developed by Dahl and others.

Homans' concept of asymmetrical power falls on the borderline between the "imbalance" notion and a third category based on unequal benefits; it thus deserves separate treatment.[43] Homans begins by defining power as asymmetrical in the sense that the behavior of one of the parties to an exchange "changes in some sense more than the behavior of the other." Homans uses the example of an exchange of advice for approval,[44] thus raising the question of how to compare a change in approval with a change in advice in the absence of a common denominator of value. Since the difficulties of comparing different scopes have already been discussed, there is no need to belabor this point.

Homans then shifts the focus of his discussion of power from the amount of behavior change to the "net reward" each party derives from the exchange. The "general condition that establishes interpersonal power," according to Homans, is that one party "gets less out of the exchange" than the other. Although one might think that the person "getting less" from the exchange is the weaker, this is not what Homans has in mind. Instead, he states – or restates – the "principle of least interest," in which "the person who is perceived by the other as the less interested, the more indifferent, to the exchange is apt to have the greater power." This principle, of course, has been discussed by Thibaut and Kelley and

---

[42] Cf. White, *Nobody Wanted War*; Robert Ardrey, *The Territorial Imperative* (New York: Atheneum, 1966); and Konrad Lorenz, *On Aggression* (New York: Harcourt, Brace, and World, 1966).

[43] The discussion that follows is based on pp. 70–83 of Homans, *Social Behavior*.

[44] This example is used often by Homans. It refers to an experienced office worker's willingness to give helpful advice to less experienced fellow workers and their willingness to give gratitude and admiration in return.

by Schelling, and many would consider it a useful empirical observation about certain kinds of bargaining situations.[45] For Homans, however, it is not merely a useful insight, it is "the one essential characteristic of power." He thus defines power as follows:

> When A's net reward – compared, that is, with his alternatives – in taking action that will reward B is less, at least as perceived by B, than B's net reward in taking action that will reward A, and B as a result changes his behavior in a way favorable to A, then A has exerted power over B.

In addition to the cumbersome wording, there are at least two difficulties with this definition. First, the role of B's perceptions is not clear. If B's perceptions of A's relative indifference are crucial, why even mention the real situation? If B's perceptions are what matter, why does Homans (p. 85) insist that "it is necessary to know the payoffs for both parties, not just for one of them?" A second difficulty is the possibility that interpersonal comparisons of subjective value are implied by the need to compare A's reward with B's. Although Homans (p. 74) explicitly denies that this problem exists, his explanation begs several questions. For example, Homans argues that objective indicators of net rewards can be found but then admits that such indicators can be manipulated by each party so as to mislead the other. Furthermore, Homans' argument that the actual participants in the power transaction can avoid direct interpersonal value comparisons is beside the point. The prohibition on such comparisons is a methodological constraint on social scientists, not on other people. In our everyday lives we can and do make methodologically unsound value comparisons all the time.

In addition to causal asymmetry, "imbalance" asymmetry, and "unequal benefit" asymmetry, some would say that power asymmetry resides in the uneven distribution of power resources. In every society some people have more power than others, and there is an implication of asymmetry in that fact. This concept is mentioned here only to show how appealing the idea of power as

[45] John W. Thibaut and Harold H. Kelley, *The Social Psychology of Groups* (New York: Wiley, 1959), p. 103; and Schelling, *Strategy of Conflict*.

inherently asymmetrical can be. When someone observes that power is asymmetrical, everyone may nod; but they do not necessarily agree on the meaning of the message.

Thus far, objections to the concept of power as inherently asymmetrical have stemmed primarily from the relative absence of counterparts to money in social exchange and the consequent need to specify scope in defining and measuring power. Nagel, however, has suggested still another objection, based on the *costs* of making influence attempts.[46] Nagel points out that many influence situations require A to reward, punish, threaten, promise, furnish information, and/or monitor in order to get B to do X. Since "these behaviors of A are caused by B's reluctance to do X (or, more generally, by the improbability of B's doing X spontaneously)," Nagel suggests, "they indicate the scope of B's power over A."[47] Thus, when the opportunity costs of A's influence attempt are taken into account, the inherently asymmetrical concept of power is further called into question.

Consider two examples that Eckstein claims are "clearly asymmetric" – "the power of a criminal over his victim or the slow driver over the queues in his wake."[48] If A must commit a criminal act in order to get B to do X, A has modified his behavior in what is likely to be a significant and costly way. Likewise, the slow driver can make those behind him late for work, but only by driving so slowly that he risks making himself late also. In such situations A influences B to do X, but B's reluctance to do X also affects A's behavior. If power costs are considered, such situations are not so "clearly asymmetric" as they appear to be.[49]

In sum, several notions of power as inherently asymmetrical

[46] Jack H. Nagel, "Some Questions About the Concept of Power," *Behavioral Science*, 13 (1968), pp. 135–7.

[47] In a later work (*Descriptive Analysis of Power*, p. 141n.), Nagel modifies his position, arguing that "the effects a weaker actor may have upon a stronger cannot generally be construed as power because they are not necessarily the consequence of the weaker actor's preferences." For purposes of this discussion, however, the fact that such effects are sometimes a consequence of the weaker actor's preferences is sufficient to call into question the notion of power as inherently asymmetrical in the "imbalance" sense.

[48] Eckstein, "Authority Patterns," p. 1150.

[49] On the importance of power costs, see chapter 5. See also, Nagel, "Some Questions"; Harsanyi, "Measurement of Social Power"; and Deutsch, *Nerves of Government*, pp. 110–16. Deutsch quotes Booker T. Washington: "The only way the white man in the South can keep the Negro in the ditch is to stay in the ditch with him."

have been examined. The causal asymmetry notion is valid but can be confusing when it is applied to power relations. The "imbalance" notion and the "unequal benefits" notion, however, have serious drawbacks. The concept of power developed by Dahl, Lasswell and Kaplan, and others involves causal asymmetry but allows for both symmetric and asymmetric power relationships. Since exchange relations connote reciprocity and the possibility – but not the necessity – of symmetry, the "imbalance" and "unequal benefits" notions of power as inherently asymmetrical are not well suited for inclusion in exchange models.[50]

POSITIVE VERSUS NEGATIVE SANCTIONS

The distinction between positive and negative sanctions has been an important obstacle to incorporating a broad concept of power into social exchange models. Exchange is often depicted as mutually rewarding and beneficial, while power relations are often portrayed as based on negative sanctions and detrimental to the object of the influence attempt. A fundamental difference between Blau and Homans on this point should be noted: On the one hand, Blau defines exchange in terms of positive sanctions and power in terms of negative sanctions.[51] Homans, on the other hand, objects to such a view:

> Who shall say that a man who offers others good pay to do his bidding, and they jump at the chance, has not exerted power over them? The trouble is that in the everyday thinking of many of us we do not consider power to be really power unless it is accompanied by orders, threats, the imposition of wills, and resistance. We believe power to be inherently evil, though sometimes necessary.

[50] For more comments on defining power in terms of asymmetry, see Cartwright, "Influence, Leadership, Control," pp. 197–8; Oppenheim, *Dimensions of Freedom*, pp. 104–6; Harsanyi, "Measurement of Social Power"; Nagel, *Descriptive Analysis of Power*, pp. 141–53; Dahl, *Modern Political Analysis*, 4th edn, pp. 43–4; and Edmund Dahlstrom, "Exchange, Influence and Power," *Acta Sociologica*, 9 (1966), pp. 237–84. It should be emphasized that no one advocates viewing power as inherently symmetrical. The fruitful alternative to the assumption of asymmetry is the assumption of non-symmetry, which allows for both symmetrical and asymmetrical power relations.

[51] Blau, *Exchange and Power*, pp. 91–2, 115–17.

Yet none of these things is essential to power as we shall define it. Indeed, if we could count up all the examples of the exertion of power, we suspect that we should find the noncoercive form to be far more common than the coercive.[52]

The initial requirements for integration of exchange analysis and power analysis are a concept of power broad enough to subsume positive sanctions and a concept of exchange broad enough to include negative sanctions. Homans, Ilchman and Uphoff, and Waldman have demonstrated that exchange models can be used to explain social interaction based on threats and/or punishments.[53] Others have shown that power can be defined so as to allow for influence attempts based on positive sanctions.[54] Such a broad concept of power has an important advantage over one based only on negative sanctions – it facilitates description of the full range of policy options available to A in making an influence attempt on B. As Harsanyi has pointed out, this is "one of the main purposes for which social scientists use the concept of A's power over B."[55] I have never come across a serious scholarly argument in favor of confining an examination of A's policy options to those based on negative sanctions. The distinction between positive and negative sanctions is useful, but it does not require us to differentiate exchange from power.

AUTHORITY

It is sometimes suggested that authority – or legitimate power – presents especially difficult analytical problems, and much futile debate has focused on the similarities and differences between power and authority. At first glance, authority relations would seem quite different from exchange relations; but closer scrutiny discredits this first impression. Indeed, social exchange theory has

---

[52] Homans, *Social Behavior*, p. 83.
[53] Homans, *Social Behavior*; Waldman, *Foundations of Political Action*; and Warren F. Ilchman and Norman T. Uphoff, *The Political Economy of Change* (Berkeley: University of California Press, 1969).
[54] See chapter 4.
[55] Harsanyi, "Measurement of Social Power," p. 69.

made some of its most impressive contributions in discussions of authority and legitimacy.[56] This is not surprising when we consider the sensitivity of all social exchange theorists to the importance of positive sanctions in social life and the importance of such sanctions in determining legitimacy. The adage that "one can do anything with bayonets except sit on them" suggests that negative sanctions are less useful for acquiring legitimacy than are positive sanctions. One rarely builds a high degree of legitimacy by terror, coercion, punishment, threats, intimidation, and harassment.

Analysis of authority in terms of exchange concepts is hardly new. Social contract theorists, such as Thomas Hobbes and John Locke, placed social exchange at the heart of their explanations of political authority. They envisioned the public as giving political leaders obedience and legitimacy in return for effective performance of governmental duties. Moreover, should political leaders prove unable to perform such services, the public has the right to withdraw its allegiance and stop obeying.

Recent social exchange theorists' treatment of authority is remarkably consistent with the traditional social contract explanation. In *Exchange and Power* (p. 209), Blau for example, describes authority relations from the perspective of the individual and of the collectivity. From the individual's standpoint, obedience to the law is exchanged for social approval from one's peers; thus, the exchange between the individual and the government is indirect. The collectivity of individuals, however, gives governmental leaders two things – prevailing compliance with lawful orders and a set of social norms that help enforce compliance – in direct exchange for the contribution to the common welfare furnished by political leaders. Thus, individual incentives to obey the law (authoritative commands) are seen as different from the incentives for the collectivity. In *Foundations of Political Action* (pp. 89–117) Waldman places less emphasis on the difference between individual and group perspectives but still views legitimacy as something conferred on governments in exchange for satisfaction of basic desires for security, welfare, and dignity. Waldman argues that his exchange analysis of legitimacy is "not inconsistent with other explanations of the phenomenon" and that it "refines and

[56] E.g., Blau, *Exchange and Power*; Waldman, *Foundations of Political Action*; and Ilchman and Uphoff, *Political Economy of Change*.

accounts for the validity of some of the classic explanations of authority."

Authority relations present no insurmountable analytical problems for exchange theorists. Explanation of authority in terms of exchange is an ancient, honorable, and still viable tradition.[57]

CONCLUSION

The purpose of this chapter is to evaluate the possibility and/or desirability of conceptual integration of two key social science terms – power and exchange. The discussion thus far has shown the possibility of using power terminology to describe exchange relations and the possibility of using exchange terminology to describe many kinds of power relations. In the remainder of the discussion I will consider Cartwright's criticisms of treating power as a kind of exchange and identify the potential *advantages* of such treatment. Proper evaluation, of course, would require identification of *disadvantages* and weighing them against the advantages. The disadvantages of using exchange models to study power, however, will not be considered here. This lacuna is not only due to space limitations but also to the principle of "comparative need," i.e., it is often implied that the advantages are nonexistent. I suspect that the final accounting will fail to yield a clear-cut answer regarding the wisdom of treating power in terms of exchange models. The concept of power may be more useful in looking at social relations from the standpoint of a single actor. Although this is a legitimate analytical focus for a social scientist, it is not the only legitimate one. The concept of exchange may be more useful when one wants to emphasize the interactive or reciprocal nature of the relationship. Thus, depending on one's analytical purpose, the relative desirability of emphasizing power or exchange may vary.

Cartwright observes that the "concept of exchange provides considerable insight into many aspects of the influence process," but he sees severe difficulties in attempting to conceive of all influence processes in this way.[58] These difficulties are as follows:

---

[57] For a discussion of the analogy between the economist's concept of "liquidity" and the political scientist's concept of "legitimacy," see chapter 2.

[58] Cartwright, "Influence, Leadership, Control," pp. 16–18.

Noncontingent means

When A's sanctions are contingent on B's compliance, it is relatively easy to think of the influence process in terms of exchange. However, when A rewards or punishes B in a noncontingent way – by turning up the heat so as to increase the probability that B will remove a sweater or by giving B money so as to increase the probability that B will go to a movie – the exchange analogy is less obvious.

Comment This is a valid criticism, which suggests that some kinds of power relations cannot be described in terms of exchange. It should be noted, however, that failure to account for influence attempts based on noncontingent means is a weakness found in many discussions of power regardless of whether or not they are based on exchange.[59]

No resource transfer

In A's attempt to influence B, "resources" may be consumed, transferred; or no change in ownership may occur.

Comment The validity of this criticism is questionable, since resources may be exchanged in subtle ways. Two examples used by Cartwright to illustrate influence without resource transfer are as follows: First, distinguished citizens who "lend their names" to fund-raising organizations are depicted as giving their names but also keeping them. Social exchange theory, however, can describe this situation quite well as a situation in which the distinguished citizens receive enhanced status in return for allowing their names to be used by fund-raising organizations. Second, the supervisor who promises an employee a favor but fails to fulfill the promise is described as keeping possession of the resource. Once again, exchange theory would explain this as an employee having

[59] Harsanyi's treatment of influence attempts based on noncontingent means is especially useful. He notes, moreover, that he has given this case extra attention because it "is often overlooked in the literature" ("Measurement of Social Power," p. 71). See also David A. Baldwim, "Inter-Nation Influence Revisited," *Journal of Conflict Resolution*, 15 (1971), pp. 471–86.

exchanged compliance in return for a promised favor. The subsequent breaking of the promise is beside the point. It is the value of the promise at the moment of exchange that matters, not its later devaluation. Exchange is not necessarily equitable; even those who get gypped are participating in an exchange.[60]

No commensurate units of value

Even when exchange may plausibly be said to occur, it is often most difficult to describe the exchange in commensurate units of value.

Comment This is true, but it does not constitute a serious weakness in exchange models. The exchange of approval for advice, of compliance for money, or of one favor for another does not require measurement in terms of commensurate units of value – at least not so long as we speak of it as direct exchange (barter). It is only when indirect exchange and the fairness of exchange are discussed that standardized measures of value begin to matter. One of the exchange theorists' most important insights concerns the way societal norms function as *primitive* measuring rods that make indirect social exchange possible.[61] How do we know how much compliance it is appropriate to give police officers? Social norms embodied in laws tell us. How do you know whether it is "fair" for your neighbor to ask to sleep with your spouse in return for lending you a lawnmower? Social norms tell you. And so on. The lack of commensurate units of value for measuring exchange is not a serious problem[62] for exchange models of power unless

---

[60] Cartwright's implication that a broken promise has no value is also unacceptable. Anyone with children knows that the breaking of last week's promise to take them to the movies makes it much harder to break this week's promise to take them. Broken promises can be valuable power resources, and not only for children.

[61] There is no contradiction here with the previous emphasis on the differences between the media of social exchange and money. Both social norms and money serve as media of exchange, but social norms are very primitive while money is very sophisticated. Social norms are like money in the same way that a horse is like a new Mercedes. Both are means of transportation, but what a difference!

[62] In a sense the lack of a standardized measure of value is a "serious problem" for all power analysis. It is not, however, a problem peculiar to exchange analysis.

they employ the notion of power as inherently asymmetrical in the "power imbalance" sense discussed previously.

Despite his criticism of the attempts to marry exchange and power, Cartwright contends that "it would be premature to conclude that the effort is necessarily doomed to failure." The fact that the effort is not doomed to fail, of course, does not justify the undertaking. Let us look at some of the potential advantages of treating power – at least some kinds of power – as exchange relationships.

Several advantages of treating power as exchange can be identified. Since most exchange theorists have thus far employed an asymmetric concept of power, however, some of these advantages are potential rather than actual. These potential advantages, then, pertain to treating the conventional social science concept of power in an exchange perspective.

First, treating power as exchange would emphasize the relational nature of power, since almost everyone thinks of exchange as relational. Second, emphasis on exchange and the possible reciprocity thereby implied should help students of organization theory in overcoming the often-lamented tendency to view power as vertical, hierarchical, asymmetrical, and unilateral.[63] Third, an exchange perspective on power should inhibit the tendency to view all power relations as exploitative. A zero-sum concept of power, in which A is the "victor" and B is the "victim," is not adequate for describing many kinds of power relationships. Fourth, an exchange orientation should help sensitize power theorists to the important role of costs. This has been a traditional blind spot for students of power, but it has been one of the social exchange theorists' strengths that they have made us aware of many of the less obvious costs associated with various human choices.[64] Fifth, the propensity of power theorists to ignore positive sanctions might be offset by the exchange theorists' emphasis on rewards. And sixth, integration of such basic concepts as power and exchange could be a step toward

[63] Cartwright, "Influence, Leadership, Control," p. 2; and Dennis J. Palumbo, "Organization Theory and Political Science," in *Handbook of Political Science*, vol. 2, ed. Fred Greenstein and Nelson Polsby (Reading, Mass.: Addison-Wesley, 1975), p. 353.
[64] Cf. Chadwick-Jones, *Social Exchange Theory*, pp. 178–80.

conceptual unification of the social sciences, thus facilitating communication among economists, political scientists, sociologists, and social psychologists.

A final and fundamental point should be of special interest to political scientists. Much contemporary thinking about politics tends to view power relations as conflictual, negative, exploitative, coercive, and unpleasant from the standpoint of the one who is influenced. Exchange relations, however, tend to be depicted as cooperative, positive, beneficial, voluntary, and pleasant. The basic conception of the relation between the people and the state that emerges from such modes of thinking is likely to emphasize autonomous individuals tolerating government as a necessary evil. By contrast, a power-exchange theory of politics, such as that proposed by G. E. G. Catlin,[65] suggests that much of the resentment, suspicion, and vilification of politics and politicians is unjustified. The political process, Catlin implies, is not nearly so asymmetric as it appears to the ordinary person. Politicians provide valuable services and should not be viewed as parasites who exploit society.

> The politician, as political capitalist, assumes responsibility and expends his energies in the labour of government in return for the interest of power. And he does this entirely legitimately insofar as the power he enjoys is the power of moulding policy which accrues to a man who has the intelligence to provide men politically with the social adjustments, securities, and facilities which they want but are unable themselves to procure. The social service of the statesman is at least as high and as much deserving of recompense as that of the financier.[66]

The question of what constitutes an "accurate" or "desirable" basic concept of the relation between the government and the governed is beyond the scope of this discussion; but if the way we think about power affects the way we conceive of this basic social relation, then the stakes involved in deciding how to treat power and exchange are far greater than first appears. The question of

[65] George E. G. Catlin, *The Science and Method of Politics* (New York: Alfred A. Knopf, 1927); and *A Study of the Principles of Politics* (New York: Macmillan, 1930).
[66] Catlin, *Principles*, pp. 184–5.

whether one agrees with Eckstein in "Authority Patterns" (p. 1159) that exchanges are elements of "dissonance" or "impurity" in the political process or whether one agrees with Dahl that exchanges "are as ubiquitous in political as in economic life"[67] deserves serious consideration by every political scientist.

[67] Dahl, *Modern Political Analysis*, 4th edn, pp. 43–4.

7

Power Analysis and World Politics:
New Trends versus Old Tendencies

From Niccolò Machiavelli and David Hume to E. H. Carr and Hans Morgenthau, power has been an important (some would say too important) variable in international political theorizing. Although some may regard power analysis as old-fashioned and outdated, recent refinements in social science thinking about power suggest the possibility of revitalizing this approach to understanding international relations.

Exact turning points in intellectual history are difficult to identify, but many would regard the publication of *Power and Society* by Harold Lasswell and Abraham Kaplan as the watershed between the older, intuitive, and ambiguous treatments of power and the clarity and precision of more recent discussions.[1] Since then, Herbert Simon, James March, Robert Dahl, Jack Nagel, and others have developed the idea of power as a type of causation.[2]

---

[1] Harold D. Lasswell and Abraham Kaplan, *Power and Society* (New Haven: Yale University Press, 1950). In an early and influential article, Herbert A. Simon described his discussion as "a series of footnotes on the analysis of influence and power by Lasswell and Kaplan." See "Notes on the Observation and Measurement of Political Power," *Journal of Politics*, 15 (1953), p. 501. See also Jack H. Nagel, "Some Questions About the Concept of Power," *Behavioral Science*, 13 (1968), p. 129.

[2] Herbert Simon, *Models of Man* (New York: Wiley, 1957); James G. March, "An Introduction to the Theory and Measurement of Influence," *American Political Science Review*, 49 (1955), pp. 431–51; Robert A. Dahl, "The Concept of Power," *Behavioral Science*, 2 (1957), pp. 201–15; and "Power," in the *International Encyclopedia of the Social Sciences*, vol. 12 (New York: Free Press, 1968), pp. 405–15; Jack H. Nagel, *The Descriptive Analysis of Power* (New Haven: Yale University Press, 1975); and Felix E. Oppenheim, "Power and Causation," in *Power and Political Theory: Some European Perspectives*, ed. Brian Barry (London: John Wiley, 1976), pp. 103–16.

This causal conception of power, according to Nagel, has proved attractive for three reasons: First, there are compelling similarities between intuitive notions of power and causation. Second, causal conceptions of power are less likely to lead to tautologies. And, third, "treatment of power as causation enables power researchers to employ methods developed for more general applications."[3]

Despite the ancient origins of the study of power, Dahl maintains that "the systematic empirical study of power relations is remarkably new."[4] He attributes the "vast improvement in the clarity" of power concepts to the fact that "the last several decades probably have witnessed more systematic efforts to tie down these concepts than have the previous millennia of political thought."[5] Even those who would dispute such assertions could agree that international political theorists might find it useful to rethink their views of power in terms of the general social power literature.[6] The purpose of this chapter is to review some scholarship in international relations with special reference to the literature on social power.[7] Topics for discussion include potential power, interdependence, military power, positive sanctions, the zero-sum concept of power, and the distinction between compellence and deterrence.

Before the discussion begins, however, one *caveat* is in order. The increased precision in recent concepts of power has threatened to overwhelm the analyst. Even those most familiar with this literature have complained of interminable theoretical distinctions

[3] Nagel, *Descriptive Analysis of Power*, pp. 9–10.

[4] Dahl, "Power," p. 414.

[5] Robert A. Dahl, *Modern Political Analysis*, 4th edn (Englewood Cliffs, N.J.: Prentice-Hall, 1984), p. 20.

[6] Two important works in international relations use Hans Morgenthau's textbook published in 1948 as their basic reference on power: Charles P. Kindleberger, *Power and Money* (New York: Basic Books, 1970), and Robert Gilpin, *U.S. Power and the Multinational Corporation* (New York: Basic Books, 1975).

[7] For a review of a different set of international relations works with regard to a different set of topics, see David Baldwin, "Inter-Nation Influence Revisited," *Journal of Conflict Resolution*, 15 (1971), pp. 471–86. For a suggestion that current "academic practitioners of international relations analysis and theory" have neglected the study of power, see Colin S. Gray, *The Geopolitics of the Nuclear Era* (New York: Crane, Russak, 1977), pp. 1–5. Gray's contention that power analysis is the only approach that "enables students to appreciate the essence of the field" of international relations, however, goes considerably beyond the argument I am presenting here.

that make a broad overview difficult to achieve.[8] For purposes of this discussion, therefore, the term "power" will be used in a broad generic sense that is interchangeable with such terms as "influence" and "control." This usage is not intended to deny the validity or the utility of distinguishing among such terms for other purposes; it is intended to imply the relevance of the following discussion for all situations in which A gets B to do something he would not otherwise do, regardless of how such situations are labeled. The primary focus will be on basic distinctions *essential* to thinking about power rather than on distinctions that are useful in some contexts but irrelevant in others. In discussing power as a type of causation, it is *essential* to specify or at least imply who is influencing whom with respect to what; in short, both scope and domain must be specified or implied.[9] Such distinctions may seem obvious and trivial at first, but I will argue that insistence on them would orient discussions of international power less toward general theories of power and more toward contextual analysis.

POWER: POTENTIAL, PROBABLE, AND ACTUAL

The frequent failure of power predictions has been noted so often by scholars, journalists, statesmen, and the "man in the street"

[8] Cartwright, "Influence, Leadership, Control," p. 4; and Robert A. Dahl, *Modern Political Analysis*, 2nd edn (Englewood Cliffs, N.J.: Prentice-Hall, 1970), p. 16.

[9] On the importance of this point, see Lasswell and Kaplan, *Power and Society*, p. 76; Dahl, "Power," p. 408; Dahl, *Modern Political Analysis*, 4th edn, pp. 26–30; and Nagel, *Descriptive Analysis of Power*, pp. 14, 115. Among students of international politics, the strongest proponents of this view have been Harold and Margaret Sprout. See their *Man–Milieu Relationship Hypotheses in the Context of International Politics*, Center of International Studies, Princeton University, Research Monograph (Princeton, 1956), pp. 39–49; "Environmental Factors in the Study of International Politics," *Journal of Conflict Resolution*, 1 (1957), pp. 309–28; *The Ecological Perspective on Human Affairs: With Special Reference to International Politics* (Princeton: Princeton University Press, 1965), pp. 83–98, 214–16; and *Toward a Politics of the Planet Earth* (New York: Van Nostrand, 1971), pp. 163–78.

One might think that the consensus on the relational nature of power and the need to specify scope and domain that has characterized the social power literature for nearly four decades would obviate the need to reiterate these points. No so! James Lee Ray and Ayse Vural dispute both the relational nature of power and the necessity of specifying scope and/or domain; see "Power Disparities and Paradoxical Conflict Outcomes," *International Interactions*, 12 (1986), pp. 318–20.

that it deserves a label – something like "the paradox of unrealized power." How is it that "weak powers" influence the "strong"? How is it that the "greatest power in the world" could suffer defeat at the hands of a "band of night-riders in black pajamas"?[10] How do we explain the "cruel and ridiculous paradox" of the "big influence of small allies"? How can the Arabs get away with defying the United States? How can tiny Israel exercise so much influence on US foreign policy? I shall consider two alternative explanations of this so-called paradox.

First, failure to translate alleged "potential power" (or power "resources") into actual power may be explained in terms of malfunctioning conversion processes. The would-be wielder of power is described as lacking in skill and/or the "will" to use his power resources effectively: "The Arabs had the tanks but didn't know how to use them." "The Americans had the bombs but lacked the will to use them." "The large states controlled the money but lacked organizational unity." And so forth.[11] Bad luck, incompetence, and pusillanimity are the most common elements in such explanations. "He had the cards but played them poorly" is the theme.

A second explanation for the failure of power predictions focuses on variations in the scope, weight, and domain of power. As Harold and Margaret Sprout have reminded us many times, the capabilities (or potential power) of an actor must be set in the context of a "policy–contingency framework" specifying who is trying (or might try) to get whom to do what.[12] From this

---

[10]   "I still believe he [President Johnson] found it viscerally inconceivable that what Walt Rostow kept telling him was 'the greatest power in the world' could not dispose of a collection of night-riders in black pajamas": Arthur Schlesinger, Jr, "The Quagmire Papers," *New York Review of Books* (December 16, 1971), p. 41.

[11]   For examples of this type of explanation, see Klaus Knorr, *Power of Nations: The Political Economy of International Relations* (New York: Basic Books, 1975), pp. 9–14; 17–18; Robert O. Keohane and Joseph S. Nye, *Power and Interdependence: World Politics in Transition* (Boston: Little, Brown, 1977), pp. 11, 18–19, 53, 225; Dahl, *Modern Political Analysis*, 4th edn, p. 31; and Ray S. Cline, *World Power Assessment: A Calculus of Strategic Drift* (Boulder, Col.: Westview Press, 1975). The inclusion of Dahl in this list is somewhat anomalous since Dahl stresses variations in the scope and domain of power.

[12]   Sprout and Sprout, *Ecological Perspective*, pp. 83–98, 214–16; and *Toward a Politics*, pp. 163–78. Actually the Sprouts' concept of a "policy–contingency framework" goes beyond specification of scope and domain to include the time, place, and means of an influence attempt. For purposes of this discussion, however, the Sprouts' insistence that

Power Analysis and World Politics

perspective, the failure of power predictions is likely to be attributed to faulty predictive techniques rather than to the actors themselves. The so-called "paradox of unrealized power" results from the mistaken belief that power resources useful in one policy–contingency framework will be equally useful in a different one. So-called "weak powers" influence so-called "strong powers" because of the power analyst's failure to account for the possibility that a country may be weak in one situation but strong in another. Planes loaded with nuclear weapons may strengthen a state's ability to deter nuclear attacks but may be irrelevant to rescuing the *Pueblo* on short notice. The ability to get other countries to refrain from attacking one's homeland is not the same as the ability to "win the hearts and minds of the people" in a faraway land. The theme of such explanations is not "he had the cards but played them poorly," but rather "he had a great bridge hand but happened to be playing poker."

In order to evaluate these alternative explanations of the "paradox of unrealized power," a closer examination of the concept of "power resources" is in order. What distinguishes power resources from other things? How fungible are power resources? What is the range of variation in the value of power resources? And what working assumptions about power resources are most suitable for international political analysis?

How are we to recognize power resources when we see them? Implicitly or explicitly, almost everyone conceives of such resources as the "means by which one person [actor] can influence the behavior of other persons [actors]."[13] One problem is that it is difficult to imagine what is excluded, since almost anything could be used to influence someone to do something in some situation or another. Another problem is that the means by which one actor can influence the behavior of another depends on who is trying to get whom to do what. A pleasant smile may suffice as a means to get the boss's attention, but a threat to quit may be required to get a raise. Diplomatic pressure may suffice to gain support on a relatively unimportant vote in the UN General Assembly, but force may be necessary to get a country to relinquish land claims. What

"policy–contingency frameworks" be specified will be treated as roughly equivalent to Dahl's insistence that scope and domain be specified.
[13] Dahl, *Modern Political Analysis*, 4th edn, p. 31.

functions as a power resource in one policy–contingency framework may be irrelevant in another. The only way to determine
whether something is a power resource or not is to place it in the
context of a real or hypothetical policy–contingency framework.[14]
Prior to the nineteenth century, neither oil nor uranium was
a power resource, since no one had any use for either. Only within
the policy–contingency framework of the past hundred years or so
have they become resources.

Although it might seem that the predictive value of power
resource inventories is impaired by insistence on prior specification of
scope and domain (or policy–contingency framework), the
opposite is true. The accuracy of our estimate of whether an
architect has "adequate" raw materials to complete his project is
likely to improve if we first ascertain whether he plans to build a
birdhouse or a cathedral.

If there were some generalized means of exercising political
power – just as money is a generalized means of exercising
purchasing power – the problem of conceiving and measuring
political power would be much simpler. Political power resources,
however, tend to be much less liquid than economic resources. The
owner of an economic resource, such as a petroleum field, has little
trouble converting it into another economic resource, such as a
factory; but the owner of a political power resource, such as the
means to deter atomic attack, is likely to have difficulty converting
this resource into another resource that would, for instance, allow
his country to become the leader of the Third World.[15] Whereas
money facilitates the exchange of one economic resource for
another, there is no standardized measure of value that serves as a
medium of exchange for political power resources.

That is not to say that some political power resources are not

---

[14] "It seems that what we call a 'resource' is such, not on its own account, but solely
because of the uses to which it can be put, and its quantitative aspect, how much resource
there is, is still more evidently determinable only in terms of the use": Frank H. Knight,
Risk, Uncertainty, and Profit (New York: Harper & Row, 1921), pp. 65–6.

[15] Ray and Vural object to this line of argument by asserting that an assumption of
"robust fungibility" has proven useful in explaining the outcomes of wars during the past
century or two. They fail, however, to point out how such war-winning ability can be
transformed into the ability to lead the Third World or to prevail in other non-military
situations. See "Power Disparities," p. 319. There is more to international politics than Ray
and Vural's myopic military perspective would suggest.

more fungible than others. One could rank-order power resources according to fungibility; that is, those most likely to be effective in most situations with regard to most people over the most scopes would rank high. Although agreement on the rank-ordering would be far from complete, one would expect money, time, information, and a reputation for making credible threats or promises, to rank generally high; while two-headed goats, smog, hula hoops, and asses' jawbones would rank generally low. Despite such variation in the fungibility of political power resources, it is important to recognize that *no political power resource begins to approach the degree of fungibility of money.*[16] As a group, political power resources are relatively low in fungibility; that is precisely why specification of scope and domain is so essential in analyzing political power.

If the range of variation in the effectiveness of power resources were relatively narrow, explaining the failure of power predictions in terms of A's inability or unwillingness to convert his resources into actual power would be less objectionable. As it is, however, even a *caveat* to the effect that power resources in one issue-area may lose some of their effectiveness when applied to another does not suffice. Power resources (or assets) in one policy–contingency framework may not only lose their effectiveness in another context; they may actually become liabilities rather than assets. Threatening voters with nuclear attack is not merely one of the less effective ways to win a mayoral election in New Haven; it is a guarantee of defeat. Possession of nuclear weapons is not just irrelevant to securing the election of a US citizen as UN Secretary-General; it is a hindrance. "First-strike weapons" may not only decline in effectiveness in deterrent situations; they may actually impair one's ability to deter.[17]

The source of this problem is the failure to insist that scope and domain be specified with regard to power resources as well as to

[16] See Joseph S. Nye, Jr, and Robert O. Keohane, "Transnational Relations and World Politics," *International Organization*, 25 (1971), p. 736; Robert O. Keohane and Joseph S. Nye, "World Politics and the International Economic System," in *The Future of the International Economic Order: An Agenda for Research*, ed. C. Fred Bergsten (Lexington, Mass.: Lexington Books, 1973), p. 121; Keohane and Nye, *Power and Interdependence*, p. 146.

[17] See Thomas C. Schelling, *The Strategy of Conflict* (Cambridge, Mass.: Harvard University Press, 1960), pp. 205–54.

power relationships. Money, tanks, bombs, information, and allies are often called "power resources"; but one can easily imagine plausible policy–contingency frameworks within which each of these becomes a liability rather than an asset. To insist that the scope and domain of power resources be specified would probably inhibit (but not prevent) the development of general theories of international power relationships and promote the development of contextual analyses of power. Such contextual power analysis is precisely what Lasswell and Kaplan were calling for:

> Failure to recognize that power may rest on various bases, each with a varying scope, has confused and distorted the conception of power itself, and retarded inquiry into the conditions and consequences of its exercise in various ways. . . .
>
> In particular, it is of crucial importance to recognize that power may rest on various bases, differing not only from culture to culture, but also within a culture from one power structure to another. . . .
>
> What is common to all power and influence relations is only effect on policy. What is affected and on what basis are variables whose specific content in a given situation can be determined only by inquiry into the actual practices of the actors in that situation. . . .
>
> Political analysis must be contextual, and take account of the power practices actually manifested in the concrete political situation.[18]

Although a contextual approach to power analysis would undoubtedly reduce the parsimony of theorizing about power, this disadvantage is less serious than it seems. Specification of scope and domain need not imply atheoretical empiricism. Policy–contingency frameworks can be defined more or less specifically to suit the purpose of the analyst. As the Sprouts put it:

> Estimates of capabilities covering all members of the society of nations in all imaginable contingencies would run to millions of combinations and permutations. No government, even more

[18] Lasswell and Kaplan, *Power and Society*, pp. 85, 92, 94.

emphatically no university or private individual, could conceivably carry out so massive a research and analysis. Nor is any such undertaking contemplated or needed by anyone. A great many contingencies – for example, Canadian–US military confrontation – are too remote to justify any consideration. By a process of elimination, one comes eventually to a hard core of contingencies that seem more or less likely to set the major patterns of international politics in the years to come, and with regard to which the relative capabilities of interacting nations are not self-evident.[19]

Emphasis on policy–contingency frameworks could improve theorizing about international politics by encouraging the development of "middle-level" theories and by forcing the acknowledgment of assumptions that are often left implicit; e.g., the assumption of war-winning capacity that is implicit in much balance-of-power theorizing.[20]

The question of whether to emphasize the fungibility or lack of

[19] Sprout and Sprout, *Toward a Politics of the Planet Earth*, p. 178. Dahl makes a similar point regarding the possibility of comparing policy–contingency frameworks: "Power comparability will have to be interpreted in the light of the specific requirements of research and theory, in the same way that the decision as to whether to regard any two objects – animals, plants, atoms, or whatnot – as comparable depends upon general considerations of classification and theoretical import. To this extent, and to this extent only, the decision is 'arbitrary'; but it is not more 'arbitrary' than other decisions that establish the criteria for a class of objects" ("The Concept of Power," p. 209). Nagel also notes that "domain and scope need not be particularistic or unique. Depending on one's purpose and the limits imposed by reality, the outcome class may contain a few similar members or many diverse elements" (*Descriptive Analysis of Power*, p. 14).

Robert O. Keohane overlooks this important qualification when he suggests that I came close to insisting on a narrowly specific definition of each policy–contingency framework. Although I would agree with his contention that no generalization is possible if each issue is defined "as existing within a unique 'policy–contingency framework,'" I do not think that such a view can be attributed to me. The qualifications in the text and in this footnote explicitly repudiate any such interpretation. See "Theory of World Politics: Structural Realism and Beyond," in *Political Science; The State of the Discipline*, ed. Ada W. Finifter (Washington, D.C.: American Political Science Association, 1983), p. 524.

[20] Two excellent yet quite different examples of power theorizing based on explicit recognition that power configurations vary from one policy–contingency framework to another are Keohane and Nye, *Power and Interdependence*; and Hayward Alker, "On Political Capabilities in a Schedule Sense: Measuring Power, Integration, and Development," in *Mathematical Approaches to Politics*, ed. Hayward Alker, Karl W. Deutsch, and Antoine Stoetzel (San Francisco: Jossey-Bass, 1973), pp. 307–73. The former work illustrates the value of "middle-level" empirical theorizing about power; the latter work demonstrates that abstract model-building is not precluded by the assumption that power is multi-dimensional.

fungibility of power resources is not a black-and-white issue. The fruitful way to pose the question is: "What working assumption about the fungibility of power resources is most useful for international political analysis during the next decade?" How one answers this question will depend partly on the extent to which one believes power resources to be fungible, and partly on the particular distortions in current thinking about international power relationships that one regards as most in need of correction. The demonstrations by Schelling[21] that even slight changes in the context of an influence attempt can convert a power asset into a power liability, the painful demonstration that the "most powerful state the world has ever known" could not achieve its goals in Southeast Asia, and the effect of the 1973 Arab oil embargo on US foreign policy suggest that political power resources are much less fungible than has often been implied. Among students of international politics there is a tendency to exaggerate the fungibility of power resources, often to the point of ignoring scope and domain; but there is hardly any example of international power analysis that exaggerates the importance of contextual variables, i.e., the policy–contingency framework. In the absence of contrary evidence, I would propose that the international political analyst start with the assumption that power resources are situationally specific. As evidence of fungibility is discovered, appropriate modifications in this working assumption can be made.[22]

Although Keohane and Nye are clearly skeptical about the fungibility of power resources, they appear unwilling to place the burden of proof on those who maintain that power resources are highly fungible. They note that "one of our most important analytical tasks is . . . to understand the exceptions and limitations to basic structural hypotheses that rest on assumptions about the fungibility of power."[23] Whereas they place the burden of proof

---

[21] Schelling, *Strategy of Conflict.*

[22] It is instructive to compare this paragraph with Ray and Vural, "Power Disparities," pp. 318–21. They seem to view this passage as a wholesale assault on the principle of parsimony rather than as a measured and qualified suggestion for a short-term research strategy addressed to scholars who think exaggeration of the utility of military force is an important weakness in current thinking. One is tempted to despair when accused of treating something as a "black-and-white issue" that one has explicitly denied should be so treated.

[23] Keohane and Nye, *Power and Interdependence,* pp. 146–7.

on those who purport to find exceptions to assumptions of *highly* fungible power, the approach advocated here would place the burden of proof on those who purport to find evidence of exceptions to assumptions that power resources tend to be *low* in fungibility. Whereas the Sprouts and Dahl[24] reject as practically meaningless any statement about influence that does not clearly indicate scope, Keohane and Nye confine themselves to the suggestion that "we may need to reevaluate the usefulness of the homogeneous conception of power."[25]

The "paradox of unrealized power," then, can be explained either in terms of inadequate conversion processes or in terms of mistaken judgments regarding the fungibility of power resources.[26] The latter explanation is preferable for two reasons. First, the emphasis on A's inability and/or unwillingness to convert his alleged power resources into actual power encourages sloppy power analysis. No matter how inept the power analyst has been at estimating A's power resources, the failure of A to influence B can always be attributed to A's lack of commitment, or incompetent execution of the influence attempt. To take it to an absurd but illuminating extreme, one can imagine a power analyst saying "I just don't understand how a country with so many two-headed goats, so much smog, and so many asses' jawbones could have lost the Third World War. It must have been due to lack of skill or commitment on the part of the leaders." To take it to an equally illuminating, more painful, but less absurd point, one frequently hears the following: "I just don't understand how a country with so many nuclear weapons and so many soldiers could have failed to accomplish its goals in Vietnam. It must have been caused by clumsy and spineless national leadership." Emphasis on skill and will in conversion processes makes it all too easy for the power analyst to avoid facing up to his mistakes. In estimating the *capabilities* of states, the probability of successful conversion should be included in the estimate. In estimating

---

[24] Dahl, "Power," p. 408; Sprout and Sprout, "Environmental Factors," p. 325.

[25] Keohane and Nye, "World Politics and the International System," p. 163.

[26] Although I consider only two ways of explaining the paradox, there are, as always, an infinite number of possible explanations. Ray and Vural erroneously attribute to me the view that *only* two explanations are possible and then treat such a view as their "most fundamental disagreement with Baldwin's approach" ("Power Disparities," p. 329).

probable power, the likelihood of sufficient commitment should also be included.

A second reason for rejecting the conversion-process explanation in favor of the relative-infungibility explanation is that the latter is more likely to focus attention on the contextual nature of power. Whereas the former approach draws attention to the skill of the would-be power wielder, the latter treats such skill as just another resource and focuses attention on the actual or postulated policy–contingency framework within which capabilities are being estimated. Thus, the conversion-process analyst is more likely to attribute the failure of A's threatened beating of B to get B to do X to A's clumsy execution of the threat, but the relative-infungibility analyst is more likely to point out that since B is a masochist, A's threat was doomed to fail from the beginning.[27]

Let us examine some examples of international power analysis from the perspective of a relative-infungibility analyst.[28] Knorr, in *The Power of Nations*, emphasizes the importance of the distinction between putative and actualized power; he notes that the frequent failure to convert the former into the latter is a source of puzzlement to many. The distinction, according to Knorr, is between power as a "means" and power as an "effect." Power as a

---

[27] The idea that power resources or "power bases" could be identified without reference to the value system of the person or group to be influenced is not found in Lasswell and Kaplan. They make it clear that power relations presuppose B's value system. See *Power and Society*, pp. 76–7, 83–4.

Ray and Vural object to both reasons without seeming to understand either. With respect to the first, they point out that "inept power analysts could hide their lack of aptitude by pointing to various idiosyncracies in the policy–contingency framework within which A's influence attempt occurred, whenever A's attempts fail" ("Power Disparities," p. 321). Not so. Inept power analysts could *attempt* to hide their lack of aptitude this way, but it would not work; for in order to do so, the inept power analyst must admit his failure to specify the correct policy–contingency framework in estimating the likely success of A's influence attempt. The reason I argue that the conversion-process explanation is more likely to encourage sloppy power analysis is my belief that people are more likely to blame their mistakes on others than on themselves. Ray and Vural object to the second reason by charging that it amounts to nothing more than an assertion that power lacks fungibility (p. 337n.). Contrary to such a misinterpretation, focusing attention on policy–contingency frameworks implies nothing whatever about the degree to which power is fungible. The point, of course, is that the success of A's influence attempt is a function of both A's actions *and* B's value system.

[28] Generally speaking, I consider this to be the perspective of all those who emphasize the importance of scope specification, policy–contingency frameworks, and/or contextual analysis, including Lasswell and Kaplan, the Sprouts, and Dahl.

"means" is something that nations "have and can accumulate."[29]

At this point, the relative-infungibility analyst is likely to ask two questions: First, why is the distinction not made in terms of potential and actual effects? That would be straightforward and would retain the basic relational quality of the concept of power.[30] The distinction between an actual and a postulated relation between A and B should be easy enough for most readers to grasp. In describing putative power as a means that can be possessed and accumulated, Knorr risks obscuring the relational nature of power and returning to the earlier concept of power as an undifferentiated quantifiable mass. A similar risk is incurred when Knorr describes putative power as "inherent in the things of value" that A is ready to give.[31] A relational concept of power assumes that actual or potential power is never inherent in properties of A, but rather inheres in the actual or potential relationship between A's properties and B's value system. Knorr views putative power as "capabilities that permit the power wielder to make effective threats."[32] These capabilities may be transformed into actual power through a conversion process in which the crucial variables are B's perceptions, values, and propensities. The problem is that such variables must be considered in determining whether A has putative power in the first place, since the effectiveness or potential effectiveness of a threat depends partially on B's perceptions of it and on B's value system. *Before* one postulates whether he is dealing with a coward or a masochist, one can say nothing whatever about the potential effectiveness of a threat. *Before* one can attribute putative power to A one must postulate a scenario or set of scenarios which specify whom A might try to influence and in what respects. Consideration of B's perceptions, values, and skills cannot be delayed until it is time to discuss A's ability to convert his putative power into actual power. If B's perceptions, values, and skills are such as to make it impossible for A to influence him, then putative power should never have been attributed to A in the first place.

A second question that might be asked is whether Knorr makes

[29] Knorr, *Power of Nations*, p. 9.
[30] Cf. Nagel, *Descriptive Analysis of Power*, pp. 172–3.
[31] Knorr, *Power of Nations*, p. 313.
[32] Ibid., p. 9.

it sufficiently clear that there are no generalized means of exercising political power. The means that work in one policy–contingency framework may be counterproductive or irrelevant in another. Although Knorr notes that actualized power differs in weight, scope, and domain,[33] he fails to apply these distinctions to putative power. There is no reason to believe, however, that statements about potential power are less subject to the requirement to specify scope and domain than are statements about actual potential power.

Cline's *World Power Assessment* represents the polar opposite of the type of contextual analysis advocated by the Sprouts and Lasswell and Kaplan. Cline's basic conceptual framework is a formula for measuring national power:

$$Pp = (C+E+M) \times (S+W)$$

where

Pp = perceived power
C = critical mass = population+territory
E = economic capability
M = military capability
S = strategic purpose
W = will to pursue national strategy.[34]

This formula is applied to forty nations, each receiving a number representing "total weighted units of perceived power."[35] The United States is assigned 35 such units; the Soviet Union gets 67.5.

---

[33] Ibid., p. 18. For further discussion of Knorr's treatment of power, see David A. Baldwin, *Economic Statecraft* (Princeton: Princeton University Press, 1985).

[34] Cline, *World Power Assessment*, p. 11. Cline's book is especially interesting as an indication of how power analysis is performed by high-level government officials. He has served as Deputy Director for Intelligence in the CIA and as Director of Intelligence and Research in the Department of State.

As Ray and Vural point out, there is another body of literature based on an assumption of "robust fungibility" of power that is ignored here. Since this literature is concerned with explaining the initiation and outcome of wars, it did not seem necessary to discuss it in the context of the much broader focus of this chapter. Ray and Vural, however, seem to think that since "big battalions" win most wars, national power is highly fungible ("Power Disparities," pp. 319ff). It is fortunate for the world – and unfortunate for Ray and Vural's argument – that nation-states influence each other in many ways other than making war.

[35] Cline, *World Power Assessment*, p. 130.

For the most part, Cline's analysis ignores questions of scope and domain. Although he defines power as the ability of one government to cause another government to do something it would not otherwise do, there is little or no indication that power resources useful in causing one government to do X may be useless or counterproductive in causing another government to do Y.[36]

Whereas the Sprouts insist that strategies (actual or postulated) be treated as *givens* in capability analysis, Cline treats strategy as a variable to be discussed *after* weights have already been assigned to the other variables. Whereas Cline assigns power weights to territory and population, the Sprouts maintain that "such data acquire political relevance only when viewed in some frame of assumptions as to what is to be attempted, by whom, when and where, *vis-à-vis* what adversaries, allies, and unaligned onlookers."[37]

In allocating weights for national strategy, Cline assigns high values to countries with "clearcut strategic plans for international aggrandizement" and low values to those without such plans. American strategy is given 0.3, while Russian strategy receives 0.8. Toward the end of the book, Cline describes his preferred strategy for the United States and admits that this strategy has been "implicit in the situation described in preceding pages of this book."[38] A relative-infungibility analyst might point out that it would have been helpful if Cline had made such policy assumptions explicit earlier in the book.

Despite the fact that one can eventually ferret out the vague and implicit policy–contingency framework underlying Cline's *World Power Assessment*, the wisdom of treating power at such an abstract general level may be questioned. If one wanted to promote the idea of power as monolithic, homogeneous, uni-dimensional, and highly fungible, it would be difficult to improve on Cline's approach.

In *Power and Money*, Kindleberger differentiates between "strength" and "power" along lines similar to the distinction

[36] Cline describes power as "a subjective factor" (*World Power Assessment*, p. 8) and uses the term "perceived power" in his formula. In a puzzling footnote, however, he indicates that "real power" is something different from "perceived power" (ibid., p. 12n.). The distinction is not developed, thus leaving one wondering about the significance of the formula.

[37] Sprout and Sprout, *Toward a Politics of the Planet Earth*, p. 177.

[38] Cline, *World Power Assessment*, pp. 134–5.

between potential and actual power. He treats strength as a means which "exists independently of whether it is used to assert or achieve control over policies of other countries" and power as strength capable of being used effectively.[39] This definition of power, he claims, "does not imply a purpose." But power divorced from purpose begins to sound like generalized or highly fungible power. In context, however, it is clear that Kindleberger intends the statement to differentiate probable from potential power in the sense that a state may have the potential power to influence the policies of another state, but may have neither the intention nor the desire actually to exercise such power. The weakness in Kindleberger's concept of power is that he implies that power can be divorced completely from goals or purposes. Although it is true that potential power does not imply actual purposes, it does imply at least a hypothetical purpose in the sense of a postulated policy–contingency framework.

In considering the "paradox of unrealized power," it has been argued that the most useful way to resolve the paradox is by tying power analysis more closely to specific contexts. I have suggested that one of the most crucial weaknesses in current thinking about international power relationships is the failure to specify scope and domain, and the consequent tendency to exaggerate the fungibility of power resources. In order to demonstrate the usefulness of contextual power analysis, I shall conclude with an examination of the problem of "worst-case" analysis from the perspective of the above discussion.

In worst-case analysis, the assumption is that preparing for the worst is wise and prudent policy. This assumption, often espoused by military thinkers, is usually associated with the idea that policy-makers should concentrate on assessing the *capability* of other actors more than (or rather than) on the *intentions* of other actors. "Why not prepare for the worst?" is a superficially appealing slogan that must be refuted each year when military appropriations are being considered. Recognition of the multidimensional nature of power and the low fungibility of power resources is vital in

---

[39] Kindleberger, *Power and Money*, p. 56. He defines power in terms of ability to use strength "efficiently" at one point (p. 56) and in terms of ability to use strength "effectively" at another point (p. 65). In the context of power analysis the difference is not trivial.

showing why worst-case analysis is not a wise and prudent basis for policy. The reason may be demonstrated by comparing political power with purchasing power.

Storing up purchasing power in order to be able to deal with unforeseen financial catastrophes is an ancient, honorable, and prudent undertaking. The existence of a common denominator of economic value that also serves as a medium of exchange (i.e., money) enables us to treat economic resources *as if* they were unidimensional, thereby allowing us to prepare *simultaneously* for small, medium, and large financial difficulties. The fact that I am indebted to druggists, farmers, the government, bankers, and insurance companies for a wide variety of goods and services hardly matters, since I can use the same purchasing power resource – money – to pay them all. This is why we say that money is highly fungible. In dealing with problems of purchasing power, more money is almost always better than less. Aside from tax problems, it is difficult (but not impossible) to imagine a situation in which too much money prevents one from exercising one's purchasing power.

Political power is quite different from purchasing power. There is no common denominator of political value corresponding to money in terms of which political debts can be discharged. The lack of fungibility of political power resources means that preparing to deal with the worst contingencies may hinder one's ability to deal with less severe ones. ("The worst may be the enemy of the bad!") Thus, preparing for a nuclear first strike may weaken a country's deterrent capability; preparing for nuclear war may weaken a country's ability to get one of its citizens elected Secretary-General of the UN; preparing for a seven-year famine may weaken a nation's ability to resist the demands of poor countries for food aid; preparing for military domination of the world may make it hard to win the hearts and minds of the people; and preparing for autarky may hurt a country's bargaining ability in international trade negotiations. Because political power is multidimensional and political power resources are low in fungibility, more power in one policy–contingency framework may mean less in another. Although in terms of purchasing power, more is almost always better than less, the same cannot be said of any particular kind of political power. Since not all contingencies are equally probable, policy-makers who prepare for the worst and ignore the intentions of other nations may wind up preparing for a very costly but unlikely contingency at the expense of preparing for a less devastating but more likely contingency. Such policy-makers are neither wise nor prudent.

POWER AND INTERDEPENDENCE

Everyone seems to agree that "interdependence" is important; but not everyone agrees on how it should be defined, or on whether it is increasing or decreasing.[40] Although many would agree that interdependence refers to a situation in which states are "significantly" affected by their interaction, there is less agreement as to how to differentiate "significant" effects from "insignificant" ones. Three possibilities may be considered. First, interaction can be equated with interdependence. It is sometimes suggested that this denotes mere interconnectedness rather than interdependence.[41] Second, interdependence can be defined in terms of interactions (or transactions) that have reciprocal costly effects.[42] The difficulty with this definition is that many forms of international interaction, such as trade, involve reciprocal costly effects but not mutual dependency. Such a conception does not seem to capture the notion of dependence underlying the use of that term in common parlance. Buying what is easy to buy elsewhere (e.g., sand) or buying what is easy to do without (e.g., caviar) are not usually considered to create dependency, although both kinds of

[40] See Oran R. Young, "Interdependencies in World Politics," *International Journal*, 24 (1969), pp. 726–50; Richard Rosecrance and Arthur Stein, "Interdependence: Myth or Reality?" *World Politics*, 26 (1973), pp. 1–27; Kenneth Waltz, "The Myth of Interdependence," in *The International Corporation*, ed. Charles Kindleberger (Cambridge, Mass.: MIT Press, 1970), pp. 205–23; Robert O. Keohane and Joseph S. Nye, "International Interdepedence and Integration," in Nelson W. Polsby and Fred I. Greenstein (eds), *Handbook of Political Science*, vol. 8, *International Politics* (Reading, Mass.: Addison-Wesley, 1975), pp. 363–414.

[41] Alex Inkles, "The Emerging Social Structure of the World," *World Politics*, 27 (1975), pp. 467–95, esp. pp. 477–86.

[42] This definition seems to be the basic concept of interdependence espoused by Keohane and Nye, *Power and Interdependence*, pp. 8–9. There is some ambiguity about this point, however, since their concept of "vulnerability interdependence" corresponds more closely with the idea of interdependence as transactions that are mutually costly to forgo.

transactions involve costs for each trading partner.[43] In conceiving of dependence or interdependence, the relevant costs are not those involved in *carrying out* the transaction, but rather those involved in *foregoing* it. Not everyone who drinks is an alcholic; not everyone who smokes is an addict; and not every international trading relationship involves dependency. The true measure of a country's dependency on imported oil is not what it has to give up in order to get it, but rather what it would have to give up in order to go without it. The smoker who can quit whenever he wants to is not an addict; the drinker who can take or leave it is not an alcoholic; and the country that can easily forgo imported oil is not dependent on it. This basic insight of the Stoics deserves reiteration in the context of discussions of interdependence.

A third way to conceive of interdependence, then, is in terms of relationships that are costly for each party to forgo.[44] This conception of interdependence has three advantages over most others. First, it captures the intuitive notion of dependency underlying most common parlance. Second, it is consistent with the theoretical treatments of dependency by Thibaut and Kelley, Emerson, and Blau.[45] Although these works are well known in the

---

[43] The pioneering work by Albert O. Hirschman, *National Power and the Structure of Foreign Trade* (Berkeley: University of California, 1945) is still the best statement of the relationship between trade and dependency: "The influence which country A acquires in country B by foreign trade depends in the first place upon the total gain which B derives from that trade; the total gain from trade for any country is indeed nothing but another expression for the total impoverishment which would be inflicted upon it by a stoppage of trade. In this sense, the classical concept, gain from trade, and the power concept, dependence on trade, now being studied are seen to be merely two aspects of the same phenomenon" (p. 18). See also Jean-Jacques Rousseau, *The First and Second Discourses*, trans. Roger D. Masters and Judith R. Masters (New York: St Martin's Press, 1964), p. 36n.; and *On the Social Contract*, trans. Judith R. Masters, ed. Roger D. Masters (New York: St Martin's Press, 1978), p. 74n.

[44] See Waltz, "Myth of Interdependence"; also Inkles, "Emerging Social Structure," pp. 483–8; Stephen D. Krasner, "State Power and the Structure of International Trade," *World Politics*, 28 (1976), pp. 317–47, at p. 320.

[45] John W. Thibaut and Harold H. Kelley, *The Social Psychology of Groups* (New York: Wiley 1959), pp. 100–25; Richard M. Emerson, "Power–Dependence Relations," *American Sociological Review*, 27 (1962), pp. 31–41; Peter M. Blau, *Exchange and Power in Social Life* (New York: Wiley, 1964), pp. 118–25, 133, 197. If a graduate student were to ask me where to begin the study of international interdependence, I should direct attention to these writers and to Hirschman's *National Power and the Structure of Foreign Trade* rather than to more recent treatments of this topic in the international relations literature.

literature on social power, they are rarely cited in discussions of international interdependence.[46] Cross-fertilization between the social power literature and the international relations literature is more likely if our fundamental concepts of dependency are compatible. A third advantage of this conception of inter-dependence is that it facilitates thinking about the links between dependency and power. In order to study dependency, one must look at opportunity costs of alternative relationships as well as at actual relationships. Likewise, in order to study power, one must look not only at what B does, but at what B would otherwise do.

Interdependence interests international theorists primarily because of its relationship to power. If A and B are mutually dependent on one another, then each could inflict costs on the other by severing the relationship. And the ability to inflict costs on the other actors is one measure of influence.[47] Thus, to say that A and B are interdependent implies that they possess the ability to influence one another in some respect. (Note that this approach does not involve the difficulty of describing a gun as a power resource only to discover that one is trying to influence someone who wants to be shot. Both the value systems and the available alternatives for each actor must be considered in determining whether severance of the relationship would entail costs.) In this sense, inter-dependence *always* implies mutual potential power of some kind. Whether either actor will be able to influence the other to a satisfactory degree, soon enough, with respect to the desired scopes, or at acceptable cost to itself, is quite another matter. As Young has pointed out, a rising level of interdependence increases both the opportunities and the costs of exercising power.[48]

If dependency and power are closely linked concepts, some of the distinctions useful in studying one may be useful in studying the other. Knorr has outlined a number of such distinctions in his discussion of interdependence.[49] Just as power relationships vary

---

[46] The extensive bibliography on interdependence compiled by Keohane and Nye for the *Handbook of Political Science* contains no entry for any of the authors cited in the preceding footnote – including Hirschman.

[47] Cf. John C. Harsanyi, "Measurement of Social Power, Opportunity Costs, and the Theory of Two-Person Bargaining Games," *Behavioral Science*, 7 (1962), pp. 67–80; and Nagel, *Descriptive Analysis of Power*.

[48] Young, "Interdependencies," pp. 746–7.

[49] Knorr, *Power of Nations*, pp. 207–10.

in scope, weight, domain, and symmetry, so do relationships of interdependency: contextual analysis may be as appropriate for the study of interdependence as it is for the study of power.

Keohane and Nye suggest that in order to understand the role of power in interdependence, we must distinguish between "sensitivity" and "vulnerability."[50] "Sensitivity interdependence" refers to the liability to incur costly effects within a given policy framework; "vulnerability interdependence" refers to the liability to incur costly effects even after the policy framework has been altered. For example, "sensitivity interdependence" could be used to refer to the costs of working within the framework of the Bretton Woods monetary regime during the late 1960s; "vulnerability interdependence" could be used to refer to the costs associated with changing to a different international monetary regime. The distinction between the two types of interdependence indicates that dependence, like power, varies from one policy–contingency framework to another. Sensitivity interdependence and vulnerability interdependence are simply labels applied to particular kinds of policy–contingency frameworks. Although Keohane and Nye use these distinctions imaginatively to generate important observations about world politics, the distinctions themselves represent no new theoretical insights. Lasswell and Kaplan, Dahl, and the Sprouts have previously pointed out that power relationships in one policy–contingency framework are likely to differ from those in another.

Instead of treating the distinction between sensitivity interdependence and vulnerability interdependence as one of many ways to differentiate among policy–contingency frameworks, Keohane and Nye maintain that the distinction is essential to understanding the "role of power in interdependence."[51] In answer to the question of how this distinction helps us to understand the relationship between interdependence and power they reply: "Clearly, it indicates that sensitivity interdependence will be less important than vulnerability interdependence in providing power resources to actors."[52] As an empirical proposition, this answer is debatable; as a logical deduction, it is a

[50] Keohane and Nye, *Power and Interdependence*, pp. 11–12.
[51] Ibid.
[52] Ibid., p. 15.

non sequitur. Consider the example of a marriage. Sensitivity interdependence could be used to refer to the costs associated with working nonviolently within the framework of the marriage, of "making the marriage work." Vulnerability interdependence could be used to refer to the costs associated with violent divorce. Although the husband might have the advantage in terms of brute force and economic ability to survive a divorce, it is not clear that this power resource would be more important than the power resources provided by sensitivity interdependence. If both husband and wife were strongly committed to nonviolent resolution of conflict within the framework of the marriage, the power resources associated with asymmetrical vulnerability interdependence might be of little or no importance compared to those associated with sensitivity interdependence. Likewise, if nation-states have a strong commitment to making a given international regime work, the power resources associated with sensitivity interdependence may be more important than those associated with vulnerability interdependence.[53] If revolution is "unthinkable," the ability to foment a revolution is not a particularly useful power resource. In the absence of information or assumptions about the degree of commitment to maintaining a given policy framework, one can say *nothing* about the relative importance of the power resources provided by sensitivity interdependence and vulnerability interdependence. Although Keohane and Nye have formulated a useful distinction, they have overestimated its importance for understanding the relation between power and interdependence.

It has been suggested that Dahl's concept of power is incapable of dealing with interdependence.[54] Since Dahl is close to the "mainstream" of contemporary thinking about social power, some consideration of this viewpoint is in order. It will be argued that Dahl's concept is capable of dealing with interdependence and that the contrary claim is based on a distorted view of Dahl's

[53] The distinction between "sensitivity" interdependence and "vulnerability" interdependence bears some resemblance to that between limited war and "total" (or not-so-limited) war. The policy constraints are obviously fewer in one situation than in the other. For a demonstration that ability to fight a "total" war may be of little help in fighting a limited war, see Charles Wolf, Jr, "The Logic of Failure: A Vietnam 'Lesson,'" *Journal of Conflict Resolution*, 16 (1972), pp. 397–401.

[54] Jeffrey Hart, "Three Approaches to the Measurement of Power in International Relations," *International Organization*, 30 (1976), pp. 297, 303.

position. Hart's argument is based on a distinction among three conceptions of power: (1) as control over resources, (2) as control over actors, and (3) as control over events and outcomes. Dahl's concept of power as the ability of A to get B to do what he would otherwise not do is classified as (2), control over actors.[55] Such a classification seriously distorts Dahl's idea, since his concept of power includes *both* actors and outcomes as necessary components. Dahl's insistence that statements about power that fail to specify scope verge on meaninglessness underscores the fact that his concept of power concerns the ability of one actor to influence another actor *with respect to certain outcomes*. In the literature on social power, Dahl's position is often referred to in terms of control over outcomes and is sometimes even classified as an "outcome definition."[56] As Nagel points out, anyone who employs a causal concept of power, such as Dahl's, must state the outcome caused.[57]

Hart's suggestion that Dahl's concept of power cannot account for the possibility of interdependence among actors is puzzling.[58] In the mutual nuclear deterrence between the Soviet Union and the United States, the security of each depends on the other. This is typically regarded as an example of interdependence and can be described in terms of simultaneous attempts by each nation to get the other one to do what it might not otherwise do – i.e., refrain from attack. In the third edition of *Modern Political Analysis*, the system of mutual deterrence is even cited by Dahl as an example of a situation of reciprocal influence.[59] The contention that Dahl's concept of power can neither account for nor deal with interdependence is unconvincing.

MILITARY POWER

Two of the most important weaknesses in traditional theorizing about international politics have been the tendency to exaggerate

[55] Ibid., p. 291. A similar line of reasoning, drawing on Hart's article, is found in Keohane and Nye, *Power and Interdependence*, p. 11.
[56] Nagel, *Descriptive Analysis of Power*, pp. 9–10, 14, 29, 114–22, 175–6.
[57] Ibid., p. 14.   [58] Hart, "Three Approaches," p. 303.
[59] Dahl, *Modern Political Analysis*, p. 50. See also Nagel, *Descriptive Analysis of Power*, pp. 142–3.

the effectiveness of military power resources and the tendency to treat military power as the ultimate measuring rod to which other forms of power should be compared.[60] Both tendencies are anathema to the approach advocated by Lasswell and Kaplan. Although these authors give "special consideration to the role of violence," they repeatedly assert that power does not rest "always, or even generally, on violence"; that "power may rest on various bases"; that "none of the forms of power is basic to all the others"; and that "political phenomena are only obscured by the pseudosimplification attained with any unitary conception of power as being always and everywhere the same."[61] Despite the vigorous efforts of Lasswell and Kaplan and the tradition of contextual power analysis they spawned, the contemporary literature on international relations often exhibits the same tendencies to exaggerate the effectiveness of military power bases as did the earlier works.

Cline's *World Power Assessment* notes the existence of various forms of power, but describes war as the "true end game" in international "chess." "A study of power," according to Cline, "in the last analysis, is a study of the capacity to wage war."[62] In a similar vein, Gilpin acknowledges that power may take many forms, "though, in the final analysis, force is the ultimate form of power." Gilpin even makes the more extreme contention that "ultimately, the determination of the distribution of power can be made *only* in retrospect as a consequence of war."[63] Phrases describing force as the "ultimate" form of power imply that all forms of power are arrayed on a single continuum of effectiveness or importance. If power is conceived of as a multidimensional phenomenon, it is harder to think in terms of such a continuum. If one thinks of power as situationally specific rather than generalized, the idea of an "ultimate" form of power does not make much sense. It may well be that there are some very important policy-

[60] No attempt to document the existence of these weaknesses is made here. Ray and Vural would surely dispute labelling such tendencies as "weaknesses"; indeed, they seem to treat them as "strengths" ("Power Disparities").

[61] Lasswell and Kaplan, *Power and Society*, pp. ix, 76, 85, 92, 94.

[62] Cline, *World Power Assessment*, p. 8.

[63] Gilpin, *US Power*, p. 24; emphasis added. The conception of war as the ultimate measuring rod of national power is also reflected in Robert Gilpin, *War and Change in World Politics* (New York: Cambridge University Press, 1981), pp. 31–3.

contingency scenarios in which force is a critically important power resource, but it would be more helpful to identify such situations than to assert that force is the "ultimate" form of power. Most states, after all, resolve most international disputes most of the time without the actual or threatened use of force.

Although Keohane and Nye continually criticize the traditional emphasis on military force, even they sometimes seem to exaggerate the effectiveness of military force as a power resource. While noting the increasing costs associated with military force and the inapplicability of force to many situations, they contend that force "dominates" other means of power.[64]

The proposition that military force is more effective than other power resources is both ambiguous and debatable. In the absence of clearly specified or implied policy–contingency frameworks, the proposition that force is more effective than other power bases has little, if any, meaning. As I argued earlier, all generalizations about power should be set in a context specifying (as a minimum) who is trying to get whom to do what. In some situations, force works very well, but in others it is actually counterproductive. Underlying the analysis of Keohane and Nye there seems to be a set of implicit assumptions as to the number of policy–contingency frameworks in which force is effective, and as to the relative importance of such frameworks. It would be helpful if the authors would spell out such assumptions, including the criteria used in assigning weights to such frameworks.

As an empirical proposition, the idea that force dominates other means of power could be formulated as a hypothesis to be tested, but it does not deserve the status of an assumption. According to Keohane and Nye, "*if* there are no constraints on one's choice of instruments" – i.e., if cost considerations are ignored – "the state with superior military force will prevail."[65] Despite the fact that *Power and Interdependence* describes several situations in which

[64] See Keohane and Nye, *Power and Interdependence*, pp. 8, 11–18, 27–9, 228. Although the authors use the term "dominates," the context indicates that they are referring to the relative "effectiveness" of force. Credence is lent to this interpretation by their use of the term "effectiveness" instead of "dominance" in an earlier similar discussion. Cf. Keohane and Nye, "World Politics and the International Economic System," pp. 125–6.
[65] Keohane and Nye, *Power and Interdependence*, p. 27; emphasis in original.

force would *not* be effective, and despite the easily demonstrable counterproductivity of military power resources in many policy–contingency frameworks, Keohane and Nye imply that military force will prevail if costs can be ignored.

Let us examine three situations referred to in *Power and Interdependence*. First, Keohane and Nye contend that "military power dominates economic power in the sense that economic means alone are likely to be ineffective against the serious use of military force."[66] Although this is a rather special situation that can hardly serve as the basis for sweeping generalizations about the relative effectiveness of economic and military power, it is neither self-evident nor manifestly true. Opinions differ, of course, but it is not obvious to me that in 1973 the American threat to use force worked better than the Arab oil embargo. Second, they indicate that "in the worst situations, force is ultimately necessary to guarantee survival."[67] That may have been a useful assumption for students of international politics prior to the atomic age – although I doubt it – but at a time of rapidly multiplying (military and nonmilitary) threats of planetary disaster, it should be treated as a hypothesis to be scrutinized carefully.[68] In today's world, the effectiveness of military force in guaranteeing survival may be steadily and rapidly declining. Third, Keohane and Nye state that "military power helps the Soviet Union to dominate Eastern Europe economically as well as politically."[69] That hypothesis may be plausible, but it also sounds plausible when stated backwards – i.e, "military power *hinders* the Soviet attempt to dominate Eastern Europe, at least in some respects." *A priori*, I have no reason to believe that the 1968 invasion of Czechoslovakia bolstered the long-run prospects for communism in Eastern Europe. *A priori*, it seems reasonable to suspect that this invasion may have generated (intensified?) some anti-Russian resentment that will not disappear quickly. Although Nye and Keohane may

[66] Ibid., p. 16.
[67] Ibid., p. 27.
[68] For a review of some of these threats, see Harold Sprout and Margaret Sprout, *Multiple Vulnerabilities: The Context of Environmental Repair and Protection*, Center of International Studies, Princeton Univerisity, Research Monograph no. 40 (Princeton, 1974).
[69] Keohane and Nye, *Power and Interdependence*, p. 28.

be right, one wishes that students of international politics would consider the possibility that the Soviet use of force in Eastern Europe was counterproductive in at least some respects.[70]

Even within the military sphere, power discussions could be fruitfully considered in a more contextual manner. The idea of "maximizing the military might" of a state does not make much sense unless military power resources are relatively fungible. In a world of widely differing military policy–contingency frameworks – nuclear war, conventional war, limited war, guerrilla war, and so forth – it might be more useful to speak about different kinds of military power.[71] This approach is especially appealing to the extent that military power assets in one policy–contingency framework become liabilities in another. Schelling's demonstration that first-strike weapons can be liabilities in certain kinds of deterrent situations is a case in point.[72]

POSITIVE SANCTIONS

Positive sanctions (rewards and promised rewards) have long been important as a means by which some states get other states to do things they would not otherwise do. Whether such relationships should be labeled "power," "influence," or "nonpower influence," need not concern us here, since we are using the term "power" in the generic sense that includes all such labels. The important thing is recognition that positive sanctions are significant resources by which international actors affect the behavior, beliefs, attitudes, or policies of other actors. Knorr has rightly pointed out the paucity of academic literature concerning the role of positive sanctions in world politics.[73] In a world in which destructive power seems to

---

[70] I do not want to push this argument too far. Jacob Viner was fond of quoting William Stanley Jevons as follows: "It is always to be remembered that the failure of an argument in favor of a proposition does not, generally speaking, add much, if any probability, to the contradictory proposition." For a discussion of Soviet domination of Eastern Europe that identifies several drawbacks to the Soviet use of force, see Christopher D. Jones, "Soviet Hegemony in Eastern Europe: The Dynamics of Political Autonomy and Military Intervention," *World Politics*, 29 (1977), pp. 216–41.

[71] On this point, see Knorr, *Power of Nations*, p. 46.

[72] Schelling, *Strategy of Conflict*, pp. 207–54.

[73] Knorr, *Power of Nations*, pp. ix, 310–11.

grow exponentially, improved understanding of the actual and potential role of positive sanctions is highly desirable.

The increased attention being focused on economic power in world politics reinforces the need for more research on positive sanctions, since economic power often takes such a form.[74] It is interesting – but not encouraging – to note that the *International Encyclopedia of the Social Sciences* (1968) includes an index entry for "threat" but none for "promise"; an article on "punishment" but none on "reward"; and an article on "military power potential" but none on "economic power potential." Knorr's consideration of military power, economic power, interdependence, negative sanctions, and positive sanctions in *The Power of Nations*, however, provides some hope that the next *International Encyclopedia* may fill such lacunae.

One of the most difficult conceptual problems in thinking about positive sanctions is the relationship between exchange and power. Despite the fact that ordinary economic exchange relations can be described in terms of Dahl's broad intuitive notion of power, many scholars resist the use of power terminology in analyzing such relations.[75] Knorr acknowledges positive sanctions as important, but his attempt to distinguish such "nonpower influence" from exchange relations adds little to the discussion.[76] On the one hand, "power influence" is described as "harmful" to B because it restricts his choices. On the other hand, "nonpower influence" is described as "beneficial" to B because it enriches his choices. Although it is useful to define positive and negative sanctions in terms of whether B *perceives* them as rewards or punishments, it seems unwise to assume that B always knows what is best for him. It is not necessarily harmful to restrict the choices available to children, drug addicts, or nation-states. Children can be rewarded with too much candy; drug addicts can be rewarded with too much heroin; and countries can be given more foreign aid

[74] See Baldwin, "Economic Power," in *Perspectives on Social Power*, ed. James T. Tedeschi (Chicago: Aldine, 1974), pp. 395–413; and *Economic Statecraft*.

[75] On this point, see Baldwin, *Economic Statecraft*. In the literature on international relations, Hirschman's *National Power and the Structure of Foreign Trade* is of fundamental importance. His treatment demonstrates that power potentially inheres in all international trade relations.

[76] Knorr, *Power of Nations*, pp. 7–8, 310–19.

than is good for them. The question of whether rewards are actually beneficial to the recipient is an important one, but it seems more useful to treat it as an empirical rather than a definitional question.

Within the category of mutually "beneficial" interaction, Knorr distinguishes between "exchange" and "nonpower influence" as follows:

> What distinguishes nonpower influence flows from . . . exchanges is that one actor gives something of value to another without condition, without any stipulated payment, now or later. For instance, A may extend economic assistance to B, exclusively in order to enable the latter to accelerate his economic development. A expects to receive nothing in return from B, and B understands this.[77]

Such a distinction seems almost impossible for researchers to apply to relations among nation-states. Stipulations regarding repayment may be unstated and may be only vaguely perceived by the actors involved. The social exchange theorists have demonstrated that exchange can be a subtle process and that feelings of indebtedness on the part of the reward recipient may be created *regardless* of the stipulations or intentions of the reward giver.[78] Furthermore, even the most altruistic benefactor may change his mind and remind the aid recipient that he owes him a favor. In strictly economic exchanges such attempts to make retroactive stipulations regarding payment are unlikely to succeed, because the original recipient can point out that the terms of the transaction were clearly specified at the time it occurred. But social and political exchange are distinguished from economic exchange partly by the vagueness of the obligations involved.[79] Even the example cited by Knorr could be regarded as a type of social

---

[77] Ibid., p. 311.

[78] See Blau, *Exchange and Power*; Alvin W. Gouldner, "The Norm of Reciprocity," *American Sociological Review*, 25 (1960), pp. 161–78; Marcel Mauss, *The Gift*, trans. Ian Cunnison (Glencoe, Ill.: Free Press, 1954); Wilton S. Dillon, *Gifts and Nations* (The Hague: Mouton, 1968); and Baldwin, *Economic Statecraft*, pp. 290–4.

[79] "Social exchange differs in important ways from strictly economic exchange. The basic and most crucial distinction is that social exchange entails *unspecified* obligations" (Blau, *Exchange and Power*, p. 93; emphasis in original).

exchange. State A could be viewed as exchanging economic assistance for state B's promise to use the money to accelerate economic development (rather than to buy weapons or swell the Swiss bank accounts of the leaders). People and countries exchange money for promises all the time; so there is nothing particularly unusual about such an interpretation of Knorr's example. As long as A places any strings at all on the use of his aid, he may be viewed as making a stipulation as to payment. After all, if the behavior (attitude, policy, or whatever) stipulated by A had no value to him, he would not make the stipulation in the first place. I have never encountered a real-world example of totally stringless aid, and I never expect to. The United States has dispersed billions of dollars to promote economic development in other countries, but it is clear that American policy-makers – rightly or wrongly – believe that faster economic development in those countries would enhance the long-run welfare and security of the United States.[80] In sum, although distinctions between power and exchange can be made, I suspect that students of international relations would find it as profitable to focus on the similarities as on the differences.

The fact that the mutual exchange of rewards is so prevalent in international relations may partly explain why the subject lacks excitement; that, in turn, may partly explain why students of international relations have focused their attention on the rarer but presumably more exciting instances in which countries have exchanged threats and/or punishments. However, the role of positive sanctions in world politics has begun to attract scholarly attention. Roger Fisher, Klaus Knorr, Johan Galtung, Richard Rosecrance, Alexander George, Richard Smoke,[81] and a few

[80] See Baldwin, *Economic Development and American Foreign Policy* (Chicago: University of Chicago Press, 1966).

[81] Roger Fisher, *International Conflict for Beginners* (New York: Harper & Row, 1969); Knorr, *Power of Nations*; Johan Galtung, "On the Effects of International Economic Sanctions, With Examples from the Case of Rhodesia," *World Politics*, 19 (1967), pp. 378–416; Richard Rosecrance (ed.), *The Future of the International Strategic System* (San Francisco: Chandler, 1972); Alexander George and Richard Smoke, *Deterrence in American Foreign Policy* (New York: Columbia University Press, 1974); Fred H. Lawson, "Using Positive Sanctions to End International Conflicts: Iran and the Arab Gulf Countries," *Journal of Peace Research*, 20 (1983), pp. 311–28; and Louis Kriesberg, "Carrots, Sticks, De-escalation: US–Soviet and Arab–Israeli Relations," *Armed Forces and Society*, 13 (1987), pp. 403–23.

others have contributed to this discussion, but much work remains to be done. I suggest that further research on this topic could be built on the earlier work of Hirschman and the social exchange theorists. Eckstein's suggestion that exchange theory has much to offer students of international politics deserves to be taken seriously.[82]

POWER AS A ZERO-SUM GAME

Traditionally, scholars of international relations have distinguished between conflict and cooperation. Power, it has often been argued, has to do with conflict but not with cooperation. The implied assumption was that we needed less conflict and more cooperation. Thomas Schelling, in *The Strategy of Conflict*, called into question the usefulness of this dichotomy by showing that most, if not all, interesting international political situations involved mixtures of both conflictual and cooperative elements. Although zero-sum games and games of pure cooperation might be useful ways to define the ends of a continuum, neither was likely to describe a real-world situation. Even war – traditionally regarded as the epitome of intense conflict – was shown by Schelling to involve significant cooperative dimensions. Although Schelling relied primarily on limited war to make his point, his logic can easily be extended to include so-called "total war." Nuclear war may not be unthinkable, but a war in which the participants would be *indifferent* to the prospects of planetary destruction is difficult to imagine. Even poker – that prototypical example of a zero-sum game – is hardly ever a zero-sum game in real life. Such values as the enjoyment of the game, concern about the player who is in over his head, and worries about whether the other players will be willing to play again in the future, almost always intrude on what is supposed to be a zero-sum game.

Despite Schelling, nuclear weapons, and ever-increasing aware-ness of the fragility of the earth's ecosystem, one still finds references to international politics as a zero-sum game in some or all respects. Stanley Hoffmann, for example, has argued that the

[82] Harry Eckstein, "Authority Patterns: A Structural Basis for Political Inquiry," *American Political Science Review*, 67 (1973), pp. 1157–9.

model of a zero-sum game is "a valid account for considerable
portions of world politics."[83] His citation of the Arab–Israeli
dispute as a case in point is instructive. Although conflict may be
the dominant mode of Arab–Israeli interaction, conceiving of the
situation as a zero-sum game virtually assures that cooperative
dimensions will be overlooked. Even Hoffmann's *caveat* – that he is
using the zero-sum model as an "ideal-type" in order to "reveal
the essence of the game" – fails to balance the perspective. In zero-
sum games, the absence of cooperative elements is not merely one
characteristic among many; it is the essential defining characteristic.
A portrayal of the Arab–Israeli dispute as a zero-sum game
strengthens neither our understanding of the situation nor the
prospects of peace.[84]

Robert Gilpin argues that international politics *always* takes the
form of a zero-sum game. After noting that "politics is the realm
of power," he states that "the essential fact of politics is that
power is always relative; one state's gain in power is by necessity
another's loss." "From this *political* perspective," he adds, "the
mercantilists are correct in emphasizing that in power terms,
international relations is a zero-sum game."[85] Regardless of what
one thinks of Gilpin's concept of power, it is important to realize
that the Dahl–Lasswell–Kaplan conception of power is not a zero-
sum view. Their conception permits us to describe situations in
which A's ability to get B to do X increases *simultaneously* with
B's ability to get A to do X.[86]

The model of the zero-sum game may be a potentially useful
conceptual tool for the student of international politics. However,
given traditional propensities to exaggerate the importance of
negative sanctions while ignoring positive ones and to concentrate
on conflictive dimensions of world politics while neglecting
cooperative ones, theorists would do well to leave this particular

[83] Stanley Hoffmann, "Notes on the Elusiveness of Modern Power," *International
Journal*, 30 (1975), p. 191.
[84] It is interesting to note that one could neither predict nor advocate Sadat's dramatic
visit to Israel on the basis of zero-sum game assumptions. The players in a zero-sum game
have no common interests – by definition. Therefore, they never have a reason to negotiate
(unless they think their opponent is stupid and can be outwitted).
[85] Gilpin, *US Power*, pp. 22–5, 34; emphasis in original; and *War and Change*, p. 94.
For other examples, see Baldwin, *Economic Statecraft*, pp. 21–2.
[86] For further discussion of this point, see chapter 2.

conceptual tool on the shelf for a few years. Mixed-motive game models almost always provide a more accurate description of real-world situations than do zero-sum models.

COMPELLENCE AND DETERRENCE

The distinction between compellence and deterrence is frequently noted by scholars in international relations – usually with reference to Schelling.[87] No instance of a challenge to the validity or the usefulness of this distinction has come to my attention. I will argue that an implicit assumption about the probability of a successful influence attempt underlies Schelling's discussion of compellence and deterrence, and that this assumption calls into question both the validity and the usefulness of the distinction.[88] There are, according to Schelling, typical differences between threats intended to make an adversary do something and threats intended to keep him from starting something. These differences concern the probability of success, the clarity of the threat, timing, and the difficulty of compliance.[89]

There is a difference between trying to discourage the Russians from launching a nuclear attack and trying to encourage the South

[87] At times such references become rather confusing. Keohane and Nye, for example, usually use the terms "positive" and "negative" power to refer to the compellence/deterrence distinction ("World Politics and the International Economic System," pp. 119, 134; *Power and Interdependence*, p. 44). But elsewhere they refer to the ability to resist influence attempts as "the negative dimension of power" ("World Politics and the International Economic System," p. 134). It seems desirable to maintain a clear distinction between deterring influence attempts and resisting them. The difference between deterring a nuclear attack and resisting one is a difference that matters.

[88] Parts of the argument that follows are drawn from Baldwin, "Bargaining with Airline Hijackers," in *The 50% Solution*, ed. I. William Zartman (New Haven: Yale University Press, 1983), pp. 404–29. One example of the extent to which students of international relations have accepted the compellence/deterrence arguments of Schelling is provided by the following passage: "Enough has already been said to indicate the disparities between American and Soviet strategic doctrines in the nuclear age. These differences may be most pithily summarized by stating that whereas we view nuclear weapons as a deterrent, the Russians see them as a 'compellant' [sic] – with all the consequences that follow" (Richard Pipes, "Why the Soviet Union Thinks It Could Fight and Win a Nuclear War," *Commentary*, 64 (July, 1977), p. 34). It will be argued here that the consequences that follow are by no means obvious.

[89] Schelling, *Strategy of Conflict*, pp. 195–9; and Schelling, *Arms and Influence* (New Haven: Yale University Press, 1966), pp. 69–91.

Africans to change their form of government, but describing that difference as the difference between keeping someone from doing something and getting someone to do something is not very helpful. From a purely semantic standpoint, any deterrent threat can be stated in compellent terms, and any compellent threat can be stated in deterrent terms. Thus, we could talk about compelling the Russians to do X (when X is anything except launching a nuclear attack) and about deterring South Africans from doing X (when X is continued white dominance). When we describe an influence attempt as deterrence, we usually have in mind a threat that is intended to *reduce* the probability of occurrence of an event that was not very likely to occur in the first place – e.g., nuclear attack, murder, or airline hijacking. When we describe an influence attempt as compellence, however, we usually have in mind a threat intended to *increase* the probability of occurrence of an event that was not very likely to occur anyway. Schelling is quite right in observing that "it is easier to *deter* than to *compel*,"[90] but that is more of a truism than an empirical observation. The person who tries to prevent unlikely things from happening will probably succeed; while the person who tries to cause unlikely things to happen will probably fail.

There are non-trivial differences between trying to do difficult things (like changing South Africa's policy of white supremacy), and trying to do easy things (like preventing the Russians from launching a nuclear attack). Almost all of the differences between compellent and deterrent threats suggested by Schelling can be accounted for by the difference in the autonomous probability of the outcome one is trying to influence.[91] The observation that

[90] Ibid., p. 100; emphasis in original. For an empirical study of deterrence and compellence that questions the relative ease of the latter, see Walter J. Petersen, "Deterrence and Compellence: A Critical Assessment of Conventional Wisdom," *International Studies Quarterly*, 30 (1986), pp. 269–94.

[91] The autonomous probability of the outcome X is defined as the probability that X would have occurred in the absence of any attempt by A to make it occur. Thus, the autonomous probability of X in a situation in which A is trying to influence B to do X is the probability that B would have done X anyway. See Karl W. Deutsch, *The Analysis of International Relations*, 3rd edn (Englewood Cliffs, N.J.: Prentice-Hall, 1988), pp. 24–31, 166. Strictly speaking, the autonomous probability of B's performance of X is not the same as the probability of success of A's attempt to get B to do X. A high autonomous probability need not indicate a high probability of success for A, and a low autonomous probability does not necessarily mean that it will be hard for A to get B to do X. B's strong dislike of A

deterrent threats are more likely to succeed than compellent threats seems less profound when one lays bare the implicit assumption that deterrent threats are used for easy tasks while compellent threats are used for hard tasks.

Most of the discussion of the different requirements in timing of deterrence and compellence can be reduced to the truism that considerable effort will be required to accomplish hard things, while one can accomplish easy things with much less effort. Why do compellent threats have to be "put in motion to be credible"?[92] Because they need a lot of credibility. Why do they need so much credibility? Because they are so unlikely to succeed in the first place!

Schelling also argues that it is likely to be especially difficult to comply with a compellent threat:

> There is another characteristic of compellent threats, arising in the need for affirmative action, that often distinguishes them from deterrent threats. It is that the very act of compliance – of doing what is demanded – is more conspicuously compliant, more recognizable as submission under duress, than when an act is merely withheld in the face of a deterrent threat. Compliance is likely to be less casual, less capable of being rationalized as something that one was going to do anyhow.[93]

Since Schelling uses the term "compellent threat" to refer to situations in which A is trying to get B to do something he is very unlikely to do, and the term "deterrent" threat to refer to situations in which A is trying to get B to do something he was likely to do anyway, the above passage is not surprising. Of course it is harder to rationalize compliance with compellent threats as something one intended to do anyhow, especially since compliance was something one had no intention of doing. It is much easier to

may make him reluctant to do X if he knows A wants him to; likewise, B's respect for A may make him eager to do X after he learns of A's desire. Other things being equal, however, it is generally harder to make unlikely events occur than it is to make likely events occur. For purposes of this essay, therefore, it will be arbitrarily assumed that influence attempts aimed at bringing about outcomes of low autonomous probability have a low probability of success; while influence attempts aimed at bringing about outcomes of high autonomous probability have a high probability of success.

[92] Schelling, *Arms and Influence*, p. 72.
[93] Ibid., p. 82.

give the appearance of doing what comes naturally if one really *is* doing what comes naturally. All of Schelling's comments about ease of compliance must be reversed if one compares the compellent threat – "Breathe or I'll shoot" – with the deterrent threat – "Don't breathe or I'll shoot." It is virtually tautological to say that the higher the autonomous probability of B's performance of X, the harder it will be to detect whether B's performance of X resulted from A's influence attempt. Schelling is quite right in saying that compliance is difficult in what he calls compellence situations. This difficulty, however, is not a characteristic of compellent threats; it is a characteristic of the particular type of influence situations that are being labeled "compellent." The difficulty of compliance with a compellent threat disappears if we change the situation from "Stand on your head and whistle Yankee Doodle or I'll shoot" to "Breathe or I'll shoot."[94] Compliance is conspicuous in some compellent threat situations; in others it is not.

Another difference between compellent and deterrent threats, according to Schelling, is that the former tend to be more ambiguous than the latter. Once again, particular kinds of situations seem to be implied:

> In addition to the question of "when," compellence usually involves questions of where, what, and how much. "Do nothing" is simple; "Do something" is ambiguous. "Stop where you are" is simple; "Go back" leads to "How far?" "Leave me alone" is simple; "Cooperate" is inexact and open-ended.[95]

"Do nothing," however, is not that simple. It leads to "What do you mean; I have to do something, don't I?" or "I can't just do nothing!" "Do nothing that will upset me" is more ambiguous than "Get the hell out of here!" "Stop where you are" is not so simple when said by a hijacker to the pilot of a plane at 30,000 feet. "Leave me alone" is not so simple when said by a tired father to a small child. It invariably leads to "Does that mean I must

---

[94] "Breathe or I'll shoot" is actually just a variation of "act normally or I'll shoot" – a compellent threat often found in TV dramas depicting the criminal hiding in the closet while the prisoner answers the doorbell.

[95] Schelling, *Arms and Influence*, pp. 72–3.

leave the room or merely that I must stop talking to you?" "Is it all right if I talk to myself?" "How about if I just listen to records?" In such a situation, "Leave me alone" is ambiguous; "Go play in the yard" is simple. Even if one accepts the distinction between deterrent and compellent threats, there is no reason to believe that one type of threat is intrinsically clearer than the other.

The alleged greater clarity of deterrent threats carries over to assurances.[96] Because the assurances associated with compellent threats tend to be ambiguous, they tend to lack credibility. Blackmailers, as Schelling says, "find the 'assurances' troublesome when their threats are compellent"; but blackmailers also find assurances troublesome *even when their threats are not compellent*. The credibility of assurances is not a function of the kind of threat being made; it is a function of the same sort of things that determine the credibility of threats and promises. The credibility of one's assurance that he will not explode a nuclear bomb if his demands are met grows out of the obvious unpleasantness of such an act, not out of the nature of the threat being made. Sadists, kidnappers, blackmailers, extortionists, and airline hijackers find that the credibility of their assurances is undermined by the obvious opportunities and incentives they have to renege on their assurance commitments, regardless of whether they have made deterrent or compellent threats.

Although the distinction between deterrence and compellence at first appears to be very helpful in analyzing world politics, further scrutiny raises serious questions about the utility of the distinction. The failure to provide a precise definition of compellence makes it hard to be sure, but a low probability of success seems to be inextricably bound up with the implied definition of this term. It is worthwhile to distinguish between threats and promises and between influence attempts with a high probability of success and those with a low probability of success. Until more precise definitions and more persuasive arguments are produced, however, students of international relations should be wary of the distinction between compellence and deterrence.[97]

---

[96] Ibid., p. 74.

[97] The closest Schelling comes to a precise definition of compellence is in *Arms and Influence*, pp. 70–1. I suspect that psychologists may have some persuasive arguments as to

CONCLUSION

A review of selected works of international relations scholarship reveals the continued existence of a number of traditional tendencies in the treatment of power. First, the tendency to exaggerate the fungibility of power resources and the related tendency to neglect considerations of scope are still with us. Despite years of exhortation by the Sprouts, discussions of national capabilities without reference to explicitly stated or clearly implied policy–contingency frameworks are common. Second, the propensity to treat military power resources as the "ultimate" power base, and the related propensity to overestimate the effectiveness of military force, have not disappeared. And third, emphasis on conflict and negative sanctions at the expense of emphasis on cooperation and positive sanctions is not uncommon.

It was suggested that the contextual analysis of power advocated by Lasswell and Kaplan, Dahl, the Sprouts, and others would provide a useful corrective for traditional weaknesses in treatments of power by students of international relations. Such contextual analysis would have a number of implications for the way scholars of international relations talk about their subjects. First, the division of the world into "great powers," "small powers," and "middle powers" would be called into question, since such terms usually connote generalized rather than situationally specific power. At the very least, users of such terms would be required to specify the issue-area they have in mind.[98] Second, the idea of a single monolithic international "power structure" would be called into question, since such a concept implies either highly fungible power resources or a single

---

why it is useful to distinguish between deterrence and compellence. Schelling does not present such arguments, however.

[98] The practice of specifying the scope and domain in terms of which "Great Powers" are defined would help to illuminate the military bias embedded in such terms. The widely read book by Paul Kennedy is a case in point: *The Rise and Fall of the Great Powers* (New York: Random House, 1987), p. 539. He defines a Great Power as "a state capable of holding its own against any other nation" – a definition as vague as it is innocuous. In a footnote, however, the reader is referred to Martin Wight's *Power Politics* (Middlesex: Penguin Books, 1979). Only by consulting Wight does one learn that "holding its own" refers to war-fighting capacity.

dominant issue-area. Students of world politics must recognize, as students of American politics have recognized, "that the notion of '*the* power structure' of a social unit is a dangerously misleading siren. There are as many power structures as there are issues fruitfully distinguished."[99] Keohane and Nye take two steps forward when they demonstrate that international power structures vary from one issue-area to another; but they slip one step backward when they imply that an overall structural approach that fails to distinguish among issue-areas and that is based on the assumption that power, like money, is highly fungible, can provide even a partial explanation of world politics.[100] It is time to recognize that the notion of a single overall international power structure unrelated to any particular issue-area is based on a concept of power that is virtually meaningless.[101] It is difficult to see how a model based on a virtually meaningless concept of power can provide even a partial explanation of international political relations. Instead of talking about *the* distribution of power resources underlying *the* international power structure, students of world politics could more profitably focus on the multiple

---

[99] Frederick W. Frey, "Comment: On Issues and Nonissues in the Study of Power," *American Political Science Review*, 65 (1971), p. 1086. See also Raymond E. Wolfinger, "Nondecisions and the Study of Local Politics," and "Rejoinder to Frey's 'Comment,'" both in *American Political Science Review*, 65 (1971), pp. 1063–80 and 1102–4, respectively.

Ray and Vural infer that this line of argument calls into question both the meaning and utility of "the classic question (in international politics as well as the world of sports) 'Who's Number One?'" ("Power Disparities," p. 320). I concur. I regard it as useless and nonsensical to assess athletic ability without reference to a specified set of athletic activities. How is one to compare a tennis player, a swimmer, a baseball player, an archer, and a weightlifter? It is equally useless and nonsensical to compare the influence of nation-states without any explicit or implicit reference to scope and domain. The implicit assumption by some students of international politics that only military force matters is akin to assuming that athletic prowess should be measured solely in terms of boxing ability.

As Dahl points out, "it is difficult enough to estimate relative influence within a particular scope and domain; it is by no means clear how we can 'add up' influence over many scopes and domains in order to arrive at total, or aggregate, influence." He adds that "an analogous problem arises when we try to compare two athletes who compete in different sports. Was Babe Ruth a better athlete than Jack Dempsey? The question seems unanswerable" (*Modern Political Analysis*, 4th edn, pp. 26–30).

[100] Keohane and Nye, *Power and Interdependence*, pp. 43–54, 222–5.

[101] Dahl, *Modern Political Analysis*, p. 27: "Any statement about influence that does not clearly indicate the domain and scope it refers to verges on being meaningless." For a similar comment, see Sprout and Sprout, "Environmental Factors," p. 325.

distributional patterns of a wide variety of resources related to a number of significant issue-areas.

The point here is not to deny either the possibility or the desirability of generalizations about power patterns within very broadly – perhaps even vaguely – defined issue-areas. It is to suggest that healthy skepticism and scholarly caution should be proportionate to the broadness and vagueness of the specification of the issue-area. Rough indicators of power hierarchies in given issue-areas can be useful, but only if the limitations and pitfalls of such an approach are clearly understood and acknowledged.[102] The important thing is recognition that the absence of a common denominator of political value in terms of which different scopes of power could be compared is not so much a methodological problem to be solved as it is a real-world constraint to be lived with. Economists, after all, did not invent money in order to solve the conceptual problem of aggregating economic values; they just happen to be luckier than political scientists. If the real world has not chosen to provide political analysts with a political counterpart to money, it would be folly to pretend that it has.

Although power analysis is probably the oldest approach to the study of world politics, it is also one of the most promising for the years ahead. Refinements in the causal notion of power since 1950 have not yet been fully integrated into the literature on international relations, but there is no reason why this should not happen. Both social power literature and social exchange theory have much to offer the student of world politics. As Hayward Alker has observed, "Far from being nearly dead, weak, or inadequate as some critics have implied, power measurement has just begun."[103]

[102] For an impressive demonstration of generalization at a high level of abstraction based on explicit acknowledgment of the importance of scope and domain and the resulting multidimensional nature of power, see Alker, "On Political Capabilities."

[103] Ibid., pp. 370–1.

8

Interdependence and Power:
a Conceptual Analysis

Priority in the use of a novel meaning of a term is no cause for pride; in fact it betrays a lack of "terminological discipline" and a want of linguistic inventiveness – for when a writer creates or modifies a concept he ought also to coin a new word to denote it, rather than corrupt the language and spread confusion.[1]

The concept of dependence – mutual or otherwise – in world politics has stimulated lively scholarly controversy. Some view it as helpful in explaining the distribution of power in the world,[2] while others condemn it as an "unhelpful" and "misleading" analytical category.[3] Many scholars complain about the lack of conceptual clarity,[4] and some even deny that there is any generally

[1] Fritz Machlup, *Essays on Economic Semantics* (Englewood Cliffs, N.J.: Prentice-Hall, 1963), p. 12.
[2] Robert O. Keohane and Joseph S. Nye, "World Politics and the International Economic System," in *The Future of the International Economic System*, ed. C. Fred Bergsten (Lexington, Mass.: Lexington Books, 1973), pp. 121–5; Robert O. Keohane and Joseph S. Nye, *Power and Interdependence: World Politics in Transition* (Boston: Little, Brown, 1977), pp. 3–19.
[3] Sanjaya Lall, "Is 'Dependence' a Useful Concept in Analysing Underdevelopment?" *World Development*, 3 (1975), p. 808.
[4] Richard Rosecrance and Arthur Stein, "Interdependence: Myth or Reality?" *World Politics*, 26 (1973), p. 2; Richard Rosecrance et al., "Whither Interdependence?" *International Organization*, 31 (1977), pp. 425–6; James A. Caporaso, "Dependence, Dependency, and Power in the Global System: A Structural and Behavioral Analysis," *International Organization*, 32 (1978), pp. 13ff; Robert Solomon with Anne Gault, *The Interdependence of Nations: An Agenda for Research*, A Report to the National Science Foundation (December, 1977), p. 6; and Robert O. Keohane and Joseph S. Nye, Jr,

accepted definition of the term.[5] The purpose of this chapter is to examine the concept of dependence, to clarify it through explication, to consider recent conceptual distinctions in analytical and historical perspective, and to address the question of whether "dependence" can be treated as part of a larger family of social science concepts sometimes called "power terms."

It is important to be clear as to what this chapter is about, but it is equally important to understand what it is *not* about. It does not offer empirical observations as to whether dependence or interdependence is increasing or decreasing. It does not offer normative observations as to whether dependence or interdependence is "good" or "bad." And it is not an attempt either to refute or to understand *dependencia* theory as recently formulated by certain Latin American scholars.[6]

CONCEPTUAL ANALYSIS: ORDER OR ANARCHY?

This chapter is an exercise in conceptual analysis. It is an attempt to clarify and explicate the concept of dependence and related concepts, such as "interdependence" and "dependency." It offers no new definition, no theory of interdependence, and no new technique of measurement. I am aware that some would deny the worth of such an undertaking and dismiss it as "mere semantics" or "pure logomachy." The advancement of knowledge, however, depends on the ability of scholars to communicate with one another; and clear concepts seem to help. If one is to theorize about interdependence or attempt to measure it, the essential first

"International Interdependence and Integration," in *Handbook of Political Science*, ed. Fred I. Greenstein and Nelson W. Polsby (Reading, Mass.: Addison-Wesley, 1975), vol. 8: *International Politics*, p. 368.

[5] Hayward R. Alker, Jr, Lincoln P. Bloomfield, and Nazli Choucri, *Analyzing Global Interdependence*, 4 vols (Cambridge, Mass.: Center for International Studies, MIT, 1974), vol. 1: *Analytical Perspectives and Policy Implications*, p. 2.

[6] For discussions primarily concerned with understanding Latin American usage, see Caporaso, "Dependence, Dependency, and Power," pp. 13–43; Raymond D. Duvall, "Dependence and *Dependencia* Theory: Notes Toward Precision of Concept and Argument," *International Organization*, 32 (1978), pp. 51–78; and C. Richard Bath and Dilmus D. James, "Dependency Analysis of Latin America: Some Criticisms, Some Suggestions," *Latin American Research Review*, 11 (1976), pp. 3–54.

step is a clear conceptualization of the nature of interdependence. As Felix Oppenheim has argued, "the elucidation of the language of political science is by no means an idle exercise in semantics, but in many instances a most effective way to solve substantive problems of political research."[7]

Conceptual analysis presupposes guidelines or "rules of the game" in terms of which such undertakings may be judged. The idea that anyone is free to define terms arbitrarily, without explanation or justification, is anathema to conceptual analysis. The "rules" or "guidelines" underlying the analysis that follows are drawn from three disparate yet surprisingly compatible sources – a nineteenth-century political economist (Thomas Malthus),[8] a twentieth-century economist (Fritz Machlup),[9] and a twentieth-century political scientist (Felix Oppenheim).[10]

Writing in 1827, Malthus noted that the tendency of different writers to attribute different meanings to the same terms had given rise to complaints about "differences of opinion among political economists." As a corrective to this situation, he offered four rules for "guidance in defining and applying the terms used in the science of political economy." These rules are as deserving of attention by political economists today as they were then, perhaps more so. First: When terms "which are of daily occurrence in the common conversation of educated persons" are employed, they should be defined "so as to agree with the sense in which they are understood in this ordinary use of them." Second: When common usage does not suffice, "the next best authority is that of some of the most celebrated writers in the science, particularly if any one of them has, by common consent, been considered as a principal founder of it."[11] Third: Recognizing that changes in meaning are

---

[7] Felix E. Oppenheim, "The Language of Political Inquiry: Problems of Clarification," in *Handbook of Political Science*, ed. Fred I. Greenstein and Nelson W. Polsby (Reading, Mass.: Addison-Wesley, 1975), vol. 1: *Political Science: Scope and Theory*, p. 284. See also Machlup, *Essays*, pp. 3–6.

[8] Rev. T. R. Malthus, *Definitions in Political Economy, preceded by An Inquiry into the Rules Which Ought to Guide Political Economists in the Definition and Use of Their Terms; with Remarks on the Deviations from these Rules in their Writings* (London: John Murray, 1827).

[9] Machlup, *Essays,*. pp. 3–6ff.

[10] Oppenheim, "Language of Political Inquiry," pp. 283–335.

[11] It is a fair inference that Malthus had Adam Smith in mind here. The contemporary relevance is illustrated by Albert O. Hirschman's contention that "no one has yet given a

sometimes justifiable, Malthus proposed that "the alteration proposed should not only remove the immediate objections which may have been made to the terms as before applied, but should be shown to be free from other equal or greater objections, and on the whole be obviously more *useful* in facilitating the explanation and improvement of the science. A change which is always itself an evil, can alone be warranted by superior utility taken in the most enlarged sense." Fourth: "Any new definitions adopted should be consistent with those which are allowed to remain."[12]

Although I find Malthus' rules eminently sensible and as applicable now as then, others may prefer the more modern criteria for evaluating concepts presented by Oppenheim in the *Handbook of Political Science*:[13] First: Concepts should be operational in the broadest sense, although this should not be interpreted as requiring quantification. Second: Concepts that establish definitional connections with other terms are to be preferred. Third: Concepts that draw attention to theoretically important aspects of the subject matter that might easily be overlooked are desirable. Fourth: Concepts should not preclude empirical investigation by making true "by definition" what had better be left open to empirical inquiry. Fifth: Concepts should remain reasonably close to ordinary language. "Ordinary language," however, does not necessarily mean the way most people would define the term, but rather the "set of rules they implicitly follow when applying it to a given situation." Sixth: The meaning of concepts should be "open" in the sense that the possibility of change is never completely ruled out.

The various criteria suggested by Malthus and Oppenheim will be discussed later with reference to recent scholarly treatments of dependence.[14] For now it suffices to point out that Machlup,

better picture of 'dependence on trade' than Adam Smith" (*National Power and the Structure of Foreign Trade* (Berkeley: University of California, 1945), p. 73).

[12] All quotations in this paragraph are from Malthus, *Definitions in Political Economy*, pp. 1–7. Alfred Marshall shared Malthus' view that economics should "conform itself to the familiar terms of every-day life, and so far as possible must use them as they are commonly used" (*Principles of Economics*, 2 vols, 2nd edn (London: Macmillan, 1891), vol. 1, p. 103).

[13] Oppenheim, "Language of Political Inquiry," pp. 297–309.

[14] In view of suggestions by Caporaso and Duvall that a clear distinction be drawn between the concepts of dependence and dependency, it should be noted that such a

Malthus, and Oppenheim all agree that, *certeris paribus*, deviations from common usage are undesirable characteristics in scientific concepts and that such deviations call for careful explanation and justification. Special care in discussing the nature and methods of conceptual analysis prior to examining the concept of interdependence is in order because much of the recent scholarly work on international and transnational dependence fails to satisfy the criteria articulated by either Malthus or Oppenheim.

What follows is an explication of the concept of dependence in its most general and fundamental sense. It should be noted at the outset that some would deny that explication of a generic concept of dependence serves a useful analytic purpose.[15] Since the arguments for and against this position were cogently stated in Robert Dahl's classic article on "The Concept of Power,"[16] there is no need to repeat them here. Dahl sought to capture the basic intuitive notion of power in the same sense that this chapter will pursue the basic intuitive notion of dependence that underlies discussions of dependence, dependency, interdependence, or independence. Thus, references to concepts of dependence in the following discussion are meant to apply, *mutatis mutandis*, to these related terms as well.

To favor the elucidation of general abstract concepts of power or dependence, however, does not commit one to the view that discussions of actual power or dependence relations should be carried on at very high levels of abstraction. It is not illogical to advocate that a clearly defined generic concept of power (or dependence) be used to develop low- and/or medium-level generalizations rather than highly abstract ones. In short, there is a difference between defining a concept and applying it.

distinction is not employed in this essay for reasons that will be explained later. Unless otherwise indicated, treatments of dependence, independence, interdependence, autonomy, and dependency are regarded as falling within the same general field of inquiry. As used here, the term "interdependence" always refers to "mutual dependence."

[15] Caporaso, "Dependence, Dependency, and Power," p. 18; Edward L. Morse, "Transnational Economic Processes," *International Organization*, 25 (1971), p. 382; Fernando Henrique Cardoso and Enzo Faletto, *Dependency and Development in Latin America* (Berkeley: University of California Press, 1979), pp. xii–xiii.

[16] Robert A. Dahl, "The Concept of Power," *Behavioral Science*, 2 (1957): 201–15, esp. p. 214. See also, Oppenheim, "Language of Political Inquiry," pp. 283ff.

THE CONCEPT OF DEPENDENCE: 1568–1968

Conventional usage is a basic reference point for evaluating scientific concepts according to Malthus, Machlup, and Oppenheim. In explicating the concept of dependence, the single most important question concerns conventional usage. Both the everyday usage by laymen and traditional scholarly usage will be examined. Since international and transnational dependence is of particular interest to the writer and likely readers of this chapter, particular attention will be devoted to usage in the context of world affairs.

Common usage

Raymond Duvall provides a useful discussion of the two basic meanings of "dependence" in ordinary language.[17] On the one hand, "dependence" is used in a causal sense to refer to situations in which an effect is contingent on or conditioned by something else. Keohane and Nye are apparently referring to this usage when they note that "in common parlance, *dependence* means a state of being determined or significantly affected by external forces."[18] On the other hand, "dependence" is also used to refer to a relationship of subordination in which one thing is supported by something else or must rely upon something else for fulfillment of a need. It is apparently this second meaning that Caporaso refers to as "the familiar, common sense" usage of the term.[19]

Duvall points out that the two basic meanings of "dependence" correspond to the distinction often made between "sensitivity interdependence" and "vulnerability interdependence."[20] Whereas

[17] Duvall, "Dependence and *Dependencia* Theory," pp. 61–8.

[18] *Power and Interdependence*, p. 8.

[19] Caporaso, "Dependence, Dependency, and Power," pp. 18–19, 24. See also, Ramsay Muir, *The Interdependent World and Its Problems* (Boston: Houghton Mifflin, 1933), p. 1; and Kenneth Waltz, *Theory of International Politics* (Reading, Mass.: Addison-Wesley, 1979), p. 143.

[20] Duvall, "Dependence and *Dependencia* Theory," pp. 62–3. Although it is customary to attribute the distinction between "sensitivity" and "vulnerability" interdependence to Keohane and Nye (see "World Politics and the International Economic System"), the distinction is also found in an earlier article by Kenneth Waltz, "The Myth of Interdependence" in *The International Corporation*, ed. Charles Kindleberger (Cambridge, Mass.: MIT Press, 1970), p. 210.

the first meaning implies mere contingency, the second implies need fulfillment that would be costly to forgo.

Duvall's discussion notes that the two basic meanings of "dependence" can be traced back for several centuries. Although Duvall offers no documentation for this, his assertions are compatible with the *Oxford English Dictionary*.[21] Perusal of the *OED*, however, furnishes additional clues relating to usage in different contexts. The preponderance of references to world affairs pertain to the second meaning.[22] The *OED* provides examples of the second meaning with regard to "depend," "dependence," "dependency," and "dependent." In every case examples concerning world affairs are included. Especially noteworthy is a seventeenth-century reference to "the effect of depending upon forraign Countries for Hemps," a reference comparable in meaning and context to contemporary discussions of "vulnerability dependence." Neither the concept of vulnerability dependence nor its usage in the context of world affairs is new. If the *OED* is taken as an authority, it would appear that this second meaning of "dependence" is more conventional than the first in discussions of world politics and economics.

Scholarly usage: general

Scholarly usage, of course, sometimes diverges from that of the layman; therefore, conventions among scholars should be considered. Conventional treatments by economists and international relations scholars are of most direct relevance to international and transnational dependence. Scholarly discussions do not always

[21] *A New English Dictionary on Historical Principles* (Oxford: Clarendon Press, 1897). (Also known as the *Oxford English Dictionary*, and hereafter cited as *OED*.) Cf. E. Littre, *Dictionnaire de la langue Francaise* (Paris: Librairie Hachette, 1883). Similar dependency terminology exists in English, Italian, French, and Spanish and can be traced back to the same Latin roots. Usage of the term in a political context to refer to relations in which one actor relies upon another for fulfillment of a need, a usage suggesting subjection or subordination, is several centuries old in each of these languages. "Vulnerability dependence" is not new! This concept of dependence seems to be implicit in the writings of the Stoic philosopher Epictetus, *The Discourses and Manual*, trans. P. E. Matheson (Oxford: Clarendon Press, 1916).

[22] This may be an overly cautious statement. Judgments as to what should be classified as "world affairs" may differ, however, and I do not wish to quibble. In my judgment, the *OED* does not contain a single example of the first meaning in the context of world affairs.

explicitly state a definition of "dependence," thus leaving the reader two basic strategies for determining what the author has in mind. First, one might reasonably assume that failure to provide an explicit definition indicates that the author is following common usage, in which case the previous discussion suggests that the second meaning is the more likely. Second, one can look for contextual clues. Since both basic meanings of "dependence" involve influence in its broadest sense, it is not much help to look for words like "affect," "change," "influence," "impinge," "induce," or "cause." The crucial difference between the first and second meaning of "dependence" has to do with the ease of breaking the relationship; "sensitivity interdependence" implies nothing about the cost of altering the relationship.[23] Thus, if one finds a relationship or its effects referred to as "necessary," "ineluctable," "inevitable," "inextricable," or "unavoidable," it is grounds for suspicion that the author has in mind a relationship that would be costly to break. Likewise, if terms such as "need," "compel," "must," "constraint," or "Hobson's choice" are used to describe the relationship, it seems fair to infer that the second meaning of "dependence" is the relevant one. If "dependence" is used with reference to "self-sufficiency," "autarky," or the ability of one actor to "do without" another, the opportunity costs of forgoing the relationship would seem to be the underlying concern.

Scholarly usage: economists

In 1972 Richard Cooper asserted that " 'economic interdependence' normally refers to the dollar value of economic transactions among regions or countries, either in absolute terms, or relative to their total transactions." He distinguished this "normal usage" from his more restricted concept of "the *sensitivity* of economic transactions between two or more nations to economic develop-

---

[23] "Costs" in this essay always refer to "opportunity costs." Although dependency may be defined in terms of the costs of "breaking" a relationship, it can also refer to alterations in the relationship short of total severance. This point is of little consequence for the argument in this essay, however; and the terms "breaking," "altering," "severing," and "forgoing" will be used interchangeably.

ments within those nations."[24] In 1973 Tollison and Willett referred to Cooper's sensitivity concept as representing "normal usage by economists."[25] Without disputing the rapid progress of the discipline of economics, "normal usage" would appear to change with remarkable speed. In 1979 Marina v. N. Whitman reiterated the assertion of Tollison and Willett that "as generally understood by economists, the term *interdependence* refers to the sensitivity of economic behavior in one country to developments or policies originating outside its own borders."[26] If such references are taken to mean that many economists think of interdependence in terms of the mutual sensitivity of economic variables, they can be supported with evidence. If, however, such references are interpreted to mean that economists since the time of Adam Smith have characteristically favored the first meaning of "dependence," based on contingency, rather than the second, based on need, supporting evidence is difficult to find.

The most important thing to note about economists' usage of "dependence" or "interdependence" is that clarity is lacking. They rarely offer an explicit definition of the concept, rarely include it in the index of a book, and often omit it from dictionaries of economic terminology.[27] Until recently, it has not been an important analytic term for most economists.

This is not to say that references to "dependence" cannot be found. In explaining the benefits of specialization and exchange, Adam Smith made it clear that dependency was a likely consequence in the sense that exchange relationships involved benefits that satisfied mutual needs and which would therefore, by

---

[24] Richard N. Cooper, "Economic Interdependence and Foreign Policy in the Seventies," *World Politics*, 24 (1972), p. 159.

[25] Robert D. Tollison and Thomas D. Willett, "International Integration and the Interdependence of Economic Variables," *International Organization*, 27 (1973), p. 259. This article not only asserts a view of "normal usage" that differs from Cooper's view of "normal usage," it even cites Cooper's article in support of this contention.

[26] Marina v. N. Whitman, *Reflections of Interdependence: Issues for Economic Theory and US Policy* (Pittsburgh: University of Pittsburgh Press, 1979), p. 265. Also in 1979, Kenneth Waltz concluded that "sensitivity interdependence" was "essentially an economist's definition" (*Theory of International Politics*, p. 139).

[27] Cf. Harold S. Sloan and Arnold J. Zurcher, *A Dictionary of Economics*, 4th edn (New York: Barnes and Noble, 1961); *The McGraw-Hill Dictionary of Modern Economics* (New York: McGraw-Hill, 1965); and John Eatwell, Murray Milgate, and Peter Newman (eds), *The New Palgrave: A Dictionary of Economics*, 4 vols (London: Macmillan, 1987).

definition, be costly to forgo.[28] Ramsay Muir has described Smith
as having "revolutionized economic science by working out the
theory of interdependence";[29] and Albert O. Hirschman has
contended that "no one has yet given a better picture of the nature
of 'dependence on trade.' "[30] Hirschman drew attention to the
intimate connection between the concept of "gain from trade" and
the concept of dependence:

> The influence which country A acquires in country B by foreign
> trade depends in the first place upon the total gain which B derives
> from that trade; the total gain from trade for any country is indeed
> nothing but another expression for the total impoverishment which
> would be inflicted upon it by a stoppage of trade. In this sense the
> classical concept, gain from trade, and the power concept,
> dependence on trade, now being studied are seen to be merely two
> aspects of the same phenomenon.[31]

It should be noted that Hirschman did not view the conceptual
linkage between "gains from trade" and "dependence" as redefining the latter concept, but rather as clarifying it. And rightly
so, for he simply provided a more precise statement of the second
basic meaning of "dependence." This concept of "dependence" in
terms of the opportunity costs of forgoing trade has been implicit
in many economists' discussions of international economic relations
both before and after Adam Smith.[32]

---

[28] *An Inquiry into the Nature and Causes of the Wealth of Nations* (1776), reprint edn
(New York: Modern library, 1937), pp. 13–16. To say that specialization and exchange
create dependency is not to say that each trading partner incurs an equal amount of
dependency, nor does it imply dependency on each trading partner. A country that increases
its economic well-being through trade becomes dependent on trade but not necessarily on
any particular product or trading partner.

[29] Muir, *Interdependent World*, p. 18.

[30] Hirschman, *National Power*, p. 73.

[31] Ibid., p. 18. Hirschman notes that the "gain from trade" refers to "that part of a
country's well-being which it is in the power of its trading partners to take away" (p. 19).
Thus, vulnerability is necessarily implied by this type of dependency. Ernst B. Haas
overlooks this point when he introduces "vulnerability interdependence" and "opportunity
cost interdependence" as two separate concepts. They are simply different labels for the
same basic concept. See "Is There a Hole in the Whole? Knowledge, Technology,
Interdependence, and the Construction of International Regimes," *International Organization*, 29 (1975), pp. 861–4.

[32] Edmond Silberner, *La guerre dans la pensée économique du XVI au XVIII siècle*
(Paris: Librairie du Recueil Sirey, 1939), pp. 11, 14–15, 94–5, 109–14, 173, 190–1, 195,

It would be a mistake to depict Hirschman's usage as "mere trade dependence." Although Hirschman's work happens to focus on trade, his explication of the concept of dependence is applicable

263ff; *The Problem of War in Nineteenth-Century Economic Thought* (Princeton: Princeton University Press, 1946), pp. 54–6ff; Rev. T. R. Malthus, *Observations on the Effects of the Corn Laws and of a Rise or Fall in the Price of Corn on the Agriculture and General Wealth of the Country* (London: J. Johnson, 1814), pp. 22–3; R. G. Hawtrey, *Economic Aspects of Sovereignty* (London: Longmans, Green, 1930), pp. 103–4; Whitney H. Shepardson, "Nationalism and American Trade," *Foreign Affairs*, 12 (April 1934), p. 407; Commission of Inquiry into National Policy in International Economic Relations, *International Economic Relations* (Minneapolis: University of Minnesota Press, 1934), pp. 11, 103–9, 132–5; Franz Eulenburg, "International Trade," *Encyclopedia of the Social Sciences*, vol. 4 (New York: Macmillan, 1937), pp. 196–200; Gottfried Haberler, *The Theory of International Trade* (London: William Hodge, 1936), pp. 239–40: A. C. Pigou, *The Political Economy of War*, rev. edn (New York: Macmillan, 1941), pp. 5–18; George A. Steiner (ed.), *Economic Problems of War* (New York: John Wiley, 1942); Hirschman, *National Power*, pp. 3–81; Jacob Viner, "The Prospects for Foreign Trade in the Post-War World," *Readings in the Theory of International Trade*, ed. American Economic Association (Philadelphia: Blakiston, 1950), pp. 527–8; J. B. Condliffe, *The Commerce of Nations* (New York: Norton, 1950), pp. 620–1; Jules Backman et al., *War and Defense Economics* (New York: Rinehart, 1952), pp. 113–38; William W. Lockwood, *The Economic Development of Japan* (Princeton: Princeton University Press, 1954), pp. 384–6; P. T. Ellsworth, *The International Economy*, rev. edn (New York: Macmillan, 1958), pp. 1–3; Thomas C. Schelling, *International Economics* (Boston: Allyn and Bacon, 1958), pp. 512–13; Michael Michaely, "Concentration of Exports and Imports: An International Comparison," *Economic Journal*, 68 (1958), pp. 722–3; Charles J. Hitch, "National Security Policy as a Field for Economics Research," *World Politics*, 12 (1960), pp. 444–5; Charles P. Kindleberger, *Foreign Trade and the National Economy* (New Haven, Conn.: Yale University Press, 1962), pp. 143–5; Paul Marer, "The Political Economy of Soviet Relations with Eastern Europe," in *Testing Theories of Economic Imperialism*, ed. Steven T. Rosen and James R. Kurth (Lexington, Mass.: Lexington Books, 1974), pp. 231–60; Jan Tinbergen et al., *RIO: Reshaping the International Order, A Report to the Club of Rome* (New York: Signet, 1976), pp. 48–50; and Fritz Machlup, *A History of Thought on Economic Integration* (New York: Columbia University Press, 1977), pp. 29, 53. This concept of dependence is grounded in the logical structure of international trade theory, as Hirschman shows. Whitman (p. 157) notes that "the idea of economic interdependence among nations has always lain at the heart of the pure theory of international trade"; but she fails to note that it is "vulnerability interdependence" that lies at the heart of trade theory, not the "sensitivity interdependence" which she elsewhere (p. 265) describes as the economists' generally understood definition of interdependence. Peter Katzenstein associates the concept of "sensitivity interdependence" with "neo-classical international trade theory" ("International Relations and Domestic Structures: Foreign Economic Policies of Advanced Industrial States," *International Organization*, 30 (1976), p. 9). Katzenstein does not explain the nature of the relationship; nor does he cite any "neo-classical trade theorists" to support his contention. John S. Chipman identifies Viner and Haberler as "neoclassical" trade theorists; but as noted above, both used the term "dependence" in a way similar to Hirschman ("A Survey of the Theory of International Trade: Part 1, The Classical Theory," *Econometrica*, 33 (1965), pp. 478–9).

to a wide range of social exchange relationships.[33] If the term
"interaction" is substituted for "trade" each time it appears in the
previous quotation, this point will become clear.

To show that economists have often used "dependence" in its
second meaning does not establish such usage as "normal";
however, it does justify a certain amount of skepticism with regard
to undocumented assertions that "sensitivity interdependence"
represents normal usage by economists.

Some economists, of course, have used "dependence" in its first
meaning to refer to contingent relations. Ellsworth, for example,
seems to employ "dependence" in this sense in discussing the
interdependence of national currencies, even though he seems to
use the second meaning of "dependence" in discussing why trade
takes place.[34] Machlup uses "interdependence" in the sense of
covariance of economic variables most of the time; but when
referring to the relationship between national power and self-
sufficiency, he seems to revert to the second meaning of "dependence."[35] And many of the essays in a volume edited by Robert
Aliber apparently employ "interdependence" to refer to the
covariance of economic variables.[36]

In the past two decades or so, economists' usage of the term
interdependence has become so confusing that a brief digression
from my main argument is in order. In addition to using
"interdependence" to refer to relations that would be mutually
costly to forgo, some economists have used it interchangeably with
"integration," "openness," and "mutual sensitivity."[37] Each of
these terms represents an analytically distinct concept, and none
corresponds to "interdependence" in the sense of relations that
would be mutually costly to break. "Openness" refers to the

[33] Cf. Peter M. Blau, *Exchange and Power in Social Life* (New York: John Wiley, 1964);
and Richard M. Emerson, "Power-Dependence Relations," *American Sociological Review*,
27 (1962), pp. 31–41.

[34] Ellsworth, *International Economy*, pp. 2–3, 318.

[35] Machlup, *Essays*, pp. 13–23; *History of Thought on Economic Integration*, pp. 15,
19–20, 29, 53, and 81.

[36] Robert Z. Aliber (ed.), *National Monetary Policies and the International Finance
System* (Chicago: University of Chicago Press, 1974).

[37] On this point, see Tollison and Willett, "International Integration," pp. 255, 259–60,
267; Marina v. N. Whitman, "Economic Openness and International Financial Flows,"
Journal of Money, Credit and Banking, 1 (1969), pp. 727–8, 745; and Cooper, "Economic
Interdependence and Foreign Policy," pp. 159–60.

degree of interaction with the outside world and is usually measured in terms of the ratio of foreign trade to GNP.[38] "Sensitivity" refers to the covariance of economic variables. And "integration," as Machlup's careful explication has shown, has as its essential defining characteristic the degree to which opportunities for efficient division of labor are used.[39] Each of these concepts has different uses and different empirical referents; thus, it is desirable to distinguish among them. This does not rule out the possibility that a particular research project might employ an *operational* definition of interdependence in terms of "openness"; but it does imply that appropriate qualifications should be stated.

In sum, economists have paid little attention to "dependence" as a scientific concept but have frequently – dare I say "normally"? – used the term in its common-sense second meaning. I have failed to locate a single economist's work that explicitly acknowledges the two basic meanings of dependence and that offers reasons for preferring the first meaning in a way that would even begin to satisfy the Reverend Malthus.[40] Indeed, conceptual analysis seems to have gone out of style among economists – with the notable exception of Machlup. With reference to the alleged propensity of economists to define interdependence in terms of "sensitivity," the following hypotheses might be considered: One is more likely to find an economist using "dependence" in this sense: (1) the more

[38] Henry C. Wallich, "Money and Growth," *Journal of Money, Credit and Banking*, 1 (1969), p. 281; and Whitman, "Economic Openness," p. 727.

[39] Machlup, *History of Thought on Economic Integration*, p. 18.

[40] After admitting that he has not "done an exhaustive survey of use of the term [interdependence] by economists," Richard Cooper nevertheless proceeds to ignore the voluminous references contained in footnote 32 of this chapter. Cooper then describes my interpretation of Hirschman as using the terms "interdependence" and "mutual dependence" interchangeably as a "dubious procedure." He fails to note, however, that most people – and most dictionaries – treat these terms as equivalent. (In personal communications with Hirschman with respect to my interpretation of his work, he has raised no such objection.) See Richard N. Cooper, "Economic Interdependence and Coordination of Economic Policies," in *Handbook of International Economics*, vol. 2, ed. R. W. Jones and P. B. Kenen (Amsterdam: Elsevier Science Publishers, 1985), pp. 1196–8.

After noting the OED definition of interdependence, Cooper rejects it in favor of an unconventional and misleading distinction between "mutual dependence" and "interdependence." Robert Gilpin embraces the "*Oxford English Dictionary* definition" which he misreads Cooper as favoring. See Robert Gilpin, *The Political Economy of International Relations* (Princeton: Princeton University Press, 1987), p. 17.

recent the reference; (2) in discussing monetary relations rather than trade relations; (3) in relatively mathematical treatments of the topic; and (4) with reference to particular economic variables rather than with reference to purposive actors, such as nation-states.

Scholarly usage: international relations

It is a peculiar fact of intellectual history that international relations scholars writing on interdependence have paid very little attention to treatments of this topic by previous generations of scholars in the same field. Keohane and Nye, for example, virtually ignore scholarly treatments of interdependence prior to the Second World War.[41] Whatever else one might say about the concept of "dependence," there can be no doubt that scholarly concern about its role in interstate relations predates the Second World War. The opposed concepts of "self-reliance" and "dependence" are basic to an understanding of Machiavelli's *The Prince*.[42] Defining dependence in terms of reliance on others, of course, implies a lack of self-sufficiency, which, in turn, implies the second basic meaning of dependence, defined in terms of benefits that would be costly for one or both parties to forgo. References to this concept of interstate dependence are found in the writings of the early Mercantilists as well as in the writings of Montesquieu and Rousseau.[43] In the twentieth century excellent scholarly

[41] Keohane and Nye, "International Interdependence and Integration," pp. 363–414. Edward L. Morse has suggested that "the analysis of interstate interdependence begins with a central political problem that arose in international economic interchange after World War II" (*Modernization and the Transformation of International Relations* (New York: Free Press, 1976), p. 117)); but he modified this statement to apply only to "recent writings" in a later publication. See "Interdependence in World Affairs," *World Politics: An Introduction*, ed. James N. Rosenau, Kenneth W. Thompson, and Gavin Boyd (New York: The Free Press, 1976), p. 663.

[42] Niccolò Machiavelli, *The Prince*, trans. James B. Atkinson (Indianapolis, Ind.: Bobbs-Merrill, 1976), pp. 68–9, 149, 163, 171, 203, 359. Although first published in 1532, *The Prince* was written about 1514.

[43] Silberner, *La guerre dans la pensée économique*, pp. 7–122; Jean-Jacques Rousseau, *The First and Second Discourses* [1750, 1755], trans. Roger D. Masters and Judith R. Masters (New York: St Martin's Press, 1964), p. 36n.; *On the Social Contract* [1762], trans. Judith R. Masters, ed. Roger D. Masters (New York: St Martin's Press, 1978), p. 74n.; and Charles-Louis de Montesquieu, *De l'esprit des lois* (1748), book XX, chap. 2, cited by Hirschman, *National Power*, p. 10n.

discussions of international interdependence have been provided by Sir Norman Angell (1914), Francis Delaisi (1925), and Ramsay Muir (1933).[44] All three works contain both conceptual explication and empirical generalizations that are well worth the attention of contemporary scholars.

The concept of interdependence, as used by international relations scholars, is often accused of having a normative bias and of being ill-defined.[45] Although specific examples are rarely cited by the accusers, some could probably be found. There is little evidence, however, that scholarly discussions of international interdependence from the time of Machiavelli to about 1960 were *characterized* by ill-defined or normatively biased concepts of dependency.

The charge of a normative bias in earlier conceptualizations of interdependence rests on a misconception of the traditional concept of the "benefits" of interdependence and a failure to distinguish between normative and factual concepts.

Keohane and Nye object to defining interdependence in terms of "mutual benefit." "In some cases," they contend, "an interdependent relationship may have such negative consequences that both parties would be quite happy to cease contact with one another entirely, forgoing any benefits that such contact may bring." They cite a "tense and rapidly escalating arms race" as an example.[46] The obvious question, of course, is why either party would continue a relationship that both would prefer to end. Arms races can be ended by either side at any time. Human beings can always break off a social relationship. Mass suicide is perhaps the most extreme option, but it is not without some historical precedent. The point, of course, is that mutually unpleasant relationships of interdependence, such as arms races, are maintained because the likely alternatives would be even more unpleasant. The only

---

[44] Sir Norman Angell, *The Foundations of International Polity* (London: William Heinemann, 1914); Francis Delaisi, *Political Myths and Economic Realities* (London: Noel Douglas, 1925); and Muir, *Interdependent World.*

[45] Edward L. Morse, *Foreign Policy and Interdependence in Gaullist France* (Princeton: Princeton University Press, 1973), p. 51; Morse, "Interdependence in World Affairs," pp. 662–3; Keohane and Nye, "Interdependence and Integration," pp. 363, 365, 368, 376–7; and Rosecrance et al., "Whither Interdependence?" p. 426.

[46] "Interdependence and Integration," p. 367. See also a similar argument in *Power and Interdependence*, pp. 9–10.

reason to continue strategic interdependence between the United States and the Soviet Union is that the alternative might be worse. The "benefits" of interdependence, thus, are simply another way of stating the opportunity costs of severing the relationship. No matter how "bad" an interdependent relationship may be, it is presumably preferable to the most likely alternative. The "benefits" implied by the traditional concept of interdependence – i.e., in its second meaning – are not defined in absolute terms, but rather in terms of likely alternative situations. Avoiding value deprivation, after all, is just as much a "benefit" as is value augmentation. Thus, contrary to the view of Keohane and Nye, defining interdependence in terms of the "mutual benefits" to the parties involved does *not* limit it to situations in which "the modernist view of the world prevails: where threats of military force are few and levels of conflict low"; and it *does not* exclude such cases as "the strategic interdependence between the United States and the Soviet Union."[47] The "benefits" of interdependence should be defined in terms of the values of the parties and the likely effects on those values of breaking the relationship. If there is little or no effect, or if the parties would actually be better off, the relationship should not be described as interdependent. It is in this sense, *and in this sense only*, that interdependence involves mutual benefits.

The charge that earlier concepts of interdependence contained or implied a normative bias is made by Morse.[48] Although he cites Ramsay Muir, it is not clear what other writers Morse has in mind. Rosecrance et al. refer to "most students" as wishing to "use interdependence in a positive sense to see higher interdependence as a fundamental force for better relations among nations."[49] Because discussions of international interdependence prior to the Second World War were often found in books advocating world government or disarmament, the attribution of normative bias is understandable – but not necessarily justifiable.

If one discounts the rhetoric and crusading tone of this

---

[47] *Power and Interdependence*, p. 9. Even states at war may be described as interdependent if each would prefer to continue the war relationship rather than incur the costs of ending that relationship, e.g., surrender, defeat, or mutual annihilation.

[48] Morse, "Interdependence in World Affairs," pp. 662–3.

[49] Rosecrance et al., "Whither Interdependence?" pp. 426–7.

literature, the concepts employed and the basic logic of the argument are not usually normative.[50] Sir Norman Angell used the following story about two men in a boat to illustrate the nature of interdependence:

> The boat was leaky, the sea heavy, and the shore a long way off. It took all the efforts of the one man to row, and of the other to bail. If either had ceased both would have drowned. At one point the rower threatened the bailer that if he did not bail with more energy he would throw him overboard; to which the bailer made the obvious reply that, if he did, he (the rower) would certainly drown also. And as the rower was really dependent upon the bailer, and the bailer upon the rower, neither could use force against the other.[51]

Sir Norman drew the conclusion from this anecdote that the degree of interdependence varies inversely with the effectiveness of force. This story is a remarkably concise summary of the basic elements of the arguments presented by Sir Norman, Muir, and Delaisi. First, the situation involves division of labor since neither man can both row and bail. Second, exchange is involved in the sense that each man trades his labor for the other's – "I will row if you will bail." Third, there are mutual benefits of this exchange in that they both stay alive. Fourth, each is dependent on the other in the sense that the opportunity costs of breaking the relationship are high. Fifth, this reciprocal dependency constrains each party's behavior with respect to the other. Sixth, dependency is portrayed as a rather unpleasant "fact of life" to be endured and adjusted to rather than as a godsend to be celebrated. And seventh, Sir Norman's conclusion about the effects of interdependence on the effectiveness of force is a plausible, empirically testable proposition. It may not be true; but it is, in principle, falsifiable.

The arguments of Sir Norman, Muir, and Delaisi are simply amplifications of the story of the leaky boat in terms of international relations. The process of international specialization and exchange is viewed as creating international interdependence

---

[50] On the nature of normative inquiry and concepts, see Oppenheim, "Language of Political Inquiry," pp. 314–28.
[51] Angell, *Foundations of International Polity*, p. 17.

(empirical observation). The world is becoming, or has become, so interdependent that without world government (or disarmament or whatever) the achievement of many values to which people now subscribe, such as peace and economic well-being, will be impeded or prevented (empirical proposition).[52] The logical implication of such arguments is that if people are willing to tolerate a world in which life is nasty, brutish, and short, world government is unnecessary. Far from presenting a rosy picture of an interdependent world, such arguments imply that such a world will be most unpleasant *unless* appropriate adaptive measures are taken – e.g., world government or disarmament. This may be mistaken or naive, but it is a line of argument that is, in principle, empirically testable.[53] It is not a normative argument, and it is not based on a normative concept of interdependence.

Although Delaisi, Muir, and Sir Norman may not present a "rigorous" definition of interdependence, it is quite clear what they mean by it. They are using the term in the same way it had been used for centuries: to refer to international relationships that would be costly to break. They have in mind the same basic concept of dependency as that employed by Machiavelli, Montesquieu, Rousseau, Adam Smith, and Malthus. Hirschman and Waltz would later use the term in this same sense.

Keohane and Nye contend that interdependence has "normally" been defined simply as a condition in which events in one part of the world covary with events in other parts of the world.[54] Such usage, as Duvall[55] has pointed out, corresponds to the first basic meaning of "dependence" – i.e., as a conditional relationship. If "normal usage" is intended to apply only to the past decade or so,

---

[52] Morse attributes to Muir the view that the growth of interdependence is a "requisite for the abolition of interstate conflict" (*Foreign Policy and Interdependence*, p. 51, and "Interdependence in World Affairs," pp. 662–3). Actually, Muir's argument is that the abolition of war is a requisite for survival in an interdependent world in the sense that an interdependent world will be very unpleasant unless war is abolished.

[53] Neither the naiveté nor the falsity of this line of argument is as obvious to this writer as it appears to some.

[54] "International Interdependence and Integration," pp. 366–7, 370. They cite Oran R. Young as an example of this "normal" usage. See "Interdependencies in World Politics," *International Journal*, 24 (1969), pp. 726–50. Waltz apparently agrees that this represents "common" usage, in *Theory of International Politics*, p. 139.

[55] Duvall, "Dependence and *Dependencia* Theory," pp. 62–3.

Keohane and Nye may well be correct; but if a longer time period is considered, the validity of their assertion is less obvious.

International relations scholars have tended to discuss dependence and interdependence with reference to self-sufficiency and the vulnerability of a state to alterations in certain kinds of international relationships, especially trade.[56] Such usage implies the second meaning of "dependence," since, by definition, the costs of severing trade relations will be lower for self-sufficient states than for dependent ones. William E. Rappard cites a rather bizarre example of mutual dependence during the First World War in which the costs of breaking off trade were so high that two states on opposing sides carried on some trade with each other.[57]

The work of Karl Deutsch is of special interest since it is frequently cited in discussions of interdependence. Deutsch's work contains examples of both basic meanings of "dependence." In 1954 Deutsch referred to "interdependence" in terms of the "interlocking relationships" arising from the "division of labor" between "highly specialized" political units. In addition, he distinguished this "interdependence" from a relationship of "mutual responsiveness" among political units that might not be dependent upon each other – i.e., might be able to do without each other's aid.[58] Although Deutsch's concept of "mutual responsiveness" does not correspond directly to the first meaning of dependence, his concept of interdependence clearly corresponds to the second meaning as elucidated by Hirschman, Sir Norman Angell, and Delaisi. [59]

[56] Parker Thomas Moon, *Imperialism and World Politics* (Toronto: Macmillan, 1926), pp. 542–58; Frank H. Simonds and Brooks Emeny, *The Great Powers in World Politics: International Relations and Economic Nationalism* (New York: American Book Co., 1935), pp. 63–94; Nicholas John Spykman, *America's Strategy in World Politics* (New York: Harcourt, Brace, 1942), pp. 35, 270, 292–317; Quincy Wright, *A Study of War*, 2nd edn (Chicago: University of Chicago Press, 1965), pp. 319, 367; *The Study of International Relations* (New York: Appleton-Century-Crofts, 1955), pp. 250, 598; Clyde Eagleton, *International Government*, rev. edn (New York: Ronald Press, 1948), pp. 8–14; and Malcolm W. Hoag, "What Interdependence for NATO?" *World Politics*, 12 (1960), p. 369. Cf. Joseph Dunner (ed.), *Dictionary of Political Science* (New York: Philosophical Library, 1964), pp. 260–1.
[57] William E. Rappard, *United Europe* (New Haven: Yale University Press, 1930), p. 261.
[58] Karl W. Deutsch, *Political Community at the International Level: Problems of Definition and Measurement* (Garden City, N.Y.: Doubleday, 1954), p. 37.
[59] Deutsch was familiar with the work of Delaisi, Hirschman, and Sir Norman Angell,

By 1966, however, Deutsch had abandoned this earlier concept of interdependence and was defining interdependence in terms of the covariance of aspects of different systems, a usage corresponding to both the first basic meaning of "dependence" and to the current concept of "sensitivity interdependence."[60] I have been unable to locate in Deutsch's writings any acknowledgment, explanation, or justification for this shift from the traditional concept of international interdependence to a fundamentally different one.

In sum, contentions that traditional international relations usage of the term "interdependence" has been normatively biased, that it has been unclear, or that it has corresponded with "sensitivity interdependence," are all questionable. The works surveyed here suggest that the concept has been reasonably clear, generally understood, factually oriented, and has corresponded with "vulnerability interdependence." Prior to 1960 one was reasonably safe in assuming that references to "dependency" by international relations scholars corresponded to the second basic meaning as explicated by Hirschman, Muir, Delaisi, and others. Since this "traditional usage" no longer seems to be "normal," a consideration of more recent treatments of dependency relations is in order.

THE CONCEPT OF DEPENDENCE SINCE 1968

The year 1968 marked the publication of Cooper's *The Economics of Interdependence*, which makes it a convenient, though somewhat arbitrary, dividing line between the old and the new "traditional usage." Since 1968 the two basic meanings of "interdependence" have been embodied in works by Cooper and Waltz. "Sensitivity interdependence," grounded in the first meaning,

---

and even cited their work in a later article. Although he criticized their empirical observations on interdependence, there was no indication of *conceptual* disagreement. See Karl W. Deutsch and Alexander Eckstein, "National Industrialization and the Declining Share of the International Economic Sector, 1890–1959," *World Politics*, 13 (1961), pp. 267–9.

[60] Karl W. Deutsch, "Power and Communication in International Society," in *Conflict in Society*, ed. Anthony de Reuck (Boston: Little, Brown, 1966), pp. 300–1. This definition is also found in Karl W. Deutsch, *The Analysis of International Relations*, 3rd edn (Englewood Cliffs, N.J.: Prentice-Hall, 1988), p. 285.

is often associated with Cooper; and "vulnerability inter-dependence," based on the second meaning, is often associated with Waltz. Katzenstein notes that Cooper's *The Economics of Interdependence* "has been central to the reformulation of international relations theory attempted by Keohane and Nye."[61] Ruggie points out that "much of the political science work with the concept [of interdependence] was stimulated" by this book.[62] Whitman refers to Cooper's "now classic book," and Morse refers to it as a "seminal study" and as a "classic study of inter-dependence."[63]

In a "classic" study of interdependence, one may expect to find some consideration of the concept of interdependence. If there is an explicitly labelled definition of "interdependence" anywhere in Cooper's book, however, it is well camouflaged. Although "interdependence" figures prominently in the title, there is no index entry for "independence," "interdependence," "dependence," or "autonomy." At times Cooper appears to use the terms "integration" and "interdependence" interchangeably.[64] But at other times he appears to use "interdependence" to refer to relationships that would be costly to forgo. Witness the following passages:

> *Divergent economic policy has become less possible* (p. 3).
> Comment: Why has it become "less possible"? Because the costs of divergence have gone up.

> [The] *United States is discovering that its policies . . . must be influenced by what happens abroad* (p. 3).
> Comment: Why "must" US policies be influenced? Because the costs of autonomy are so high.

> *International economic intercourse . . . confines the freedom of countries . . . by embedding each country in a matrix of constraints* (p. 4).

[61] Katzenstein, "International Relations and Domestic Structures," p. 9n.

[62] John Gerard Ruggie, "Collective Goods and Future International Collaboration," *American Political Science Review*, 66 (1972), p. 875n.

[63] Whitman, *Reflections of Interdependence*, p. 161; Morse, "Interdependence in World Affairs," p. 633; and *Modernization and the Transformation of Society*, p. 117.

[64] This point is noted by Keohane and Nye, "International Interdependence and Integration," pp. 401–2.

Comment: Why are countries constrained? Because the costs of forgoing international economic intercourse are so high.

The competitive firm, if it finds the environment too constraining, can go out of business; the nation does not even have that option (p. 4).
Comment: Why does the nation "not have that option?" Because it would be too costly.

Such passages, together with Cooper's frequent references to the "need" for cooperation (p. 11), suggest that he has in mind the opportunity costs of self-sufficiency. "Mutual sensitivity" does not capture the meaning of the above passages. Relations of "mutual sensitivity" can always be severed – except when they are "necessary" in the sense that it would be costly to extricate oneself or one's country from them. "Compel," "must," "need," and "constraint" imply more than mere sensitivity or influence; they imply something about the cost of one's other options.

One of the most revealing passages in Cooper's discussion of interdependence is the following:

As with marriage, the benefits of close international economic relations can be enjoyed only at the expense of giving up a certain amount of national independence.[65]

Although it is not specifically acknowledged, the concept of interdependence as relations that would be mutually costly to forgo is embedded in this passage. If the benefits of marriage can be acquired *only* by a loss of independence, it follows that dissolving the marriage will entail a loss of such benefits. Cooper's explication of the "gains from marriage" exactly parallels Hirschman's explication of the relationship between the "gains from trade" and "dependency."[66]

Cooper's book is not really "about interdependence" at all, at least not if that implies a major concern with describing the *nature* of interdependence. That the world is highly interdependent is not so much a hypothesis to be tested as it is an assumption to use as a springboard for what really interests Cooper – i.e., the policy

[65] Cooper, *Economics of Interdependence*, p. 4.
[66] Hirschman, *National Power*, p. 18.

implications and consequences of interdependence. Cooper makes this clear at the end of his introduction, when he notes that "the remainder of the book discusses the problems created by a growing economic interdependence and explores some of the possible ways for solving these problems."[67] Now, discussing the nature of power is one thing; discussing its effects is another; just as discussing the nature of sovereignty is one thing and discussing its consequences is another. Likewise, discussing the nature of interdependence and discussing the problems it creates are two separate issues. The key to understanding this alleged "classic study of interdependence" is the realization that it is *not* about interdependence, but rather about the consequences of interdependence.

Two years after the publication of Cooper's *Economics of Interdependence*, Waltz published an article disputing what he perceived as a widely held contention that international interdependence was high, growing, and/or likely to promote peace.[68] He pointed out that the cost of disengagement from a given relationship was a measure of dependency. There is no indication in the article that Waltz perceived himself as inventing a new or unusual concept of dependency; yet other scholars repeatedly credit him with having "proposed,"[69] "developed,"[70] or "introduced"[71] this notion. Indeed, Waltz himself has apparently been convinced, since he has described himself as "offering" this

---

[67] Cooper, *Economics of Interdependence*, p. 22.

[68] Waltz, "The Myth of National Interdependence." Shortly after the publication of this article, Morse criticized it for failure to provide an explicit definition of interdependence and depicted Waltz as opposed to "conceptualizing international politics in terms of notions of interdependence" (Morse, "Transnational Economic Processes," pp. 380–1). These are puzzling charges. Waltz's concept of interdependence as relations that would be mutually costly to break is simple, straightforward, and clear; it is even contained in a section subtitled "The Meaning of Interdependence." The observation that Waltz objects to analyzing international politics in terms of interdependence is even more baffling. Waltz objects to the "rhetoric of interdependence" and to certain generalizations about the magnitude and implications of interdependence in today's world; but he does not deny the utility of the concept in analyzing world politics .

[69] Tollison and Willett, "International Integration," p. 259n.

[70] Ibid., p. 255.

[71] Kal J. Holsti, "A New International Politics? Diplomacy in Complex Interdependence," *International Organization*, 32 (1978), p. 518. Rosecrance and Stein (p. 2) say the concept "comes from" Waltz.

concept as an alternative to the "common" conception of sensitivity interdependence.[72]

Although Waltz does not refer to Hirschman's *National Power and the Structure of Foreign Trade*, the concept of dependence he "introduced" in 1970 was basically the same as the one that Hirschman explicated in 1945. The concept of "gains from trade" is just another name for the opportunity costs of forgoing trade.

From a conceptual standpoint the period since 1968 has contributed very little to thinking about international interdependence. Although scholars seem to vie with one another to invent yet another definition of "interdependence," the need for new concepts has not been demonstrated. Concepts and theories developed by earlier generations of scholars are often more relevant than is generally recognized. For example, John Ruggie lists a number of world developments that have caused students of international organization to predict that "nation-states will have to accept a degree of international regulation and control over their nominally domestic activities that goes well beyond the situation today."[73] This, however, is essentially the same argument presented by Muir, Delaisi, and others before the Second World War. When Ruggie asks what it means to say that these limitations on state autonomy "will have to be accepted,"[74] one might appropriately answer that it means that such states are interdependent; and this, in turn, means what it has meant for the past two, three, or four centuries – i.e., that the opportunity costs of autonomy are prohibitively high. Ruggie describes his application of the theory of collective goods to international collaboration as posing "the basic problem of international organization as one of national *choice under constraints*: that is, given the structure of the contemporary interstate system, what are the general conditions under which states, with differing objectives and different capabilities, choose to collaborate with others?"[75] This, however, is

[72] Waltz, *Theory of International Politics*, p. 139. In fairness to Waltz, it should be noted that he explicitly points to the correrspondence between his concept of "interdependence as mutual vulnerability" and "everyday usage" (p. 143).

[73] Ruggie, "Collective Goods," pp. 874–5.

[74] Ibid., p. 875.

[75] Ibid.

basically the same question addressed by the British classical economists with respect to foreign trade. If one substitutes "trade" for "collaborate," one has an excellent characterization of international trade theory. This theory constitutes a powerful conceptual tool for the student of international politics that should not be overlooked. It should not be necessary to develop a separate theory to cover each issue-area of international exchange relations.[76]

INTERDEPENDENCE: "SENSITIVITY" VERSUS "VULNERABILITY"

The distinction between "sensitivity interdependence," defined in terms of mutual "effects," and "vulnerability interdependence," defined in terms of the opportunity costs of disrupting the relationship, has become widely accepted and is usually attributed to Keohane and Nye.[77] The question to be addressed here is whether this distinction should be maintained, reformulated, or perhaps relabeled. The arguments in favor of retention of the distinction will be considered first.

The first, and most important reason to maintain the distinction is that it differentiates quite different phenomena. Sensitivity and vulnerability do not necessarily covary to the same degree or even in the same direction.[78]

Second, as Duvall[79] has noted, the distinction corresponds to the two basic meanings of "dependence" for the past four hundred years. It thus seems to be more fundamental than such distinctions as "strategic interdependence," "systemic interdependence," or "public goods interdependence."[80]

---

[76] The best source for broadening one's view of "exchange relations" is Blau's *Exchange and Power in Social Life*. Trade is only one of many forms of exchange among countries.
[77] Keohane and Nye, "World Politics and the International Economic System," pp. 121–5.
[78] On this point, see Cooper, "Economic Interdependence and Foreign Policy," pp. 178–9; "Economic Interdependence and Coordination," p. 1198; and Waltz, *Theory of International Politics*, p. 142.
[79] Duvall, "Dependence and *Dependencia* Theory," pp. 62–3.
[80] These "forms of interdependence" are identified by Morse, "Interdependence in World Affairs," pp. 666–71.

And third, there is a tradition of a decade or so of "conventional usage," at least by students of international relations.

The arguments against maintaining the distinction concern conventional usage, the possibility of confusion, and alternative ways of making the distinction.

The first objection to the distinction is that it contravenes common usage. As Caporaso, Waltz, Muir, and the *OED* have pointed out, "vulnerability interdependence" corresponds to everyday usage, at least with reference to world affairs.[81] Contrary to Keohane and Nye, in common parlance "dependence" does *not* mean a state of being "significantly affected by external forces."[82] A person that has been "significantly affected" by the "external force" of alcohol is called a "drunk," not an "alcoholic"; there is a difference. The Internal Revenue Service does not allow one to claim as "dependents" everyone on whom one has significant effects. When the "man-in-the-street" refers to American "dependence" on foreign oil, he has in mind the opportunity costs of doing without it, not the elasticity of prices.[83] Price sensitivity of oil would not matter one whit to the man in the street if he had affordable alternative ways to heat his house and run his car. The price of caviar in the US may be "sensitive" to price changes in other countries, but no one has suggested that America is "dependent" on caviar.

Although scholarly usage during the past decade favors retention of the distinction, the case is less persuasive if one examines scholarly usage during the past two or three centuries. The works surveyed earlier in this chapter suggest that "vulnerability interdependence" has a superior claim to the mantle of conventionality, at least in international relations, and perhaps even in economics.

A second objection to the distinction is that it is factually

[81] Caporaso, "Dependence, Dependency, and Power," pp. 18–19, 24; Waltz, *Theory of International Politics*, p. 143; Muir, *Interdependent World*, p. 1.

[82] Cooper, *Power and Interdependence*, p. 8.

[83] Those who would like to submit this proposition about the views of the mass public to empirical testing might frame questions along the following lines: "If you lived within easy walking distance of ten drugstores, would you feel dependent on any one of them?" "If there were only one drugstore within fifty miles of your home, would you feel dependent on it?" The "man in the street" may not speak in terms of "the opportunity costs of forgoing a relationship," but he has a firm grasp of the underlying concept.

misleading. Cooper identifies the problem in the following passage:

> The value of trade to a country, in terms of its contribution to national welfare [i.e., the gains from trade], may depend neither on the sensitivity nor on the magnitude of the flows, although it is more likely to be related to the magnitude than to the sensitivity. Indeed, value and sensitivity are inversely related in one important respect: high sensitivity results precisely from the capacity of a country to substitute domestic for foreign production or investment, in response to relatively small margins of advantage; yet when such substitution is easily possible at relatively low cost, the value per dollar of trade or investment to the country is correspondingly diminished.[84]

In effect, Cooper is admitting that what he calls "interdependence" may be *inversely* related to what Hirschman has called "interdependence." It is bad enough to ignore and/or to distort conventional usage; but it is worse to introduce a concept that is *inversely* related to common usage.

The third, and perhaps the most telling, argument against maintaining the "sensitivity/vulnerability" distinction is that other terms are available for making the desired distinction. As Duvall has observed, statements about dependence in its first sense are so broad as to be almost devoid of substantive content; they tell us that two variables covary, but that is about all.[85] Many terms can be used to convey the idea of covariance – e.g., "influence," "affect," "impinge," "change," "induce," or "cause." It is fine for Cooper to emphasize the importance of "the *sensitivity* of economic transactions between two or more nations to economic developments within those nations";[86] but why call this "interdependence"? Terms like "mutual influence," "mutual responsiveness," or "mutual sensitivity" convey the idea at least as well without debasing the time-honored, and still useful, concept of vulnerability interdependence.

In sum, there is a distinction between drug users and drug

---

[84] Cooper, "Economic Interdependence and Foreign Policy," pp. 178–9.
[85] Duvall, "Dependence and *Dependencia* Theory," p. 63.
[86] "Economic Interdependence and Foreign Policy," p. 159.

addicts, between drinkers and alcoholics, between being sensitive to others and being dependent on them, between influence in general and dependence as a special type of influence. It is a distinction that has been recognized and understood by scholars and laymen alike for centuries. It is a distinction that the concept of "sensitivity interdependence" blurs, but which is captured with precision and parsimony by the Hirschman–Waltz concept of dependence. Let us retain the concept of "sensitivity interdependence" but change the label to something less misleading, such as "mutual sensitivity."

"DEPENDENCE" VERSUS "DEPENDENCY"

Caporaso and Duvall have suggested that a fundamental distinction should be made between "dependence" and "dependency."[87] Whereas "dependence" refers to "external reliance on other actors," "dependency" refers to "the process of incorporation of less developed countries (LDCs) into the global capitalist system and the 'structural distortions' resulting therefrom."[88] Although both Caporaso and Duvall admit some similarity between the concepts, they emphasize the differences. "Dependence," as used by Caporaso, corresponds to "common sense" usage and to "vulnerability dependence."[89] "Dependency," however, has no basis in conventional usage, "can only be understood (i.e., its original and intended meaning is preserved) only within a certain body of historical, political, and sociological thought," and perhaps cannot be reduced to a concept at all.[90]

All of this sounds rather mystifying until one considers the purpose of the essays by Caporaso and Duvall. Duvall's purpose is to promote and facilitate a "dialogue" between what he calls "First World" scholars committed to "rigorous empirical social

[87] Caporaso, "Dependence, Dependency, and Power," pp. 18–20ff; and Duvall, "Dependence and Dependencia Theory," pp. 52–68ff.

[88] James A. Caporaso, "Introduction to the Special Issue of *International Organization* on Dependence and Dependency in the Global System," *International Organization*, 32 (1978), p. 1.

[89] Caporaso, "Dependence, Dependency, and Power," pp. 19, 31.

[90] Ibid.

science"[91] and "Third World" scholars, mostly Latin American, committed to "*dependencia* theory." Caporaso states his purpose more broadly, but he is also obviously interested in "understanding" *dependencia* theory. After stating the need to differentiate between "dependence" and "dependency," he justifies it as follows:

> What I am saying is that, should one want to use the concept of dependency and be reasonably faithful to the meaning of those [Latin American] scholars who in a sense invented and contributed most to this line of thought, then one has to respect the complexity in that thought.[92]

This, then, is the first and most important reason for defining "dependence" and "dependency" in fundamentally different ways – it facilitates understanding of the writings of a group of Latin American scholars during the past thirty years. Obviously, if one wants to understand someone's discussion of dependency, it helps to know what they mean by the term.

A second and related justification for the distinction implies that the concept of dependency was "invented" in Latin America; and this, in turn, leads to the assertion that the concepts of dependence and dependency "have different intellectual ancestries."[93] This interpretation ignores the etymology of the two concepts. The *OED* clearly indicates that the concepts of dependence and dependency have *fundamentally similar* ancestries stretching back several hundred years, i.e., dependency is the state or condition of being dependent.

[91] Duvall, "Dependence and *Dependencia* Theory," pp. 51–61. It is not clear who gets to claim the dubious distinction of being committed to "lax empirical social science." Duvall names only himself, Bruce Russett, and Caporaso as representatives of the "rigorous empirical" tradition.

[92] Caporaso, "Dependence, Dependency, and Power," p. 19. The title of the special issue of *International Organization* on Dependence and Dependency in the Global System can easily mislead one as to the contents. With a few notable exceptions, this volume is definitely slanted toward Latin America. As Richard Fagen points out, "despite the efforts of the editor to cast the theoretical net as widely as possible . . . the bulk of the writings in this volume respond in some fashion to . . . 'the [Latin American] dependency way of framing the question of development and underdevelopment.' It could hardly be otherwise, for the majority of authors represented here have had their primary research experience in or on Latin America" ("A Funny Thing Happened on the Way to the Market: Thoughts on Extending Dependency Ideas," *International Organization*, 32 (1978), p. 287).

[93] Caporaso, "Dependence and Dependency," pp. 19–20.

The first objection to defining "dependency" à la Latin America is that it constitutes a sharp deviation from several centuries of common usage. Although Caporaso[94] admits this divergence, there is no indication that he sees it as a drawback of the proposed redefinition of "dependency." To admit this redefinition of "dependency," however, is to start down the proverbial "slippery slope." What if scholars in the Philippines and Russia propose new concepts of "dependency?" Must we then speak of Filipino-dependency," "Russo-dependency," "Latino-dependency," and "Gringo-dependency?" To redefine "dependency" in terms of "a certain body of historical, political, and sociological thought" is to open the floodgates for numerous redefinitions based on different bodies of "[H]istorical, political, and sociological thought." It is, in short, a corruption of language.

Corrupting conventional language, however, can sometimes be justified – if the benefits outweigh the costs and if alternative means of achieving the benefits are unavailable. It may well be that a group of Latin American scholars have used the term "dependency" (or "*dependencia*") in a sense that is fundamentally different from the long body of common usage, but it does not necessarily follow that other scholars should therefore redefine their terms to bring their usage into line with these Latin American scholars. We must first ask whether the phenomena these authors wish to describe can be analyzed without the concept of dependency. The answer is almost certain to be "yes." In the first place, the "process of incorporation of less developed countries into the global capitalist system and the 'structural distortions' resulting therefrom" can be described adequately without reference to "dependency." In the second place, according to Caporaso and Duvall, the concept of "dependency" is *not* an important analytical tool for the *dependentistas*, but rather a mere "label for a body of theory."[95] Unless one is prepared to deny the well-known hypothesis about roses, odors, and names, it would appear

---

[94] Ibid., pp. 18–19, 24. It should be noted that the divergence from common usage involved here is not confined to English, but also applies to Italian, French, and Spanish.

[95] Ibid., p. 22; Duvall, "Dependence and *Dependencia* Theory," p. 63. Bath and James have suggested that "it might be better to change the name from 'dependency theory' to 'linkage politics'" ("Dependency Analysis," p. 33).

that *"dependencia* theory" can get along quite well without the concept of "dependency."

Redefinition of "dependency" would also violate Oppenheim's criterion of establishing definitional connections, since it would no longer be possible to define it as a state of being "dependent."[96] And Malthus would surely point out the violation of his fourth rule, that new definitions must be consistent with the remaining terms – e.g., "independence," "dependence," and "interdependence."

Two additional objections to redefining "dependency" along the lines proposed by Duvall and Caporaso are directly related to the *dependencia* literature. The argument, in effect, is that understanding this literature is so important that other social scientists should change their concept of dependency. Yet the *dependencia* literature contains vague, contradictory, and ambiguous concepts, objections *in principle* to precise concept definition, objections *in principle* to generalization, and objections *in principle* to the criterion of empirical falsifiability.[97] The scientific advantages of adapting a well-known and generally understood concept to conform with such a literature are not self-evident.

An additional objection is that despite the arguments of Caporaso and Duvall, it is not yet clear that the *dependencia* theorists always use "dependency" in a sense that diverges fundamentally from ordinary language. In a literature so fraught with ambiguity, inconsistency, and vagueness, it is difficult to say with assurance precisely what *is* meant by "dependency." It is a safe assumption that those who first began to use the term in the

---

[96] Oppenheim, "Language of Political Inquiry," pp. 303–4.

[97] For documentation and further references regarding these points, see especially the incisive and telling critique by Robert A. Packenham, "The New Utopianism: Political Development Ideas in the Dependency Literature," *Working Paper*, no. 19, Latin American Program, Woodrow Wilson International Center for Scholars, Washington, D.C. (1978). See also, Robert A. Packenham, "Latin American Dependency Theories: Strengths and Weaknesses," paper presented before the Harvard–MIT Joint Seminar on Political Development, Cambridge, Mass., February 6, 1974; Lall, "Is 'Dependence' a Useful Concept," pp. 799–810; Duvall, "Dependence and *Dependencia* Theory," pp. 52–7; 68n.; Caporaso, "Dependence, Dependency, and Power," pp. 22–4, 43; Cardoso and Faletto, *Dependency and Development*, pp. vii–xiv; Fernando Henrique Cardoso, "The Consumption of Dependency Theory in the United States," *Latin American Research Review*, 12 (1977), pp. 7–24, esp. pp. 15–16; and Tony Smith, "The Underdevelopment of Development Literature: The Case of Dependency Theory," *World Politics*, 31 (1979), pp. 247–88.

context of *dependencia* theory were aware, at least in a general way, of its common-sense denotations and connotations. Furthermore, some students of *dependencia* theory have suggested that it is concerned with asymmetrical power relations.[98] Since both Caporaso and Duvall[99] view "dependence," but *not* "dependency," as closely related to the standard social science concept of power, such interpretations of *dependencia* theory suggest that the conceptual gap may be narrower than Caporaso and Duvall imply. Indeed, if all the ambiguities, inconsistencies, obfuscation, and emotional biases could be eliminated from *dependencia* theory, I suspect that the Latin American usage of "dependency" might often turn out to be closer to the Hirschman–Waltz version of the concept than is generally supposed. Thus, Tony Smith argues that the international economic system

> has at its disposal sanctions for transgressing its basic rules which are all the more powerful since their greatest force comes *not from an active threat of intervention* so much as *from a threat of withdrawal,* which would abandon these dependent regimes to civil and regional conflict. . . . So far as I am aware, this last point has not been made by any of the dependency theorists. Nevertheless, it is clearly implicit in their form of analysis.[100]

This, of course, sounds very much like Hirschman's concept of dependence, which brings us back to the special issue of *International Organization*. Hirschman's description of himself as the "founding grandfather" of dependency theory should at least make one suspicious of assertions that his concept of dependency is fundamentally different from that of the *dependentistas*.[101]

---

[98] Fagen, "A Funny Thing Happened," p. 288; Robert A. Packenham, "Trends in Brazilian National Dependency since 1964," in Riordan Rvett (ed.), *Brazil in the Seventies* (Washington, D.C.: American Enterprise Institute, 1976), p. 91; Smith, "Underdevelopment," pp. 249, 251, 282–3, 288; and Johan Galtung, "A Structural Theory of Imperialism," *Journal of Peace Research*, 2 (1971), pp. 81–117.

[99] Caporaso, "Dependence, Dependency, and Power," pp. 28–9; Duvall, "Dependence and *Dependencia* Theory," pp. 60–1, 65.

[100] "Underdevelopment," p. 251.

[101] Albert O. Hirschman, "Beyond Asymmetry: Critical Notes on Myself as a Young Man and on Some Other Old Friends," *International Organization*, 32 (1978), p. 45.

DEPENDENCE AS POWER

References to the literature on social power are sparse in both the Latin American *dependencia* theory and the North American literature on interdependence. Except for the article by Caporaso and an occasional passing reference to Bachrach and Baratz, both sets of literature are almost bereft of references to the social power literature.[102] Galtung asserts that imperialism is a kind of power relationship but proceeds to ignore the social power literature altogether. Packenham, on the other hand, declares that one advantage of treating dependence as a form of power is that it "allows the literature on power to teach us something about what dependency means."[103] It is in this spirit that the issue will be considered here. It will be argued that dependency can be treated as part of a large family of social science "power terms" *without distorting the basic common sense meaning of the term* and that such treatment would eliminate much conceptual confusion, thus making dependency terms more useful tools for social science research. I will discuss seven dimensions of power with reference to dependency relationships. Although these dimensions are well known to power analysts, each of them has been virtually ignored by either *dependencia* theory or North American writers on interdependence, and often by both. The dimensions to be discussed include the relational nature of power, the multi-dimensional nature of power, actual versus potential power, actors' intentions, costs, power resources, and reciprocity.

Power as relation

One of the most important elements of social power analysis since 1950 has been the relational definition of power. Instead of defining power as a property of the power wielder, it has been defined in terms of an actual or postulated relationship between two or more actors. Thus, to treat dependency as a power term is

---

[102] Peter Bachrach and Morton S. Baratz, "Decisions and Non-Decisions: An Analytical Framework," *American Political Science Review*, 57 (1963), pp. 632–42; and Caporaso, "Dependence, Dependency, and Power," pp. 27–31.

[103] Packenham, "Trends in Brazilian National Dependency," p. 91.

to imply the existence of at least one other actor. Thus, when an individual or a state is described as "dependent," the obvious question is, "with respect to whom?" It should be specifically noted that the actor on whom one is dependent may be another state or it may be a rather vague conglomeration of other actors, such as "other countries," "the rest of the world," or "the international capitalist system."[104]

Power as multidimensional

Power relationships vary on many dimensions. Some of these dimensions are essential to specifying a power relation, while others are simply useful ways to distinguish one kind of power relation from another. Thus, a *complete* description of a power relation would include who is trying to get whom to do what, by what means, where, when, how, at what cost, with what degree of success, and so on; but a *minimum* specification of a power relation requires less detail. There is general agreement in the social power literature that a *minimum* specification of a power relation must include both scope and domain.[105] The implication of this multidimensional characteristic of power is that the same actor can be simultaneously strong and weak – e.g., powerful with respect to some scopes of some actors and weak with respect to other scopes of other actors. The same state may be strong with regard to deterring nuclear attack on its homeland by other nuclear states but weak with regard to "winning the hearts and minds" of Third World peoples.

Dahl has taken an unambiguous position on the importance of specifying scope and domain.

> Any statement about influence that does not clearly indicate the domain and scope it refers to verges on being meaningless. When one hears that A is highly influential, the proper question is: Influential over what actors with respect to what matters? The

[104] Cf. Caporaso, "Dependence, Dependency, and Power," p. 29.
[105] Harold D. Lasswell and Abraham Kaplan, *Power and Society*, (New Haven: Yale University Press, 1950), pp. 75–6; Robert A. Dahl, *Modern Political Analysis*, 4th edn (Englewood Cliffs, N.J.: Prentice-Hall, 1984), pp. 23–30; and Jack H. Nagel, *The Descriptive Analysis of Power* (New Haven: Yale University Press, 1975), p. 14.

failure to insist on this simple question often leads political observers astray.[106]

The same could be said about statements of dependency. When one hears that a nation-state is highly dependent, the proper question is: Dependent on what actors with respect to what matters? The United States may be dependent on Saudi Arabia with respect to oil, but it is not dependent on Saudi Arabia with respect to Strategic Arms Limitations Talks. Discussions of dependency relations in world politics seldom specify scope and domain. No single change in scholarly writing habits would bring a more dramatic improvement in the clarity and precision of such discussions than the practice of specifying who is dependent on whom with respect to what.

In addition to scope and domain, power relations vary in weight or amount. This dimension concerns the degree to which A causes a change in the probability of B's behavior with respect to a given scope. For our purposes the important implication of this dimension is that power becomes a matter of degree. Dahl has labeled the tendency to ignore variations in the degree of power as "the lump-of-power fallacy."[107] Likewise, one might identify the "lump-of-dependence fallacy." In each case differences of degree are ignored, and arbitrary and misleading dichotomies are introduced.[108] Dividing all the states in the world into the dependent and non-dependent, while ignoring differing degrees of dependency among states, is likely to obfuscate more than it clarifies.[109]

Actual versus potential power

The distinction between actual and potential power is essential but

---

[106] Dahl, *Modern Political Analysis* 4th edn, p. 27.

[107] Ibid., pp. 20–1.

[108] Cf. Lall, "Is 'Dependence' a Useful Concept," p. 803.

[109] Cardoso and Faletto, *Dependency and Development*, p. xii, argue that there is "little sense in attempting to measure 'degrees of dependence.'" Duvall, "Dependence and *Dependencia* Theory," p. 56, implies that if dependency is conceived of as a "situation," it cannot be a matter of degree. This seems contrary to common usage, however, since we often refer to "situations" as "good or bad," "pleasant or unpleasant," "political or nonpolitical," "dangerous or safe," and so on, all of which are matters of degree.

often confusing.[110] Both are relational concepts in that one refers to actual social relations while the other refers to potential social relations; and both vary in scope, weight, and domain. The primary difference concerns the motivation of the actual or potential power-wielder. The distinction allows for the common phenomenon of unused power resources; an actor may have the ability to get B to do X but lack the desire to do so.

The distinction between actual and potential power is helpful in understanding dependency because vulnerability dependence implies potential power but not necessarily actual power. Thus, Hirschman has argued that dependent countries may be able to offset their disadvantage in terms of *potential* power because they are more strongly motivated than the dominant country.[111] In a similar vein, Holsti has pointed out that one of the strong points of Keohane and Nye's *Power and Interdependence* is that "it does *not* assume, as do dependency theorists, dependency-as-vulnerability researchers, and many traditional international relations scholars, that disparities in economic capabilities or vulnerability *necessarily* lead to inequitable bargaining outcomes, much less to permanent hierarchy."[112] I agree with Holsti's assessment.

Intentions

In addition to motivation, the role of intentions in power relations is relevant to discussions of dependency. There is some dispute among students of social power as to whether the exercise of power must always be intentional on the part of the power-wielder.[113] This dispute need not be addressed here; but the possibility of unintended or undesired influence should be noted. Dependency implies something about the vulnerability of B to an influence attempt by A, but it implies little or nothing about the

---

[110] Nagel, *Descriptive Analysis of Power*, pp. 172–4; and Dorwin Cartwright, "Influence, Leadership, Control," in *Handbook of Organizations*, ed. James March (Chicago: Rand McNally, 1965), pp. 7–8.

[111] "Beyond Asymmetry," pp. 47–8.

[112] Holsti, "A New International Politics?" p. 520. Italics mine.

[113] Cartwright, "Influence, Leadership, Control," pp. 10–11; Nagel, *Descriptive Analysis of Power*, pp. 12–34; Dennis H. Wrong, "Some Problems in Defining Social Power," *American Journal of Sociology*, 73 (1968), pp. 676–7; and Felix E. Oppenheim, "'Power' Revisited," *Journal of Politics*, 40 (1978), pp. 597–601.

desires or intentions of A. The dependence of B on A may or may not be the result of A's preferences. Indeed, A may be rather unhappy with the situation. If some states find themselves dependent in some respects on other states, it does not follow that this situation is attributable to the preferences of the dominant states.[114] The dependency of children on their parents with respect to livelihood is probably caused more by biology and society than by the preferences of the parents. Concepts of power that allow for the possibility of unintended influence may be more useful to the student of dependency and autonomy than other power concepts.

It is also possible for the intentions or preferences of A to influence B without any specific attempt by A to make this happen – and perhaps even without A's awareness that it has happened! This phenomenon, known as "the rule of anticipated reactions," refers to situations in which "one actor, B, shapes his behavior to conform to what he believes are the desires of another actor, A, without having received explicit messages about A's wants or intentions from A or A's agents."[115] "Anticipated reactions" could be helpful in understanding dependency relations in which the dependent actor's behavior is modified despite the absence of any explicit demand by the dominant actor. Thus, if Japan were dependent on Saudi Arabia with respect to oil, it might modify its position on the Arab–Israeli dispute without any explicit request or demand by Saudi Arabia. Some things "go without saying." Likewise, some influence attempts "go without making."

Power costs

The concept of cost is particularly relevant to analyzing dependency, since dependency implies that the opportunity costs of forgoing the relationship are high. If state B must forgo warm homes, fully employed factories, adequate transportation systems, and high

[114] In *The Social Contract* Rousseau explicitly pointed out the disadvantages of dominance: "If one of two neighboring peoples could not do without the other, the situation would be very hard for the former and very dangerous for the latter. In such a case, any wise nation will very quickly try to relieve the other of its dependency" (p. 74n.).

[115] Nagel, *Descriptive Analysis of Power*, p. 16. There is a rich scholarly literature treating "anticipated reactions," which could be useful to students of dependency. For a thorough discussion and bibliography, see Nagel.

living standards, when state A stops exporting oil, state B is dependent on state A for oil. If, on the other hand, state B can easily get its oil elsewhere or if it is indifferent to warm homes, etc., it is not very dependent on state A with respect to oil.

Caporaso notes Emerson's definition of dependence:

> The dependence of actor B upon actor A is 1) directly proportional to B's *motivational investment* in goals mediated by A, and 2) inversely proportional to the *availability* of those goals to B outside the A–B relation.[116]

Caporaso points out that "a full specification of the structural existence of dependence . . . would include: 1) the magnitude of B's interest in or desire for a good (x); 2) the extent of control of x by another actor A; and 3) the ability of B to substitute for x or A." Although both Emerson and Caporaso provide useful explications of dependency relations, both are compatible with describing such relations in terms of the magnitude of the opportunity costs of severing the relationship. Indeed, the latter concept subsumes *all* of the components identified by Emerson and Caporaso.[117] If one seeks a parsimonious way to explain dependency relations, it is difficult to improve upon the idea of the opportunity costs of breaking the relationship.

Another reason the concept of costs is helpful in treatments of dependency is that policy alternatives can be discussed more sensibly. Discussions of dependency often portray the dependent actor as "having no alternatives," or as having "alternatives closed off." "This kind of rhetoric," as the Sprouts observe, "*never* means what it appears to mean. The statesman always has

[116] Emerson, "Power-Dependence Relations," p. 32, paraphrased in Caporaso, "Dependence, Dependency, and Power," p. 21. Caporaso and Emerson use "A" to refer to the dependent actor and "B" to refer to the dominant one. In the quote I have reversed this usage in order to maintain congruence with the more common practice in the social power literature.

[117] Emerson, "Power–Dependence Relations" (p. 32), notes the similarity between opportunity costs and the possibility of alternative relations but does not recognize that B's motivational investment is also subsumed by the concept of opportunity costs. The magnitude of the opportunity costs to B of breaking a relationship with A varies directly with the magnitude of B's desire for the good or service involved. Thus, "cornering the market" for Brussels sprouts is not likely to be a very effective way to make others dependent on you.

alternatives."[118] When someone says that the United States has no alternative to importing oil or that Canada has no alternative to trading with the United States, they really mean that alternatives involve costs that the parties are unwilling or unable to pay. Clearer understanding of dependency relations would be achieved if alternative relations were described as more or less costly rather than as existent or nonexistent.

Power resources

As the previous chapter showed, the concept of power resources has generated much confused and tautologous thinking about power relations. Since it has been suggested that dependency can be viewed as a type of power resource, wariness and caution are in order. Power resources are usually defined as the means by which one actor can influence the behavior of other actors.[119] By definition, then, those with the most power resources will have the most *potential* power or *ability* to get others to do things they would not otherwise do. If possession of such resources did not give one the ability to influence others, they would never have been classified as power resources in the first place. Thus, most statements that "explain" variations in the distribution of potential power in terms of variations in the distribution of power resources are tautological.[120] Since power resources often go unused, however, it is not tautological to explain variations in the distribution of *actual* power in terms of variations in the distribution of power resources.

[118] Harold Sprout and Margaret Sprout, *Toward a Politics of the Planet Earth* (New York: Van Nostrand Reinhold, 1971), p. 98.

[119] Cf. Dahl, *Modern Political Analysis*, 4th edn, p. 31.

[120] I refer to "most" rather than "all" such statements because some avoid tautology in a technical sense by excluding one or two items – usually "skill" or "bargaining ability" – from the list of power resources. Skill is similar to other power resources in that it may not be used in some situations. Parents who play games with their children, for example, rarely use all the skill they possess. Since skill is obviously one of the means by which an actor can influence the behavior of other actors, its arbitrary omission from the power resource category should at least be explained. Dahl admits that skill could be treated as a power resource, but his only explanation for not treating it as such is that "it is generally thought to be of critical importance in explaining differences in the power of different leaders." The same could be said, of course, for a number of other power resources (Robert A. Dahl, "Power," in *International Encyclopedia of the Social Sciences*, vol. 12 (New York: Free Press, 1968), p. 409).

Keohane and Nye suggest that "a parsimonious way to conceptualize diverse sources of power – and *therefore to explain distributions of power-resources among actors in world politics* – is to regard power as deriving from patterns of asymmetrical interdependence between actors in the issue-areas in which they are involved with one another."[121] Caporaso cites this passage by Keohane and Nye as identifying one of the "two primary links between dependence and power."[122] The difficulty with this position is that patterns of interdependence are *defined* in terms of two basic dimensions, one of which is the *relative power resources of the actors.*[123] Thus, to some extent, at least, distributions of power resources are being "explained" in terms of distributions of power resources.

The idea of regarding B's dependence on A with respect to X as a power resource for A can be interesting and useful, but only if we are careful to avoid tautology. If dependency is defined in terms of the magnitude of the opportunity costs of severing the relation, then – by definition – A has the ability to inflict costs on B. If the ability to inflict costs on another actor is considered a measure of potential power, then all dependency relations *are* power relations in the following sense: To the extent that A can make B go without oil by severing the relation between A and B, A has potential power over B with respect to the consumption of oil. This is precisely what it means to say that B is dependent on A with respect to oil consumption.

It does not follow, however, that all statements linking dependency to power are tautologies. Although dependency relations are a form of influence relations,[124] it is quite possible, and even probable, that one form of influence can serve as the basis (or power resource) for a different form of influence.[125] Thus

[121] "World Politics and the International Economic System," pp. 122–3. Italics added.

[122] Caporaso, "Dependence, Dependency, and Power," p. 28.

[123] Ibid.; and Keohane and Nye, "World Politics and the International Economic System," pp. 122–3.

[124] Lasswell and Kaplan, *Power and Society* (p. 84), define a "form of influence" as a "kind of influence relationship specified as to base value and scope."

[125] A table in which Lasswell and Kaplan, *Power and Society* (p. 87), portrayed various forms of power is often criticized for listing power as a power resource (base value). This is a misinterpretation of the table. The point that Lasswell and Kaplan were making is that "power over some values often constitutes the condition for influence or power over other values" (p. 86).

A's ability (potential power) to make B go without oil can serve as the basis for A's influence on B with respect to other activities. Saudi Arabia, for example, might use its ability to make Japan reduce its oil consumption as the basis for influencing Japan's position on the Arab–Israeli dispute. The effectiveness of an explicit or implicit threat to cut off Japan's oil supply unless it withholds support for Israel is likely to be greater if Japan really is dependent on the threat-issuing state with respect to oil. A threat by Egypt to stop exporting oil to Japan would probably not be very effective as a means of changing Japanese behavior.

The proposition that dependency (specified as to scope and domain) can serve as a power resource (specified as to scope and domain) is useful and non-tautologous. As long as one is careful to specify scope and domain, tautology can be avoided. The foregoing arguments suggest that dependency is simply a particular type of potential power relation.

Variations in the fungibility of power resources are also a frequent source of confusion. As has been pointed out many times in this book, political power resources are much less fungible than economic power resources. Any particular economic power resource can usually be converted into another kind of economic power resource. Money, as a highly liquid medium of exchange that also serves as a standard of value, facilitates such resource conversions. In the political realm, however, there is no close counterpart to money; therefore, it is much more difficult to convert one kind of power resource into another. This lack of fungibility of political power resources, together with the multi-dimensional nature of power relations, increases the probability that an actor may control large amounts of potential power with respect to some scopes but relatively small amounts of potential power with respect to other scopes. Thus, a nation may be powerful with respect to deterring nuclear attack but weak with respect to getting one of its citizens elected Secretary-General of the United Nations.

If there were a standarized measuring rod in terms of which the power to deter attack could be compared with the power to secure foreign aid, political power analysis would be much easier – almost as easy as economic analysis.

Dependency poses a similar problem in that a state can be

dependent on another state with respect to cultural enrichment or
industrial machinery but may not be dependent with respect to
military security or oil. Caporaso notes the question of whether
"dependence" is to be regarded as an "issue-specific concept or a
multi-issue 'net' property," but fails to face up to its implications.[126]
He apparently believes the issue has been resolved, however, since
later references depict dependence as "net reliance on others."[127]
His observation that "our uncertainty about a 'net' figure is in part
an uncertainty about the facts" misses the essential point – i.e.,
that the uncertainty is inherent in the nature of the problem. No
amount of fact-gathering will enable us to overcome what Catlin
has called the "*supreme difficulty*" of a science of politics – i.e., the
absence of a political counterpart to money.[128] Caporaso implies
that the problem can be solved by Harsanyi's utility analysis,
which Caporaso views as converting "power" from a "series of
observed measurement readings, registered in quantities representing
amount [i.e., weight] of power, scope, and extent [i.e., domain]" into
a "generalized production function."[129] This, however, is
tantamount to a game of "let's pretend." It is easy to "solve" the
problem of comparing different scopes of dependency or power by
imagining a political counterpart to money, but it is not very
helpful.

To the extent that one is concerned with economic dependency,
money may be a useful measure for comparing dependency in one
issue-area with dependency in another issue-area. Difficulties
arise, however, when dependency involves costs that are not easily
measured by money. When costs are political, psychological, or
cultural, there is no generally agreed upon common denominator
of value in terms of which they can be measured and compared.
While some kinds of dependency relations are easy to compare,
others are not. As Dahl has reminded us, "the problem of how to

---

[126] Caporaso, "Dependence, Dependency, and Power," p. 20.

[127] Ibid., p. 22.

[128] G. E. G. Catlin, *The Science and Method of Politics* (New York: Alfred A. Knopf,
1927), p. 251 (italics mine). Blau (pp. 94–5) points out that "in contrast to economic
commodities, the benefits involved in social exchange do not have an exact price in terms of
a single quantitative medium of exchange. . . . . It is essential to realize that this is a
substantive fact, not simply a methodological problem."

[129] Caporaso, "Dependence, Dependency, and Power," p. 31.

'add up' an actor's influence with respect to different scopes . . . has proved intractable."[130] To treat "dependence" as a "net" concept is to run head-on into this intractable problem.

Reciprocity

Reciprocity is a possibility in both power relations and dependency relations.[131] Neither power nor dependency is inherently asymmetrical if that term is meant to rule out mutual influence or dependence. States may be *simultaneously* dependent on each other with respect to similar kinds of scopes, such as cultural enrichment, military security, tariff levels, standards of living, or recreation. States may also be *simultaneously* dependent on each other with respect to different kinds of scopes. Thus, state B may be dependent on state A with respect to oil; but state A may be dependent on state B with respect to food. Wrong uses the term "intercursive power" to describe situations in which the control of one person or group over another with respect to a particular scope is "balanced" by the control of the other in a different scope.[132]

> In a stable social relation (where there is a recurrent interaction between the parties rather than interaction confined to a single occasion) a pattern may emerge in which one actor controls the other with respect to particular situations and spheres of conduct – or *scopes*, as they have often been called – while the other actor is regularly dominant in other areas of situated activity. Thus a wife may rule in the kitchen, while her husband controls the disposition of family income.

Of course, whether ruling over the kitchen "balances" ruling over the disposition of family income depends on whose wife one has in mind! One wife may view such a situation as "balancing out"; another may not. A wife who regards ruling over the kitchen as lower in status and importance than ruling over the checkbook is likely to view the situation described by Wrong as "unbalanced."

---

130 Dahl, *Modern Political Analysis*, 4th edn, p. 28.
131 For discussion and further references on this point, see chapter 6.
132 Wrong, "Some Problems in Defining Social Power," pp. 673–4.

Similarly, state A may depend on state B for raw materials and foodstuffs, while state B depends on state A for manufactured goods and technology, a situation that could be labeled "intercursive dependency." Some states may view this as "balanced" dependency, but others may regard it as "unbalanced."

CONCLUSION

This chapter concludes as it began, with a review of Oppenheim's criteria for judging scientific concepts.

   1   *Operationalization*. In explicating the concept of power, Dahl noted that to define it "in a way that seems to catch the central, intuitively understood meaning of the word must inevitably result in a formal definition that is not easy to apply in concrete research problems. . . . In practice, the concept of power will have to be defined by operational criteria that will undoubtedly modify its pure meaning."[133] The same could be said about "dependence." Both the concept of power and the concept of opportunity costs involve counterfactual conditions, and this makes both concepts hard to operationalize. Since opportunity costs are the basic defining characteristic of dependence, at least in its second meaning, the difficulty also applies to research on dependency.[134] This is an awkward situation; but then, no one has ever seriously suggested that power analysis or dependency analysis is easy.

   2   *Definitional connections*. By this criterion the dependency analyst has a potentially easier task than the power analyst. In the English language, at least, there is no verb form of the word "power"; but "dependency" has one, along with several closely related and potentially useful semantic cousins: "dependent," "dependence," "independence," and "interdependence." All of these terms share the underlying intuitive notion of relations in which the opportunity costs of severance are high (low in the case "independence") for at least one of the actors. Such a family of

---

[133] Dahl, "The Concept of Power," pp. 202, 214.

[134] Caporaso's admission that with only one exception "a serious explanation of counterfactuals was not taken up" by the contributors to the special issue of *International Organization* is, in effect, admitting that the heart of the matter was virtually ignored ("Introduction," p. 11).

related terms can provide the dependency theorist with a useful vocabulary as long as the underlying conceptual unity is preserved.

3 *Factual connections.* Defining interdependence in terms of mutual sensitivity merely draws attention to the fact that one thing affects another, a fact that is obvious and can be established without the concept of sensitivity interdependence. Defining interdependence in terms of opportunity costs, however, directs attention to "certain features of the subject matter which are of theoretical importance but often not readily apparent."[135] Counterfactual conditions, such as the opportunity costs of altering a relationship, are an example *par excellence* of facts that are not readily apparent.

4 *Not precluding empirical investigation.* Defining power and dependency in terms that allow for variations in scope, weight, and domain might be viewed as necessitating a "pluralist" view of social relations as opposed to a view emphasizing monolithic power structures. Such is not the case. Insisting that power and dependency relations be specified as to scope, weight, and domain *allows for the possibility* that the pluralists might be right, but it does not prejudge the truth or falsity of their position. If, indeed, dependency relations do not vary significantly in scope, weight, or domain, this will become apparent and will provide support for the monolithic dependency structure position.[136]

5 *Ordinary language.* The main body of this chapter has emphasized conventional usage, especially with respect to the "sensitivity/vulnerability" and "dependence/dependency" distinctions. The most salient weakness in the literature of these distinctions is the complete absence of any work that (a) acknowledges alternative definitions, (b) treats unnecessary deviations from common usage as an undesirable characteristic in scientific concepts, or (c) considers both the costs and benefits of introducing a new distinction or redefining an old concept. If one's definition diverges significantly from conventional usage, it is not enough to make one's definition clear; nor is it enough to note the divergence. It is not even enough to cite advantages of one's own

---

[135] Oppenheim, "The Language of Political Inquiry," p. 305.

[136] The weakness of the position of Cardoso and Faletto is that their approach precludes empirical investigation of certain dimensions of dependency (*Dependency and Development*, pp. viii–ix). Cf. Nagel, *Descriptive Analysis of Power*, pp. 5–6, 177.

definition. One must show that these advantages are not offset by accompanying disadvantages and that alternative means of achieving these alleged advantages are either unavailable or less acceptable. It is a formidable hurdle; and it should be, in order to prevent needless debasement of the language. If there is a single scholarly work on "sensitivity interdependence" or on "dependency" as the process of incorporating the less developed countries into the global capitalist system that meets these requirements, it has not yet come to the attention of this writer.

6   *Openness of meaning.* Scientific concepts must be allowed to evolve and should never be fixed for all time, but this does not relieve scholars of the need to justify new definitions. The tradition of using the second meaning of dependence in discussions of international and transnational relations is hundreds of years old. Although I believe this concept of dependence is still enormously useful, I am prepared to accede to any reformulations that are in accordance with basic principles of scientific inquiry. However, there is not much to be said in favor of simply "drifting" into new definitions of "dependence." Instead, let us *choose* our concepts in accordance with clearly specified criteria, such as those set forth by Malthus and Oppenheim. All those genuinely commited to scholarly communication – whether they are behaviorists, empiricists, formal modelers, conservatives, liberals, Marxists,[137] Mercantilists, or whatever – should share an interest in the explication of the concept of interdependence, which has borne such a heavy analytical burden in recent years. One does not have to agree with Adam Smith, Hirschman, or Waltz in order to use the concept of dependence they explicated.

Understanding interdependence is no mere semantic exercise. Unless the inhabitants of this shrinking planet improve their understanding of interdependence and its perils, mankind's survival is endangered. Conceptual analysis can help by clarifying the nature of interdependence, but it cannot answer questions

---

[137] The concept of interdependence used by Karl Marx seems to correspond with that used by Adam Smith, Montesquieu, and Rousseau. Cf. Karl Marx, *The Communist Manifesto* (1848), reprinted edn (Chicago: Henry Regnery, 1954), p. 14; Walter C. Clemens, Jr, *The USSR and Global Interdependence* (Washington, D.C.: American Enterprise Institute, 1978), p. 1; and R. N. Berki, "On Marxian Thought and the Problem of International Relations," *World Politics*, 24 (1971), pp. 101–4.

regarding the magnitude, rate of change, direction of change, or consequences of interdependence. Only empirical research can do that. The important thing is not to lose sight of what we are talking about as we employ our necessarily imperfect operational definitions of the abstract concept of interdependence.

Index

aid, foreign, in power relations 64, 103, 156, 157–8
Aliber, Robert 180
Alker, Hayward 137n., 168
analysis, conceptual 7–9, 170–3, 181
Angell, Norman 183, 185–7
'anticipated reactions, rule of' 205
Arab–Israeli dispute 160, 205, 209
arms negotiations 5–6
arms race 183
assurances 67, 165
authority, and social exchange theory 121–3
autonomy
  and costs of power 96–8, 192
  individual 37
Ayres, Clarence 43

Bachrach, Peter and Baratz, Morton S. 53, 61, 64, 201
balance of power 137
Baldwin, David A. 7n., 99n., 130n.
banking, political 38–9
bargaining theory 55–7
barter 18–19, 23, 28, 42, 110–11, 125
  political 19–20

bases, power, *see* power resources
Bath and James 198n.
blackmail 78–9
Blau, Peter M. 27, 147
  on costs of power 95–6
  on sanctions 59–60, 80, 120
  on social exchange 101, 104–5, 110–12, 114–16, 122, 193, 210n.
bluff, and threat 87–8
Boulding, Kenneth E. 31, 34n., 47–8, 60n., 78, 108n.
Burke, Edmund 16

Caporaso, James A. 172n., 174, 194, 196–200, 201, 206, 208, 210
Cardoso and Faletto 203n.
Cartwright, Dorwin 68, 74
  on costs of power 83.
  on social exchange theory 123–6
Catlin, G. E. G. 10–11, 12, 16, 27–8, 43, 127, 210
causation, power as 7–8, 113–14, 119–20, 129–31, 168
Chadwick-Jones, J. K. 105n.
Chandler, Lester V. 16n., 18n.

Index compiled by Meg Davies